WORLD ENGLISHES

'The refusal to collude with cosy myths is a great strength of this book. The texts and exercises are very carefully chosen to be interesting and intellectually challenging and should work well with students from different levels and ranges of experience.'
Mark Sebba, *University of Lancaster, UK*

'This book provides an excellent, informative introduction to the vexed question of English as a world language. It assesses the modern spread of the English language factually in an unbiased fashion and presents students with a wealth of exciting practical work that will enable them to develop a balanced perspective of the "global" language English.'
Richard Watts, *University of Berne, Switzerland*

Routledge English Language Introductions cover core areas of language study and are one-stop resources for students.

Assuming no prior knowledge, books in the series offer an accessible overview of the subject, with activities, study questions, sample analyses, commentaries and key readings – all in the same volume. The innovative and flexible 'two-dimensional' structure is built around four sections – introduction, development, exploration and extension – which offer self-contained stages for study. Each topic can also be read across these sections, enabling the reader to build gradually on the knowledge gained.

World Englishes:

❑ is a comprehensive introduction to the subject
❑ covers the major historical and socio-political developments in World Englishes, from the reign of Queen Elizabeth I to the present day
❑ explores the current debates in World Englishes, from English in postcolonial America and Africa and Asian Englishes in the Outer Circle, to creole development in the UK and US, and the best way to teach and test World Englishes
❑ draws on a range of real texts, data and examples, including articles from the *New York Times* and *The Economist*, emails and transcripts of speech
❑ provides classic readings by the key names in the discipline including Achebe, Ammon, d'Epie, Graddol, Li, Milroy, Modiano, Pennycook, Ngũgĩ wa Thiong'o and Widdowson.

The accompanying website can be found at
http://www.routledge.com/textbooks/0415258065

Jennifer Jenkins is a Senior Lecturer in the Department of Education and Professional Studies, Kings College London, UK. She is the author of *The Phonology of English as an International Language* (2000).

Series Editor: Peter Stockwell
Series Consultant: Ronald Carter

ROUTLEDGE ENGLISH LANGUAGE INTRODUCTIONS

SERIES EDITOR: PETER STOCKWELL

Peter Stockwell is Senior Lecturer in the School of English Studies at the University of Nottingham, UK, where his interests include sociolinguistics, stylistics and cognitive poetics. His recent publications include *Cognitive Poetics: An Introduction* (Routledge, 2002), *The Poetics of Science Fiction, Investigating English Language* (with Howard Jackson), and *Contextualized Stylistics* (edited with Tony Bex and Michael Burke).

SERIES CONSULTANT: RONALD CARTER

Ronald Carter is Professor of Modern English Language in the School of English Studies at the University of Nottingham, UK. He is the co-series editor of *Routledge Applied Linguistics*, series editor of *Interface*, and was co-founder of the Routledge *Intertext* series.

OTHER TITLES IN THE SERIES:

Sociolinguistics
Peter Stockwell

Pragmatics and Discourse
Joan Cutting

Grammar and Vocabulary
Howard Jackson

Psycholinguistics
John Field

Practical Phonetics and Phonology
Beverley Collins & Inger Mees

Stylistics
Paul Simpson

FORTHCOMING:

Language in Theory
Mark Robson & Peter Stockwell

Child Language
Jean Stilwell Peccei

WORLD ENGLISHES

A resource book for students

A
B
C
D

JENNIFER JENKINS

Routledge
Taylor & Francis Group

LONDON AND NEW YORK

First published 2003
by Routledge
2 Park Square, Milton Park, Abingdon, Oxon, OX14 4RN

Simultaneously published in the USA and Canada
by Routledge
270 Madison Ave, New York, NY10016

Reprinted 2005 (twice), 2006 (three times)

Routledge is an imprint of the Taylor & Francis Group, an informa business

© 2003 Jennifer Jenkins
Typeset in 10/12.5 pt Minion by Graphicraft Limited, Hong Kong
Printed and bound in Great Britain by TJ International Ltd, Padstow, Cornwall

British Library Cataloguing in Publication Data
A catalogue record for this book is available from the British Library

Library of Congress Cataloging in Publication Data
Jenkins, Jennifer
    World Englishes : a resource book for students / Jennifer Jenkins.
      p. cm. — (Routledge English language introductions series)
    Includes bibliographical references and index.
    1. English language—Variation—English-speaking countries. 2. English
language—Variation—Commonwealth countries. 3. English language—Variation—Foreign
countries. 4. English language—English-speaking countries. 5. English
language—Commonwealth countries. 6. English language—Foreign countries. I. Title. II.
Series.

PE2751 .J46 2003
427—dc21
                          2002036788

ISBN 10: 0-415-25805-7 (hbk)
ISBN 10: 0-415-25806-5 (pbk)

ISBN 13: 978-0-415-25805-0 (hbk)
ISBN 13: 978-0-415-25806-7 (pbk)

HOW TO USE THIS BOOK

The Routledge English Language Introductions are 'flexi-texts' that you can use to suit your own style of study. The books are divided into four sections:

A Introduction – sets out the key concepts for the area of study. The units of this section take you step-by-step through the foundational terms and ideas, carefully providing you with an initial toolkit for your own study. By the end of the section, you will have a good overview of the whole field.

B Development – adds to your knowledge and builds on the key ideas already introduced. Units in this section might also draw together several areas of interest. By the end of this section, you will already have a good and fairly detailed grasp of the field, and will be ready to undertake your own exploration and thinking.

C Exploration – provides examples of language data and guides you through your own investigation of the field. The units in this section will be more open-ended and exploratory, and you will be encouraged to try out your ideas and think for yourself, using your newly acquired knowledge.

D Extension – offers you the chance to compare your expertise with key readings in the area. These are taken from the work of important writers, and are provided with guidance and questions for your further thought.

You can read this book like a traditional text-book, 'vertically' straight through from beginning to end. This will take you comprehensively through the broad field of study. However, the Routledge English Language Introductions have been carefully designed so that you can read them in another dimension, 'horizontally' across the numbered units. For example, Units A1, A2, A3 and so on correspond with Units B1, B2, B3, and with Units C1, C2, C3 and D1, D2, D3, and so on. Reading A5, B5, C5, D5 will take you rapidly from the key concepts of a specific area, to a level of expertise in that precise area, all with a very close focus. You can match your way of reading with the best way that you work.

The Glossarial Index at the end, together with the suggestions for further reading at the end of Section D, will help to keep you orientated. Each textbook has a supporting website with extra commentary, suggestions, additional material and support for teachers and students.

WORLD ENGLISHES

The *World Englishes* volume has eight units, each following the above four-part structure. Section A units introduce the key topics in World Englishes from the sixteenth century to the present time and beyond. Section B develops these issues with additional detail and discussion. Section C offers opportunities for further study and your own research, by following through the latest work and controversies in the field. Finally, the readings in Section D take up all the strands throughout the book, and are accompanied by suggestions for further study and discussion.

The eight horizontal strands begin with the historical, social and political context (in A1, B1, C1 and D1). Strand 2 explores pidgins and creoles; strand 3 follows the debate about English today; strand 4 investigates variation in Englishes across the world. The units in A5, B5, C5 and D5 examine the issue of standardisation; strand 6 explores English as an international language; strand 7 focuses on Asian and European Englishes; and the final strand looks to the future of English and Englishes in the world. Further material and activities can also be found on the website which accompanies the book: http//:www.routledge.com/textbooks/0415258065

CONTENTS

CONTENTS **CROSS-REFERENCED**

FIGURES

TABLES

ACKNOWLEDGEMENTS

D. Crystal, *English as a Global Language* © Cambridge University Press, 1997.

J. Fishman (ed.), *Handbook of Language and Ethnic Identity* © Oxford University Press Inc., 1999.

L. Hinton, 'Trading tongues: loss of heritage languages in the United States', *English Today* 15/4 © Cambridge University Press, 1999.

A. Pennycook, *English and the Discourse of Colonialism*, extracts from pages 133–44 © Routledge, 1998. Reprinted by permission of Taylor & Francis.

B. Payton, 'English spoken here, by African Americans', *The Oakland Tribune*, 21 December 1996. Reprinted by permission of Brenda Payton.

N.A. Lewis, 'Jesse Jackson ridicules acceptance of Black English', *International Herald Tribune*, 24–25 December 1996, originally appeared in *The New York Times*. Reprinted by permission of The New York Times Syndicate, Paris.

T. Golden, 'Oakland scratches plan to teach black English', *The New York Times*, 14 January 1997. Reprinted by permission of The New York Times Agency.

Editorial unsigned (in line with editorial policy), *The Economist*, 4 January 1997 © The Economist Newspaper Limited, London, 1997.

Charles Alobwede d'Epie, 'Banning Pidgin English in Cameroon', *English Today* 14/1 © Cambridge University Press, 1998.

P. Chamoiseau, *School Days*, Granta Books, 1998.

B. Kachru (ed.), *The Other Tongue: English Across Cultures*. Copyright © 1982, 1992 by the Board of Trustees of the University of Illinois. Used with permission of the University of Illinois Press.

T. McArthur, *The English Languages* © Cambridge University Press, 1998.

M. Modiano, 'International English in the global village', *English Today* 15/2 © Cambridge University Press, 1999.

M. Modiano, 'Standard English(es) and educational practices for the world's lingua franca', *English Today* 15/4 © Cambridge University Press, 1999.

B. Kachru, 'Liberation linguistics and the Quirk concern', *English Today* 25 © Cambridge University Press, 1991.

H. Widdowson, 'Pragmatics and the pedagogic competence of language teachers', in T. Sebbage and S. Sebbage (eds) *Proceedings of the 4th International NELLE Conference*. Reproduced by permission of H.G. Widdowson.

H. Widdowson, 'The ownership of English', *Annual Conference Report* 1993, IATEFL. Reproduced by permission of H.G. Widdowson.

A. Maley, 'I so blur, you know', *IATEFL Newsletter 1997*.

C. Achebe, *Morning Yet On Creation Day*, copyright © 1975 by Chinua Achebe. Used by permission of Doubleday, a division of Random House, Inc.

Ngũgĩ wa Thiong'o, *Decolonising the Mind: The Politics of Language in African Literature*, James Currey, 1986.

P. Trudgill, 'Standard English: what it isn't', in Bex and Watts (eds) *Standard English*, Routledge, 1999. Reprinted by permission of Taylor & Francis.

L. Milroy, 'Bad Grammar is Slovenly', from L. Bauer and P. Trudgill (eds) *Language Myths*, Penguin, 1998. Copyright © Laurie Bauer & Peter Trudgill, 1998.

A. Lee, 'English to get English lessons', *The Straits Times*, 15 May 2001.

D. Crystal, *Cambridge Encyclopedia of the English Language* © Cambridge University Press, 1995.

M. Modiano, 'International English in the global village', *English Today* 15/2 © Cambridge University Press, 1999.

L. Todd, 'Global English', *English Today* 15/2 © Cambridge University Press, 1999.

A.S. Kaye, 'On the term "international English"', *English Today* 15/2 © Cambridge University Press, 1999.

M. Modiano, 'Standard English(es) and educational practices for the world's lingua franca', *English Today* 15/4 © Cambridge University Press, 1999.

D. Li, 'Incorporating L1 pragmatic norms and cultural values in L2: developing English language curriculum for EIL in the Asia-Pacific Region', in *Asian Englishes* 1/1 © David Li, 1998.

U. Ammon, 'Towards more fairness in international English: linguistic rights of non-native speakers?', in R. Phillipson (ed.) *Rights to Language: Equity, Power and Education* © Lawrence Erlbaum Associates, 2000.

A number of people far and near have contributed to this book in various ways. First all those who gave me food for thought through discussion (even if we did not always agree) and by providing useful material – especially Janina Brutt-Griffler, Clare Canton, Jenny Cheshire, Simon Elmes, Tony Hung, Ho Wah Kam, Thiru Kandiah, Constant Leung, Masaki Oda, Anne Pakir, Robert Phillipson, Edwin Thumboo, Chris Tribble, Henry Widdowson and Ann Williams. Special thanks to the second year undergraduates at King's College, London who studied World Englishes with me in 2001/2 and provided extensive feedback on the first draft: Natasha Ahuja, Chris Babidge, Laura Bolt, Emma Brown, Simon Felstein, Mark Gilbert, Rasheed Hassan, Beth Houghton, Mel Huntly, Hui Lai Ching (Chrissie), Becky Manley, Andy Mercer, Michelle O'Brien, Kristina Olsson, Bryony Rust and Huby Saroukhanoff. The book also benefited from the insights and constructive criticism of several readers, particularly Mark Sebba, Barbara Seidlhofer and Richard Watts. My thanks, too, to Susan Fearn and her many bilingual colleagues in the Language Section of the BBC World Service who gave generously of their time. I am greatly indebted to Louisa Semlyen, Christy Kirkpatrick and Liz O'Donnell at Routledge for their constant flexibility and patience, and to Ron Carter and Peter Stockwell, the series editors, who provided encouragement and useful comments throughout, and much practical help in the final stages. The writing of this book coincided with my move from the Language Centre to the Department of Education and Professional Studies. I would like to express my appreciation to colleagues in both departments for their support during this period, and especially to Sara Garcia-Peralta, Tony Thorne and Deryn Watson. Finally, as always, my immense gratitude to my family, John, Harriet and Nick. The book is dedicated to the memory of my husband, John, who died shortly before it went to press.

Every effort has been made to obtain permission to reproduce copyright material. If any proper acknowledgement has not been made, we would invite copyright holders to inform us of the oversight.

SECTION A

INTRODUCTION
KEY TOPICS IN WORLD ENGLISHES

THE HISTORICAL, SOCIAL AND POLITICAL CONTEXT

Introduction to World Englishes

In the period between the end of the reign of Queen Elizabeth I in 1603 and the later years of the reign of Queen Elizabeth II at the start of the twenty-first century, the number of speakers of English increased from a mere five to seven million to somewhere between one-and-a-half and two billion. Whereas the English language was spoken in the mid-sixteenth century only by a relatively small group of mother-tongue speakers born and bred within the shores of the British Isles, it is now spoken in almost every country of the world, with its majority speakers being those for whom it is not a first language.

Currently, there are approximately seventy-five territories where English is spoken either as a first language (L1), or as an official (i.e. **institutionalised**) second language (L2) in fields such as government, law and education. Crystal (1997) lists these territories, along with their approximate numbers of English speakers, as follows (those countries where the variety of English spoken is a pidgin or creole are indicated by an asterisk):

Table A1.1 English-speaking territories

Territory	Usage estimate		Population (1995)
	L1	L2	
American Samoa	2,000	56,000	58,000
Antigua and Barbuda*	61,000	2,000	64,000
Australia	15,316,000	2,084,000	18,025,000
Bahamas*	250,000	25,000	276,000
Bangladesh		3,100,000	120,093,000
Barbados*	265,000		265,000
Belize*	135,000	30,000	216,000
Bermuda	60,000		61,000
Bhutan		60,000	1,200,000
Botswana		620,000	1,549,000
British Virgin Islands*	17,000		18,000
Brunei	10,000	104,000	291,000
Cameroon*		6,600,000	13,233,000
Canada	19,700,000	6,000,000	29,463,000
Cayman Islands	29,000		29,000
Cook Islands	1,000	2,000	19,000
Dominica	3,000	12,000	72,000
Fiji	5,000	160,000	791,000
The Gambia*		33,000	1,115,000
Ghana*		1,153,000	16,472,000
Gibraltar	25,000	2,000	28,000
Grenada*	91,000		92,000
Guam	56,000	92,000	149,000
Guyana*	700,000	30,000	770,000
Hong Kong	125,000	1,860,000	6,205,000
India	320,000	37,000,000	935,744,000
Ireland	3,400,000	190,000	3,590,000
Jamaica*	2,400,000	50,000	2,520,000
Kenya		2,576,000	28,626,000

Table A1.1 (*continued*)

Territory	Usage estimate		Population (1995)
Kiribati		20,000	80,000
Lesotho		488,000	2,050,000
Liberia*	60,000	2,000,000	2,380,000
Malawi		517,000	9,939,000
Malaysia	375,000	5,984,000	19,948,000
Malta	8,000	86,000	370,000
Marshall Islands		28,000	56,000
Mauritius	2,000	167,000	1,128,000
Micronesia	4,000	15,000	105,000
Montserrat*	11,000		11,000
Namibia	13,000	300,000	1,651,000
Nauru	800	9,400	10,000
Nepal		5,927,000	20,093,000
New Zealand	3,396,000	150,000	3,568,000
Nigeria*		43,000,000	95,434,000
Northern Marianas*	3,000	50,000	58,000
Pakistan		16,000,000	140,497,000
Palau	500	16,300	17,000
Papua New Guinea*	120,000	2,800,000	4,302,000
Philippines	15,000	36,400,000	70,011,000
Puerto Rico	110,000	1,746,000	3,725,000
Rwanda		24,000	7,855,000
St Kitts and Nevis*	39,000		39,000
St Lucia*	29,000	22,000	143,000
St Vincent and the Grenadines*	111,000		112,000
Seychelles	2,000	11,000	75,000
Sierra Leone*	450,000	3,830,000	4,509,000
Singapore	300,000	1,046,000	2,989,000
Solomon Islands*	2,000	135,000	382,000
South Africa	3,600,000	10,000,000	41,465,000
Sri Lanka	10,000	1,850,000	18,090,000
Suriname*	258,000	150,000	430,000
Swaziland		40,000	913,000
Tanzania		3,000,000	28,072,000
Tonga		30,000	100,000
Trinidad and Tobago*	1,200,000		1,265,000
Tuvalu		600	9,000
Uganda		2,000,000	18,659,000
United Kingdom	56,990,000	1,100,000	58,586,000
UK Islands (Channel Islands, Isle of Man)	217,000		218,000
United States	226,710,000	30,000,000	263,057,000
US Virgin Islands*	79,000	10,000	98,000
Vanuatu*	2,000	160,000	168,000
Western Samoa	1,000	86,000	166,000
Zambia	50,000	1,000,000	9,456,000
Zimbabwe	250,000	3,300,000	11,261,000
Other dependencies	18,000	12,000	30,000

Source: Crystal (1997: 60)

The total numbers of L1 and L2 English speakers amount here to 337,407,300 and 235,351,300 respectively, and together these speakers constitute almost a third of the total population of the above territories (2,024,614,000 in total). However, as Crystal (1997: 61) points out, the L2 total is conservative:

> The total of 235 million . . . does not give the whole picture. For many countries, no estimates are available. And in others (notably India, Pakistan, Nigeria, Ghana, Malaysia, Philippines and Tanzania, which had a combined total of over 1,300 million people in 1995) even a small percentage increase in the number of speakers thought to have a reasonable (rather than a fluent) command of English would considerably expand the L2 grand total.

He goes on to conclude that the widely accepted figure of 350 million L2 speakers is likely to be accurate.

The number of L2 speakers discussed here also excludes one other important grouping: L2 speakers for whom English has no official function within their countries. Until recently, these speakers of English, who probably number around one billion, and whose proficiency levels range from reasonable to bilingual competence, were described as speakers of **English as a Foreign Language** (**EFL**) to distinguish them from L2 speakers for whom English serves country-internal functions, that is, speakers of **English as a Second Language** (**ESL**). Since the mid-1990s, it has become increasingly common to find EFL speakers referred to as speakers of **English as an International** Language (**EIL**) or, most recently, as speakers of **English as a *Lingua Franca*** (**ELF**), reflecting the fact that these English users from, for example, Europe and Japan, speak English more frequently as a contact language among themselves than with native speakers of English.

A further complication arises from the difficulty in categorising World English speakers as ENL (English as a Native Language), ESL or EFL/EIL. In a number of the so-called ESL countries such as Singapore and Nigeria, many English speakers learn the language either as their first language (L1) or as one of two or more equivalent languages within their bi- or multilingual repertoires. Again, there are so-called EFL/EIL countries such as the Netherlands and Scandinavia where English is increasingly being used for *intra*national (i.e. country internal) purposes rather than purely as a foreign or international language.

A theme which recurs throughout the book and which it will therefore be useful to highlight from the start, is that of value judgements of these different Englishes. The negative **attitudes** which persist today towards certain varieties of English have their roots in the past and, especially, in the two dispersals of English (see next section). The British establishment still harbours the view of the superiority of British over American English. For example, in launching the British Council's English 2000 project in March 1995, Prince Charles was famously reported in the British press as follows:

> The Prince of Wales highlighted the threat to "proper" English from the spread of American vernacular yesterday as he launched a campaign to preserve the language as world leader. He described American English as "very corrupting" and emphasised

the need to maintain the quality of language, after giving his backing to the British Council's English 2000 project [. . .] Speaking after the launch, Prince Charles elaborated on his view of the American influence. "People tend to invent all sorts of nouns and verbs, and make words that shouldn't be. I think we have to be a bit careful, otherwise the whole thing can get rather a mess."

(The Times, 24 March 1995)

It should by now be clear that there is scope for substantial disagreement as to whether the metamorphosis of *English* into *World Englishes* is a positive or negative phenomenon. As can be seen from the previous page, the use of English around the world has not proved uncontroversial or even, necessarily, beneficial. One of the purposes of this book, then, is to approach the controversies surrounding World Englishes from a wide range of perspectives in order to enable readers to draw their own conclusions.

The two dispersals of English

We can speak of two dispersals, or **diasporas**, of English. The **first diaspora**, initially involving the migration of around 25,000 people from the south and east of England primarily to America and Australia, resulted in new mother-tongue varieties of English. The **second diaspora**, involving the colonisation of Asia and Africa led, on the other hand, to the development of a number of second-language varieties, often referred to as 'New Englishes'. This is to some extent a simplification for, as was pointed out above, it is not always an easy matter to categorise the world's Englishes so neatly. And, as we also noted, the whole issue was further complicated in the twentieth century by the dramatic increase in the use of English first as a foreign and subsequently as an international language (respectively EFL and EIL).

The first dispersal: English is transported to the 'new world'

The first diaspora involved relatively large-scale migrations of mother-tongue English speakers from England, Scotland and Ireland predominantly to North America, Australia and New Zealand. The English dialects which travelled with them gradually developed into the American and Antipodean Englishes we know today. The varieties of English spoken in modern North America and Australasia are not identical with the English of their early colonisers, but have altered in response to the changed and changing sociolinguistic contexts in which the migrants found themselves. For example, their vocabulary rapidly expanded through contact with the indigenous Indian, Aboriginal or Maori populations in the lands which they colonised, to incorporate words such as Amerindian *papoose*, *moccasin* and *igloo*.

Walter Raleigh's expedition of 1584 to **America** was the earliest from the British Isles to the New World, though it did not result in a permanent settlement. The voyagers landed on the coast of North Carolina near Roanoke Island, but fell into conflict with the native Indian population and then mysteriously disappeared altogether, leaving behind only a palisade and the letters CRO carved on a tree. In 1607, the first permanent colonists arrived and settled in Jamestown, Virginia (named respectively after James I and Elizabeth 1, the Virgin Queen), to be followed in 1620 by a group of

Puritans and others on the *Mayflower*. The latter group landed further north, settling at what is now Plymouth, Massachusetts, in New England. Both settlements spread rapidly and attracted further migrants during the years that followed. Because of their different linguistic backgrounds, there were immediately certain differences in the accents of the two groups of settlers. Those in Virginia came mainly from the west of England and brought with them their characteristic rhotic /r/ and voiced /s/ sounds. On the other hand, those who settled in New England were mainly from the east of England, where these features were not a part of the local accent.

During the seventeenth century, English spread to southern parts of America and the Caribbean as a result of the slave trade. Slaves were transported from West Africa and exchanged, on the American coast and in the Caribbean, for sugar and rum. The Englishes which developed among the slaves and between them and their captors were initially contact pidgin languages but, with their use as mother tongues following the birth of the next generation, they developed into creoles (see strand 2). Then, in the eighteenth century, there was large-scale immigration from Northern Ireland, initially to the coastal area around Philadelphia, but quickly moving south and west. After the Declaration of American Independence in 1776, many Loyalists (the British settlers who had supported the British government) left for Canada.

Meanwhile, comparable events were soon to take place in Australia, New Zealand and South Africa (see Gordon and Sudbury 2002 on all three). James Cook 'discovered' **Australia** in 1770, landing in modern-day Queensland and the First Fleet landed in New South Wales in 1788. From then until the ending of transportation in 1852, around 160,000 convicts were transported to Australia from Britain and Ireland, and from the 1820s large numbers of free settlers also began to arrive. The largest proportion of settlers came from London and the south-east, although in the case of the convicts, they were not necessarily born there. Others originated in regions as widely dispersed as, for example, south-west England, Lancashire, Scotland and Ireland. The result was a situation of **dialect mixing** which was further influenced by the indigenous aboriginal languages.

New Zealand was first settled by European traders in the 1790s, though there was no official colony until after the British–Maori Treaty of Waitangi in 1840. Immigrants arrived in three stages: in the 1840s and 1850s from Britain, in the 1860s from Australia and Ireland, and from 1870 to 1885 from the UK, when their number included a considerable proportion of Scots. As in Australia, there was a dialect-mix situation, this time subject to a strong Maori influence especially in terms of vocabulary.

Although **South Africa** was colonised by the Dutch from the 1650s, the British did not arrive until 1795 when they annexed the Cape, and did not begin to settle in large numbers until 1820. The majority of Cape settlers originated in southern England, though there were also sizeable groups from Ireland and Scotland. Further settlement occurred in the 1850s in the Natal region, this time from the Midlands, Yorkshire and Lancashire. From 1822, when English was declared the official language, it was also learnt as a second language by blacks and Afrikaans speakers (many of whom were mixed-race) and, from the 1860s, by Indian immigrants to the territory.

The second dispersal: English is transported to Asia and Africa

The second diaspora took place at various points during the eighteenth and nineteenth centuries in very different ways and with very different results from those of the first diaspora.

The history of English in colonial Africa has two distinct patterns depending on whether we are talking about West or East Africa. English in **West Africa** is linked to the slave trade and the development of pidgin and creole languages. From the late fifteenth century onwards, British traders travelled at different times to and from the various coastal territories of West Africa, primarily Gambia, Sierra Leone, Ghana, Nigeria and Cameroon. However, there was no major British settlement in the area and, instead, English was employed as a *lingua franca* both among the indigenous population (there being hundreds of local languages), and between these people and the British traders. English has subsequently gained official status in the above five countries, and some of the pidgins and creoles which developed from English contact, such as Krio (Sierra Leone) and Cameroon Pidgin, are now spoken by large numbers of people, especially as a second language.

East Africa's relationship with English followed a different path. The countries of Kenya, Uganda, Tanzania, Malawi, Zambia and Zimbabwe were extensively settled by British colonists from the 1850s on, following the expeditions of a number of explorers, most famously, those of David Livingstone. These six countries became British protectorates or colonies at various points between the late nineteenth and early twentieth centuries, with English playing an important role in the major institutions such as government, education and the law. From the early 1960s, the six countries one after another, achieved independence. English remains the official language in Uganda, Zambia, Zimbabwe and (along with Chewa) Malawi, and has large numbers of second language speakers in these places, although Swahili is more likely than English to be used as a *lingua franca* in Uganda, as it is in Kenya and Tanzania.

English was introduced to the sub-continent of **South Asia** (India, Bangladesh, Pakistan, Sri Lanka, Nepal and Bhutan) during the second half of the eighteenth century although, as McCrum *et al.* (1992: 356) point out, 'the English have had a toehold on the Indian subcontinent since the early 1600s, when the newly formed East India Company established settlements in Madras, Calcutta, and later Bombay'. The company's influence increased during the eighteenth century and culminated in a period of British sovereignty (known as 'the Raj') in India lasting from 1765 to 1947. A key point was the Macaulay 'Minute' of 1835, which proposed the introduction in India of an English educational system. From that time, English became the language of the Indian education system. Even today, when Hindi is the official language of India, English is an 'associate official language' used alongside Hindi as a neutral *lingua franca*, and has undergone a process of Indianisation in which it has developed a distinctive national character comparable to that of American and Australian English (see C7).

British influence in **South-East Asia** and the **South Pacific** began in the late eighteenth century as a result of the seafaring expeditions of James Cook and others. The main territories involved were Singapore, Malaysia, Hong Kong and the Philippines. Papua New Guinea was also, for a short time a British protectorate

(1884 to 1920), and provides one of the world's best examples of an English-based pidgin, **Tok Pisin**.

Stamford Raffles is the name most closely associated with British colonialism in Southeast Asia. An administrator of the British East India Company, he played an important role in the founding of Singapore as part of the British colonial empire in 1819. Other major British centres were founded around the same time in Malaysia (e.g. Penang and Malacca), and Hong Kong was added in 1842. After the Spanish–American War at the end of the nineteenth century, the US was granted sovereignty over the **Philippines** which, although gaining independence in 1946, have retained a strong American-English influence.

In recent years, the use of English has increased in Singapore and a local variety has begun to emerge. On the other hand, the use of English declined in **Malaysia** as a result of the adoption of the local language, **Bahasa Malaysia**, as the national language and medium of education when Malaysia gained independence in 1957. While still obligatory as a subject of study at school, English was regarded as useful only for international communication. However, there has recently been a change of policy, with English-medium education being reintroduced from 2003. And even before this development, the situation was complex with, for example, radio stations using English and Bahasa together for a local audience (Sebba, personal communication). Nowadays English is also learnt in other countries in neighbouring areas, most notably Taiwan, Japan and Korea, the latter two having recently begun to consider the possibility of making English an official second language.

Between 1750 and 1900 these English-speaking settlements of the second diaspora all underwent three similar and major changes. Up until 1750, as Strevens (1992: 29) has pointed out, the British settlers thought of themselves as 'English speakers from Britain who happened to be living overseas'. After this time, Strevens continues:

> First, the populations of the overseas NS English-speaking settlements greatly increased in size and became states with governments – albeit colonial governments – and with a growing sense of separate identity, which soon extended to the flavour of the English they used. Second, in the United States first of all, but later in Australia and elsewhere, the colonies began to take their independence from Britain, which greatly reinforced the degree of linguistic difference [. . .] And third, as the possessions stabilized and prospered, so quite large numbers of people, being non-native speakers of English, had to learn to use the language in order to survive, or to find employment with the governing class.

These Englishes have much in common, through their shared history and their affinity with either British or American English. But there is also much that is unique to each variety, particularly in terms of their accents, but also in their idiomatic uses of vocabulary, their grammars and their discourse strategies.

Since 1945, most of the remaining colonies have become independent states, with English often being retained in order to provide various internal functions and/or to serve as a neutral *lingua franca*.

THE ORIGINS OF PIDGINS AND CREOLES

Definitions and development

In an article describing the development of English during the colonial period, Leith (1996) identifies three types of English colony:

> In the first type, exemplified by America and Australia, substantial settlement by first-language speakers of English displaced the precolonial population. In the second, typified by Nigeria, sparser colonial settlements maintained the precolonial population in sub-jection and allowed a proportion of them access to learning English as a second or additional language. There is yet a third type, exemplified by the **Caribbean** islands of Barbados and Jamaica. Here, a precolonial population was *replaced* by new labour from elsewhere, principally West Africa.
>
> (Leith 1996: 181–2)

The first two types of English colony were the theme of A1. In A2 and its further strands, we move on to look at the third type, whose linguistic consequences, as Leith points out, are the most complex of all: pidgins and creoles.

Until very recently, pidgins and creoles were regarded, especially by non-linguists, as inferior, 'bad' languages (and often not as 'languages' at all). In the later years of the twentieth century, linguists working in the field of second-language acquisition began to realise what could be discovered about first and second-language learning from the way pidgins and creoles developed; meanwhile linguists working in the field of sociolinguistics began to appreciate the extent to which these languages reflect and promote the lifestyles of their speakers.

Nevertheless, as will be clear from the text on Cameroon Pidgin English in D2, this view is not by any means universal, even today, and even among linguists themselves. McArthur quotes from a review in *The Economist* of 11 May 1996 of the psycholinguist Aitchison's book *The Seeds of Speech*, in which she argues that pidgins are illuminations of linguistic evolution. This is how the (anonymous) reviewer responds:

> An examination of Tok Pisin [a variety of pidgin English spoken widely in Papua New Guinea], Ms Aitchison claims, illuminates the general story of linguistic evolution. But her claim is arguably mistaken. Pidgins and creoles do not clarify that story because they do not recapitulate that process. They are, instead, examples of a differ-ent process, one that can begin only from an already evolved language. For pidgins are corruptions – in the sense of simplifying adaptations – of existing languages. They offer evidence of degenerative change in existing languages under certain pressures, not of how language evolved . . . [P]idgins [are] simple, clumsy languages incapable of nuance, detail, abstraction and precision.
>
> (McArthur 1998: 161)

This is not a very long way from views such as that expressed by a Monsieur Bertrand-Boconde in 1849, by coincidence quoted in an earlier book of Aitchison's:

> It is clear that people used to expressing themselves with a rather simple language
> cannot easily elevate their intelligence to the genius of a European language . . . the
> varied expressions acquired during so many centuries of civilization dropped their
> perfection, to adapt to ideas being born and to barbarous forms of language of half-
> savage peoples.
>
> (Quoted in Aitchison 1991: 183)

While there is still a fair degree of disagreement among the wider population and
even among linguists as to the relative merits of pidgins and creoles, there is close
agreement as to basic definitions of these languages. The sociolinguist, Wardhaugh,
for example, defines them as follows:

> A *pidgin* is a language with no native speakers: it is no one's first language but is a
> *contact language*. That is, it is the product of a multilingual situation in which those
> who wish to communicate must find or improvise a simple language system that
> will enable them to do so. [. . .] In contrast to a pidgin, a **creole**, is often defined
> as a pidgin that has become the first language of a new generation of speakers [. . .]
> A creole, therefore, is a 'normal' language in almost every sense.
>
> (Wardhaugh 2002: 60–1)

A pidgin arises in the first place to fulfil restricted communication needs between
people who do not share a common language. This happened in the past mainly (though
not exclusively) as a result of European expansion into Africa and Asia during the
colonial period, with pidgins arising as a result of contact between speakers of a
'dominant' European language and speakers of mutually unintelligible indigenous
African and Asian languages.

In the earlier stages of contact, communication tends to be restricted to basic trans-
actions for which a small vocabulary is sufficient and in which there is little need for
grammatical **redundancy**. For example, Todd (1990: 2) provides the example of the
English phrase 'the <u>two</u> big newspaper<u>s</u>'. Here, the plural marking -s on 'newspapers'
is redundant, since plurality is established by the word 'two'. In the French equivalent, 'le<u>s</u> deux grand<u>s</u> journ<u>aux</u>', there is still more redundancy (the marking of plurality not only on the word 'journaux' but also on 'les' and 'grands'). Cameroon pidgin,
on the other hand, eliminates redundancy by rendering the phrase as 'di <u>tu</u> big pepa'.

In theory, a creole arises when the children of pidgin speakers use their parents'
pidgin language as the mother tongue. In other words, a creole has native speakers.
The simple structure of the pidgin is the starting point for the creole, but now that it
is being acquired as a first language, its vocabulary expands and its grammar increases
in complexity so that it is capable of expressing the entire human experience of its
mother-tongue speakers. In practice, however, there are pidgin languages, such as
Cameroon pidgin and some varieties of Tok Pisin, that have developed in this way
without any intervention from child L1 learners.

In multilingual areas where a pidgin is used as a *lingua franca* for speakers of a
number of mutually unintelligible languages, it is likely to develop over time and be
used for an increasing number of functions. In this case, the early pidgin goes through
a series of stages, becoming progressively more complex over one or two generations.
This process is outlined in *Type 3* opposite. However, **creolisation** (the development

Type 1	Type 2	Type 3
Jargon	Jargon	Jargon
↓	↓	↓
↓	Stabilized Pidgin	Stabilized Pidgin
↓	↓	↓
↓	↓	Expanded Pidgin
↓	↓	↓
Creole	Creole	Creole
e.g.: Hawaiian Creole English	Torres Straits Broken	New Guinea Tok Pisin

Figure A2.1 Pidgin lifespan
Source: Mühlhäusler (1997: 9)

of a pidgin into a creole) can occur at any point in a pidgin's lifespan, as shown in
Type 1 and Type 2.

A final stage occurs if the creole continues to move in the direction of the
standard dominant language, in other words, to become 'decreolised'. The process of
decreolisation occurs when a creole comes into extensive contact with the dominant language as is the case, for example, with **African American Vernacular English**
(**AAVE**, commonly known nowadays as **Ebonics** – see C2). On the other hand,
among younger speakers especially, the decreolised creole may show signs of moving
back towards the creole, as is the case with the British-based patois known as 'London
Jamaican' (see C2).

There are several hypotheses as to the origin of the terms 'pidgin'. Romaine (1988:
12–13) lists five:

❑ a Chinese corruption of the English word 'business' as in 'gospidgin man' ('god-
    business-man') i.e. priest
❑ a Chinese corruption of the Portuguese word 'ocupação' ('business')
❑ from the Hebrew word 'pidjom' (meaning 'barter', 'exchange', 'trade')
❑ from the word 'pidian' (meaning 'people') in Yago, a South American Indian
    language spoken in an area colonised by Britain
❑ from the two Chinese characters 'pei' and 'ts'in', meaning 'paying money'.

Aitchison (1991) suggests that these similar terms may have originated independently
in different places and then reinforced each other, merging into the term 'pidgin' as
we know it. Mühlhäusler (1997), on the other hand, rules out all but the first two
as likely origins of the word. The origin of the term 'creole' is equally obscure. Many
authorities believe that it comes from the Portuguese word 'criar' meaning 'to nurse,
breed, nourish, bring up'. But, as Mühlhäusler (1997: 6) points out, the original meaning of the word 'crioulo' was 'white man or woman originating from the colonies',

and it has subsequently acquired further meanings such as 'slave born in a colony' and 'locally-bred, non-indigenous animal'.

Theories of origin

Many theories have been advanced to explain how pidgin and creole languages arose in the first place, and there is still no final agreement. Here there is space for no more than a brief summary of some of the more prominent theories broadly following Todd's (1990) account.

The earliest theory of pidgin origins to be advanced was that of the 'primitive native'. This belief is reflected in the quote from Bertrand-Boconde on p. 10. The attitude expressed is clearly naïve and no longer taken seriously by the majority of linguists, although it probably still represents the popular view.

Most other theories can be divided into three groups depending on whether they regard pidgins as having a single origin (**monogenesis**) or independent origin (**polygenesis**), or as deriving from universal strategies. Of the theories outlined below, the first two are polygenetic, the third monogenetic, and the final two universal:

1   The independent parallel development theory

According to this theory, pidgins and creoles arose and developed independently, but developed in similar ways because they shared a common linguistic ancestor (European languages and hence an Indo-European origin) and, in the case of the Atlantic pidgins, they also shared West African languages. In addition, pidgins and creoles were formed in similar social and physical conditions.

2   The nautical jargon theory

This theory is based on the fact that European ships' crews were composed of men from a range of language backgrounds and therefore had to develop a common language in order to communicate with each other. According to the nautical jargon theory, the sailors' *lingua franca* was then passed on to the African and Asian peoples with whom they came into contact. The nautical jargon formed a nucleus for the various pidgins, which were subsequently expanded in line with their learners' mother tongues. Evidence for this theory is provided by the nautical element in all pidgins and creoles with European lexicons (e.g. the words 'hivim', 'kapsait' and 'haisim' meaning heave, capsize and hoist).

3   The theory of monogenesis and relexification

According to this theory, all European-based pidgins and creoles derive ultimately from one proto-pidgin source, a Portuguese pidgin that was used in the world's trade routes during the fifteenth and sixteenth centuries. This pidgin is thought to have derived, in turn, from an earlier *lingua franca*, Sabir, used by the crusaders and traders in the Mediterranean in the middle ages. It was then, the theory goes, relexified by Portuguese in the fifteenth century. In other words, Portuguese lexis was introduced into Sabir grammar. This Portuguese version of Sabir would then have been used by the Portuguese in the fifteenth century when they sailed along the coast of West Africa, and would have been the first European language acquired by the indigenous population. Subsequently Portuguese influence decreased in the area and the pidgin began to be used increasingly in contact situations in which the dominant language could be English, Spanish, French or Dutch. Evidence for this theory is provided by the many linguistic similarities, both lexical and syntactic, between present-day Portuguese pidgins and creoles, and pidgins and creoles related to other European languages. For example, all pidgin and creole Englishes have a form of the Portuguese 'saber' meaning 'to know' (e.g. 'savi', 'sabi') and of 'pequeno' meaning 'little' or 'offspring' (e.g. 'pikin', 'pikinini').

4   The baby-talk theory

This theory arose because of similarities that were identified between the early speech of children and the forms in certain pidgins, such as the large proportion of content words, the lack of structural words, the lack of morphological change, and the approximation of the standard pronunciation. It was also suggested that speakers of the dominant language, in using what is known as **foreigner talk** (simplified speech) with L2 speakers, themselves promoted the use of this type of speech among the latter.

5   A synthesis

Todd (1990) takes the 'baby-talk' theory much further in her proposal of a 'synthesis'. She argues that instead of searching for a common origin in the past, we should approach the concept of common origin from a different perspective altogether: by seeking universal patterns of linguistic behaviour in contact situations. In her view, pidgins and creoles are alike because languages and **simplification processes** are alike. She cites as evidence the fact that speakers from different L1s simplify their language in very similar ways, be they children learning their L1, adults learning an L2, and even proficient speakers employing ellipsis (as in informal speech, e.g. 'Got a light?', creators of newspaper headlines, e.g. 'Air crash – fifty dead', and so on). In particular, Todd argues, these speakers all appear to have an innate ability to simplify by means of redundancy reduction when communication of the message is more critical than the quality of the language used. This suggests to Todd that there are inherent universal constraints on language.

   The synthesis approach has the advantage of being able to account for the existence of pidgins in different types of contact situation, and both the independent origin of some pidgins and the related origin of others. This is because in each case people have responded to what Todd calls 'an innate behavioural blueprint'. Although it is not possible to prove this theory, given that it focuses on mental properties, Todd provides substantial evidence in its support:

❏   all children from all L1s go through the same stages in the mastery of speech (babble → intonational patterns of the speech community → individual words → short combinations of words)

❏   children produce regular patterns across L1s which are not the same as adult norms, e.g. negator + sentence as in 'No I sit'

❏   this type of simplified language is used in all speech communities by proficient to less proficient speakers, e.g. by parents to children, native speakers to non-fluent non-native speakers.

The fact that languages are simplified in similar ways suggests that all languages have a **simple register**, but that children swiftly move on from this register because of pressure to conform to the adult version of the language. Children of pidgin speakers, on the other hand, did not have this possibility, since there were no speakers of the non-simple register available to provide input. Hence, these children drew on their **innate bioprogram** (the genetic program for language that all children are believed to be born with and which they adapt to the language they hear around them) to transform the pidgins into creoles with minimum interference from adult language. In other words, this theory, of which the strongest case is provided by **Bickerton's** (1981, 1984) **Language Bioprogram Hypothesis**, is simultaneously monogenetic and polygenetic: monogenetic in that creoles developed from pidgins by means of a single linguistic bioprogram common to all human beings, and polygenetic because of their independent origin in separate locations (see also Sebba 1997: 77–8, 95–7).

A3 WHO SPEAKS ENGLISH TODAY?

ENL, ESL and EFL

The spread of English around the world is often discussed in terms of three distinct groups of users, those who speak English respectively as:

- ❏ a native language (ENL)
- ❏ a second language (ESL)
- ❏ a foreign language (EFL).

When we come to look more closely at this three-way categorisation and, especially, when we consider the most influential models and descriptions of English use, we will find that the categories have become fuzzy at the edges and that it is increasingly difficult to classify speakers of English as belonging purely to one of the three. Nevertheless, the three-way model provides a useful starting point from which to move on to the present, more complicated situation.

English as a Native Language (or **English as a Mother Tongue** as it is sometimes called) is the language of those born and raised in one of the countries where English is historically the first language to be spoken. Kachru (1992: 356) refers to these countries (mainly the UK, USA, Canada, Australia and New Zealand) as 'the traditional cultural and linguistic bases of English'. Their English speakers are thought to number around 350 million. English as a Second Language refers to the language spoken in a large number of territories such as India, Bangladesh, Nigeria, and Singapore, which were once colonised by the British (see A1). These speakers are also thought to number around 350 million. English as a Foreign Language is the English of those for whom the language serves no purposes within their own countries.

Historically, they learnt the language in order to use it with its native speakers in the US and UK, though nowadays they are more likely to use it for communication with other non-native speakers. The current number of EFL speakers is more difficult to assess, and much depends on the level of competence which is used to define such a speaker. But if we use the criterion of 'reasonable competence', then the number is likely to be around one billion (although it should be said that this figure is not uncontroversial).

Even before we complicate the issue with changes that have occurred in the most recent decades, there are already a number of difficulties with this three-way categorisation. McArthur (1998: 43–6) lists six provisos which I summarise as follows:

1   ENL is not a single variety of English, but differs markedly from one territory to another (e.g. the US and UK), and even from one region within a given territory to another. In addition, the version of English accepted as 'standard' differs from one ENL territory to another.
2   Pidgins and creoles do not fit neatly into any one of the three categories. They are spoken in ENL settings, e.g. in parts of the Caribbean, in ESL settings, e.g. in many territories in West Africa, and in EFL settings, e.g. in Nicaragua, Panama and Surinam in the Americas. And some creoles in the Caribbean are so distinct from standard varieties of English that they are considered by a number of scholars to be different languages altogether.
3   There have always been large groups of ENL speakers living in certain ESL territories, e.g. India and Hong Kong, as a result of colonialism.
4   There are also large numbers of ESL speakers living in ENL settings, particularly the US and, to a lesser extent, the UK as a result of immigration.
5   The three categories do not take account of the fact that much of the world is bi- or multilingual, and that English is often spoken within a framework of **code mixing** (blending English with another language, e.g. 'Spanglish' in the US) and **code switching** (switching back and forth between English and another language).
6   The basic division is between **native speakers** and **non-native speakers** of English, that is, those born to the language and those who learnt it through education. The first group have always been considered superior to the second regardless of the quality of the language its members speak. This is becoming an ever more controversial issue and will be taken up in B3.

Models and descriptions of the spread of English

The most influential model of the spread of English has undoubtedly been that of Kachru (1992: 356) which is reproduced below. In accordance with the three-way categorisation described in the previous section, Kachru divides World Englishes into three concentric circles, the Inner Circle, the Outer Circle and the Expanding Circle. The three circles 'represent the types of spread, the patterns of acquisition, and the functional allocation of English in diverse cultural contexts', as the language travelled from Britain, in the first diaspora to the other ENL countries (the **Inner Circle**), in the second diaspora to the ESL countries (the **Outer Circle**) and, more recently, to the EFL countries (the **Expanding Circle**). The English spoken in the Inner Circle is

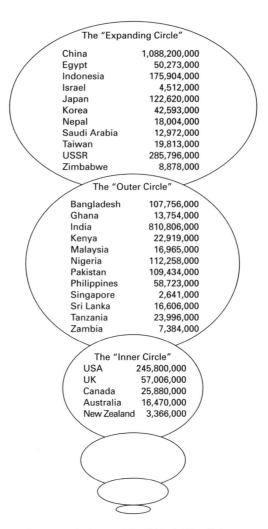

Figure A3.1 Kachru's three-circle model of World Englishes
Source: Kachru (1992: 356)
Note: In this, the most frequently cited version of the model, the circles are oval rather than circular, and presented vertically rather than concentrically, with the lowest circles representing earlier versions of English. Note also that the model was first published in 1988 and thus the figures (which are for whole populations rather than English speakers alone) are now out of date.

said to be 'norm-providing', that in the Outer Circle to be 'norm-developing' and that in the Expanding Circle to be 'norm-dependent'. In other words, English-language standards are determined by speakers of ENL, but while the ESL varieties of English have become institutionalised and are developing their own standards, the EFL varieties are regarded, in this model, as 'performance' varieties without any official status and therefore dependent on the standards set by native speakers in the Inner Circle.

Kachru argues that the implications of this sociolinguistic reality of English use around the world have gone unrecognised, and that attitudes, power and economics have instead been allowed to dictate English language policy. This situation, he maintains, has been facilitated by a number of 'fallacies' about the users and uses of English in different cultures around the world. We will look further at this issue, which developed in the early 1990s into a major debate carried out in the pages of the journal *English Today*, in B3.

Despite its major influence, with many scholars including Kachru himself still citing this model as the standard framework in the early twenty-first century, it is not without its problems. Some of these relate to recent changes in the use of English while others relate to any attempt at a three-way categorisation of English uses and users. The most serious problems are the following:

❏ The model is based on geography and genetics rather than on the way speakers identify with and use English. Some English users in the Outer Circle speak it as their first language (occasionally as their *only* language) e.g. in Singapore. Meanwhile an increasing number of speakers in the Expanding Circle use English for a very wide range of purposes including social, with native speakers and even more frequently with other non-native speakers from both their own and different L1s, and both in their home country and abroad.

❏ There is often a grey area between the Inner and Outer Circles: in some Outer Circle countries, English may be the first language learnt for many people, and may be spoken in the home rather than purely for official purposes such as education, law and government.

❏ There is also an increasingly grey area between the Outer and Expanding Circles. Approximately twenty countries are in transition from EFL to ESL status, including: Argentina, Belgium, Costa Rica, Denmark, Sudan, Switzerland (see Graddol 1997: 11 for the others).

❏ Many World English speakers grow up bilingual or multilingual, using different languages to fulfil different functions in their daily lives. This makes it difficult to describe any language in their repertoire as L1, L2, L3 and so on.

❏ There is a difficulty in using the model to define speakers in terms of their proficiency in English. A native speaker may have limited vocabulary and low grammatical competence while the reverse may be true of a non-native speaker. The fact that English is somebody's second or third language does not of itself imply that their competence is less than that of a native speaker.

❏ The model cannot account for **English for Special Purposes** (e.g. English for science and technology). Within such domains, English proficiency may be similar regardless of which particular circle speakers come from.

❏ The model implies that the situation is uniform for all countries within a particular circle whereas this is not so. Even within the Inner Circle, countries differ in the amount of **linguistic diversity** they contain (e.g. there is far more diversity in the US than in the UK). In the Outer Circle, countries differ in a number of respects such as whether English is spoken only by an élite, as in India, or is widespread, as in Singapore; or whether it is spoken by a single L1 group leading to one variety of English as in Bangladesh, or by several different L1 groups leading to several varieties of English as in India.

❑ Finally, the term 'Inner Circle' implies that speakers from the ENL countries are central to the effort, whereas their world-wide influence is in fact in decline. (Note, though, that Kachru did not intend the term 'Inner' to imply any sense of superiority.)

A number of other scholars have proposed different models and descriptions of the spread of English, sometimes in an attempt to improve on Kachru's model by taking account of more recent developments. Tripathi (1998: 55), for example, argues that the 'third world nations' should be considered as 'an independent category that supersedes the distinction of ESL and EFL'. Yano (2001: 122–4) proposes that Kachru's model should be modified in order to take account of the fact that many varieties of English in the Outer Circle have become established varieties spoken by people who regard themselves as native speakers with native speaker intuition. He therefore suggests glossing the Inner Circle as 'genetic ENL' and the Outer as 'functional ENL'. His model also takes account of the social dialectal concept of **acrolect** (standard) and **basilect** (colloquial) use of English, with the acrolect being used for international communication, and for formal and public intranational interaction, and the basilect for informal intranational communication. This is problematic in that it does not allow for the possibility of basilect use in international communication, whereas such use is becoming increasingly common. On the other hand, the attempt to remove the genetic element from the definition of 'native speaker' is very welcome.

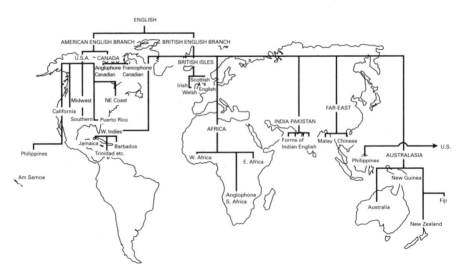

Figure A3.2 Strevens's world map of English
Source: Strevens (1992: 33)

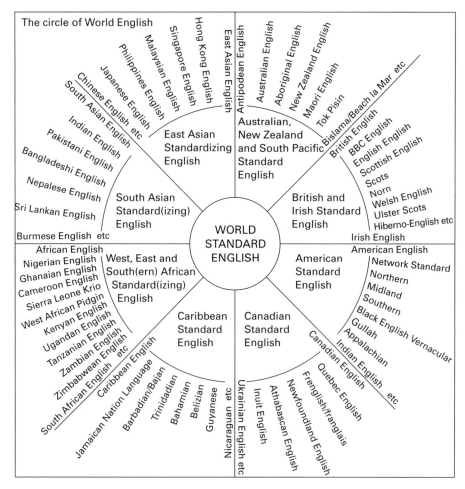

Figure A3.3 McArthur's circle of World English
Source: Crystal (1995: 111)

The oldest model of the spread of English, even predating Kachru's three circles, is that of Strevens. His world map of English (see p. 18), first published in 1980, shows a map of the world on which is superimposed an upside-down tree diagram demonstrating the way in which, since American English became a separate variety from British English, all subsequent Englishes have had affinities with either one or the other.

Later in the 1980s, both McArthur and Görlach proposed new circle models of English: McArthur's (1987) 'Circle of World English' and Görlach's (1988) 'circle model of English'. These are similar in a number of ways. Görlach's circle (not shown here) places 'International English' at the centre, followed by (moving outwards): regional standard Englishes (African, Antipodean, British Canadian, Caribbean, South Asian, US), then semi-/sub-regional standard Englishes such as Indian, Irish, Kenyan, Papua New Guinean, then non-standard Englishes such as Aboriginal English, Jamaican English,

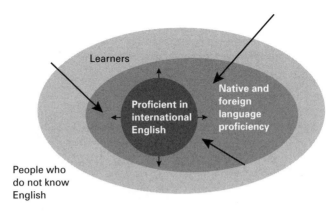

Figure A3.4 Modiano's centripetal circles of international English
Source: Modiano (1999a: 25)

Yorkshire dialect and, finally, beyond the outer rim, pidgins and creoles such as Cameroon Pidgin English and Tok Pisin.

McArthur's circle (see p. 19) has at its centre 'World Standard English' which, like Görlach's 'International English' does not exist in an identifiable form at present. Moving outwards comes next a band of regional varieties including both standard and standardising forms. Beyond these, divided by spokes separating the world into eight regions, is what McArthur (1998: 95) describes as 'a crowded (even riotous) fringe of subvarieties such as *Aboriginal English, Black English Vernacular* [now known as "African American Vernacular English" or "Ebonics"], *Gullah, Jamaican Nation Language, Singapore English and Ulster Scots*'.

A much more recent attempt to take account of developments in the spread of World Englishes is that of Modiano (1999a). He breaks completely with historical and geographical concerns and bases the first of his two models, 'The centripetal circles of international English', on what is mutually comprehensible to the majority of proficient speakers of English, be they native or non-native. The centre is made up of those who are proficient in international English. That is, these speakers function well in cross-cultural communication where English is the *lingua franca*. They are just as likely to be non-native as native speakers of English. The main criterion, other than proficiency itself, is that they have no strong regional accent or dialect. Modiano's next band consists of those who have proficiency in English as either a first or second language rather than as an international language. In other words, they function well in English with, respectively, other native speakers (with whom they share English as an L1) or other non-native speakers from the same L1 background as themselves. The third circle is made up of learners of English, i.e. those who are not yet proficient in English. Outside this circle is a final band to represent those people who do not know English at all.

Although it makes good sense to base a modern description of users of English on proficiency and to prioritise (as McArthur and Görlach had done earlier) the use of English as an international or world language, there are certain problems with

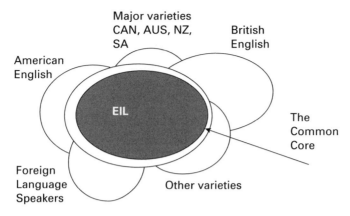

Figure A3.5 Modiano's English as an international language (EIL) illustrated by those features of English which are common to all native and non-native varieties
Source: Modiano (1999b: 10)

Modiano's model. In particular, where do we draw the line between a strong and non-strong regional accent? Presumably a strong regional accent places its owner in the second circle, thus categorising them as not proficient in international English. But at present, we have no sound basis on which to make the decision. And who decides? Again, given that international English is not defined, what does it mean to be proficient in 'international English' other than the rather vague notion of communicating well? Where do we draw the line between proficient and not proficient in international English in the absence of such a definition?

A few months later, Modiano redrafted his idea in response to comments which he had received in reaction to his first model. This time he moves away from intelligibility *per se* to present a model based on features of English common to all varieties of English. At the centre is EIL, a core of features which are comprehensible to the majority of native and competent non-native speakers of English. The second circle consists of features which may become internationally common or may fall into obscurity. Finally, the outer area consists of five groups (American English, British English, other major varieties, local varieties, foreign varieties) each with features peculiar to their own speech community and which are unlikely to be understood by most members of the other four groups.

There are still problems. For example, the difficulty of distinguishing between core and non-core varieties remains. In addition, some will find unpalatable the fact that Modiano equates native speakers with 'competent' non-natives, implying that all native speakers of English are competent users of English, which is patently untrue. There may also be objections to the designation of all the native varieties as 'major' but established Outer Circle varieties such as Indian English as 'local'.

We will return to Modiano in strand 6, when we look in detail at English as an International Language.

A4 **TYPES OF VARIATION ACROSS ENGLISHES**

'New Englishes' and 'new Englishes'

The vast majority of Englishes (all except British English) belong to one of two groups: the **new Englishes** which resulted from the first diaspora, and the **New Englishes** which resulted from the second. The former group consists primarily of North America (the US and Canada), Australia, New Zealand and South Africa. The Englishes in these territories developed independently of, and differently from, English in Britain partly because of the original mixtures of dialects and accents among the people who settled in these areas, and partly because of the influence of the languages of the indigenous populations. Nevertheless, because of their direct descendence from British English, and because they were spoken as mother tongues, there is a strong element of continuity in the use of these Englishes from pre-colonial days.

On the other hand, the latter group of Englishes, those commonly described as the 'New Englishes' (even though some of them predate the first group) were, and still are, for the most part, learnt as second languages or as one language within a wider multilingual repertoire of acquisition. This group includes, for example, Indian English, Philippine English, Nigerian English and Singaporean English (the latter being one of the few New Englishes which is increasingly being spoken as a mother tongue). This unit will not be concerned with the Englishes of the Expanding Circle, such as European Englishes and Japanese English, as these are the focus of strand 6.

The main reason for looking at a range of varieties of New English before tackling the complex issue of Standard English, is to give a clear signal that the New Englishes should be considered in their own right, and not in terms of their differences from a standard variety. This point is widely accepted in terms of American English, which is nowadays considered in the popular mind to be one of the world's two prestige varieties of English (the other being British English). Meanwhile, as you will see in A5, the other Inner Circle Englishes are only now beginning to lose the negative connotations attached to their differences from British English. However, the situation has not improved even to this extent for the Englishes of the Outer Circle. This is partly, though not entirely, because many of them are not yet fully described and in a position to identify and codify their standard forms, an issue that will be taken up in B5.

Defining a New English

The term 'New Englishes' covers a large number of varieties of English which are far from uniform in their characteristics and current use. They nevertheless share certain features. According to Platt *et al.* (1984: 2–3), a New English fulfils the following four criteria:

1   It has developed through the education system. This means that it has been taught as a subject and, in many cases, also used as a medium of instruction in regions where languages other than English were the main languages.
2   It has developed in an area where a native variety of English was *not* the language spoken by most of the population.
3   It is used for a range of functions *among* those who speak or write it in the region where it is used.

4   It has become 'localised' or 'nativised' by adopting some language features of its own, such as sounds, intonation patterns, sentence structures, words, and expressions.

English was initially spoken in Africa and Asia only by the native English speaking colonisers from Britain and North America. They set up schools to teach first English, and then other subjects through English, in order to provide a local workforce able to communicate in the language. As time went on, and the number of students increased, the English-medium schools began to recruit local non-native teachers. Their English was, inevitably, different from that of their own native-speaker teachers and the differences grew still more marked among the children who were taught by non-native speakers. Students were thus exposed to the language for several years during which time they used it for an ever increasing number of functions. In this way, the New Englishes evolved into varieties which served a wide or even full range of purposes and, at the same time, developed their own character.

Levels of variation

The main levels on which the new and New Englishes differ from the English of what Chinua Achebe has described as 'its ancestral home', i.e. Britain, and from each other, are the following: pronunciation, grammar, vocabulary/idiom, and discourse style. Although you should bear in mind that the different varieties of new and New Englishes are not internally uniform, nevertheless, as with British English, in the vast majority of cases there is sufficient in common for us to be able to talk about a particular national English, be it Nigerian English, Indian English, American English or whatever.

Pronunciation

Consonant sounds

The dental fricative sounds /θ/ and /ð/ as in the words <u>th</u>in and <u>th</u>is when spoken with a British English **Received Pronunciation (RP)** accent (with the tongue tip vibrating against the upper teeth), are pronounced in various ways by speakers of New Englishes. For example, speakers of Indian, and West Indian Englishes use instead the sounds /t/ and /d/, so that these words are pronounced 'tin' and 'dis'.

On the other hand, speakers of Lankan (= Sri Lankan), Malaysian, Singaporean, and many African Englishes often use the sounds /tθ/ and /dð/, so that the same words sound closer to 't-thin' and 'd-this'. These substitutions would have started life as attempts to produce the 'correct' L1 English sound. However once L2-English-speaking teachers began to be employed, the sounds would have been produced as classroom models and imitated by pupils. Over time, they gradually became regarded as local variants, rather than incorrect attempts to conform, and in many cases are now in the process of being codified.

The same is true of a host of other consonant sounds of which the following are among those most frequently described:

❏   /w/ is pronounced as /v/ in Lankan and some Indian Englishes so that 'wet' sounds like 'vet'.

❏ The voiceless sounds /p/, /t/ and /k/ are pronounced at the beginnings of words without **aspiration** (a small puff of air) by speakers of Indian, Philippine, Malaysian and other New Englishes, so that they sound to an outsider more like their voiced equivalents, /b/, /d/ and /g/, making the words 'pin', 'tin' and 'cap' sound closer to 'bin', 'din' and 'gap'.

❏ Consonants at the ends of words tend to be unreleased or replaced with glottal stops in Englishes such as Ghanaian, West Indian, and colloquial Singaporean, so that a word such as 'cat' may be pronounced either ca(t) with an unreleased final consonant, or ca' with a final **glottal stop**. The word-final glottal stop to replace a consonant sound, especially /t/, is also, of course, a feature of some non-standard varieties of British English such as Estuary English and Cockney.

❏ Several of the New Englishes, including Indian, West African, and Papua New Guinean, use **voiceless** word-final consonants (that is, without vibration of the vocal cords) where RP would have a **voiced** one. Words such as 'feed', 'gave' and 'rob' may thus sound to an outsider as if they end in the consonants t, f and p, that is, as 'feet', 'gafe' and 'rop'.

Finally, two consonant features which occur less widely among the New Englishes (although, as you will see in A6, they feature in some of the International Englishes of the Expanding Circle):

❏ there is a lack of distinction between /r/ and /l/ in Hong Kong, Singapore (of Chinese origin) and some East African Englishes (including Ngũgĩ's mother tongue, Gĩkũyũ), so that words such as 'red' and 'led' are interchangeable.

❏ /ʃ/ is pronounced as /s/ by speakers of some East African Englishes, and some (generally less well-educated) speakers of Hong Kong English, so that 'ship' sounds like 'sip'.

Vowel sounds

Vowel sounds vary across the New Englishes in terms of both their quality and their quantity; in other words, according to how high/low and forward/back the tongue is in the mouth, and the degree to which the lips are rounded or spread (these factors all relate to **vowel quality**), and to how long the sound is actually maintained (this factor relates to **vowel quantity**). Some of the main differences in vowel sounds across the New Englishes are as follows:

❏ many of the New Englishes, e.g. Singaporean, Indian and African Englishes, distinguish only minimally if at all between the short and long vowels /ɪ/ and /i:/ as in the RP pronunciation of the words 'sit' and 'seat', tending to pronounce both as /ɪ/.

❏ Many New Englishes pronounce RP /a:/ without its length, e.g. Lankan, Singaporean, Indian, Philippine and Jamaican Englishes, so that the word 'staff', for example, sounds closer to 'stuff' to an outsider.

❏ African Englishes tend to produce the **schwa** sound /ə/ as the full vowel [a] at the ends of words, so that 'matter' is pronounced [mata] instead of [matə].

❏ Diphthongs have a tendency to be pronounced both shorter and as monophthongs in several New Englishes including Indian, Lankan, Malaysian and African. For example, the diphthong /eɪ/ in the RP pronunciation of the word 'take' loses its second element, to become [e·] or the shorter [e] so that it sounds more like 'tek'. Similarly, in Lankan English the diphthong /əʊ/ in the word 'coat' tends to be pronounced either [oː] (by more educated speakers) or [ɔ] (by less educated speakers) so that, especially in the latter case, it sounds like RP 'cot'.

Grammar

Platt *et al.* (1984: Chapter 4) sum up the main grammatical tendencies of the New Englishes in referring to people, things and ideas as follows:

❏ a tendency not to mark nouns for plural
❏ a tendency to use a specific/non-specific system for nouns rather than a definite/indefinite system, or to use the two systems side by side
❏ a tendency to change the form of quantifiers
❏ a tendency not to make a distinction between the third person pronouns *he* and *she*
❏ a tendency to change the word order within the noun phrase.

The following is a selection from the many examples which Platt *et al.* (1984) cite for the five categories listed above. In each case, consider what the standard British/American English equivalent would be.

Activity

❏ lack of plural marking:

> up to twelve *year* of schooling (India)
> and they know all four *dialect* (Jamaica)
> Pilipino is only one of the *subject* (Philippines)

❏ specific/non-specific system:

> Everyone has *car* (India)
> I'm not on *scholarship* (East Africa) ⎫ non-specific
> I'm staying in *one* house with three other (India)
> There! Here got *one* stall selling soup noodles (Singapore) ⎬ specific

❏ quantifiers:

> Don't eat so *much sweets* (Singapore)
> *Some few fishermen* may be seen (West Africa)
> I applied *couple of places* in Australia (India)

❏ Pronouns:

> When I first met my husband, *she* was a student (East Africa)
> My mother, *he* live in kampong (Malaysia; a 'kampong' is a small settlement)

❏ Word order:

> A *two-hour exciting* display (Ghana)
> Dis *two last* years (Papua New Guinea)
> *Ninety over* cheques (Singapore/Malaysia)

Moving on to verbs, these are the main tendencies that Platt *et al.* (1984: Chapter 5) observe in many of the New Englishes:

❑ limited marking of the third person singular present tense form:

> She *drink* milk (Philippines)
> Every microcosm *consist* of many cells (India)

❑ limited marking of verbs for the past tense:

> Mandarin, I *learn* it privately (Hong Kong)
> My wife she *pass* her Cambridge (Singapore)

❑ tendency to use an aspect system (which shows whether an action is finished or still going on) rather than a tense system (which shows the time an action takes place):

> I still eat (= I am/was eating in Malaysian English)
> I have worked there in 1960 (with use of has/have + past participle to indicate a time in the past in Indian English)

❑ a tendency to extend the use of be + verb + ing constructions to stative verbs, e.g:

> She *is knowing* her science very well (East African English)
> Mohan *is having* two houses (Indian English)

❑ the formation of different phrasal and prepositional verb constructions:

> Her name *cropped* in the conversation (East African English)
> I'm going to *voice out* my opinion (West African English)

Vocabulary/idiom

There are several respects in which we could study New English vocabulary, but we will restrict examples to: locally coined words/expressions; borrowings from indigenous languages; and idioms. (The examples come from both Trudgill and Hannah (2002) and Platt *et al.* (1984).)

Locally coined words/expressions

The creative capacity of speakers of New Englishes tends to be overlooked by speakers of Inner Circle varieties, with creativity often being classified as error. This is an issue which you will be asked to respond to in B4. **Coinages** most commonly arise in one of two ways: by the addition of a prefix or suffix to an existing (British or indigenous) word, and by compounding.

Examples of the first kind of coinage are:

sting<u>ko</u>	colloquial Singaporean Eng. 'smelly'
spac<u>y</u>	Indian Eng. 'spacious'
heat<u>y</u>	Singaporean/Malaysian Eng. for foods which make the body hot, e.g. the stingko fruit, durian.
teacher<u>ess</u>	Indian Eng. 'female teacher'
jeep<u>ney</u>	Philippine Eng. 'a small bus' (army jeeps having been converted to buses)
<u>en</u>stool	Ghanaian Eng. 'to install a chief'
<u>de</u>stool	Ghanaian Eng. 'to depose a chief'

Examples of the second kind of coinage are:

peelhead	Jamaican Eng. 'a bald-headed person'
bushmeat	West African Eng. 'game'
dry coffee	East African Eng. 'coffee without milk and sugar'
key-bunch	Indian Eng. 'bunch of keys'
basket-woman	Lankan Eng. 'coarsely behaved woman'
high hat	Philippine Eng. 'a snob'

Borrowings from indigenous languages
East African English

chai	'tea'
duka	'shop'
manamba	'labourer'

Indian English

bandh	'a total strike in an area'
crore	'ten million'
swadeshi	'indigenous, native, home-grown'

Philippine English

boondock	'mountain'
kundiman	'love song'

Idioms
Platt *et al.* (1984) distinguish between learners' unsuccessful attempts to use the idioms of native speakers of English, and stabilised New English idioms. They discount the first kind altogether, a policy on which you might or might not agree with them. However, they cite examples such as Singaporean English 'gift of the gap' (for British English 'gift of the gab') and 'in lips and bounce' (for 'in leaps and bounds'), where the variation from the native speaker version is regular on account of pronunciation differences.

Some New English idioms are direct translations from indigenous idioms. For example, Singaporean and Malaysian English 'to shake legs' comes from the Malay idiom 'goyang kaki', meaning 'to be idle'. Some New English idioms are based on native speaker English, e.g. the East African idiom 'to be on the tarmac', meaning 'to be in the process of seeking a new job'. Others combine elements from native speaker English and indigenous forms, e.g. the Nigerian 'to put sand in someone's gari', meaning 'to threaten someone's livelihood' ('gari' being a type of flour). Still other idioms are variations on native speaker ones. For example, the British English idiom 'to have your cake and eat it' becomes, in Singaporean English 'to eat your cake and have it'. Presumably this began life as an unsuccessful attempt at the 'correct' British version and gradually became common Singaporean usage. Another example from Singaporean English is 'to be in hot soup', which has the same meaning as, and is a combination of, two British English idioms, 'to be in hot water' and 'to be in the soup' (i.e. to be in trouble). This highlights the difficulty in distinguishing between New English **creativity** and **incorrectness**, and it is important to keep in mind the fact that all innovation begins life as an 'error' in the standard form.

Discourse style

A feature of several New Englishes is that they have a more formal character than the Inner Circle Englishes. In particular, their vocabulary and grammatical structure are more complex. Indian English, in particular, favours 'lengthy constructions, bookish vocabulary and exaggerated forms which make even a formal style appear "more formal" to a speaker of another variety of English' (Platt *et al.* 1984: 149). Formality is, of course, a relative construct and, as the previous quotation implies, the language will only seem 'bookish' and 'exaggerated' to those who habitually use different forms.

Some Indian English stylistic features are logical extensions of British English strategies. For example, 'could' and 'would' are used in Indian English where British English would use 'can' and will', as in 'We hope that you <u>could</u> join us' or 'We hope that the Vice-Chancellor <u>would</u> investigate this matter' (Trudgill and Hannah 2002: 132). In both these cases, the past tense is used because it is felt to be more tentative and therefore more polite. The same strategy is regularly employed in British English. For example, in an instruction to a non-intimate, if the speaker wishes to appear more polite, he or she is likely to say 'Could you open the door' rather than 'Can you open the door'.

On the other hand, both Indian and African Englishes use a discourse style which cannot be found in Inner Circle Englishes, and here the indigenous culture is at least in part an influence. For example, certain aspects of Indian culture lead to expressions of thanks, deferential vocabulary and the use of blessings which would seem redundant or overdone to a speaker of an Inner Circle English: 'I am bubbling with zeal and enthusiasm to serve as a research assistant', or 'I offer myself as a candidate for the post of Research Assistant. Thanking you' (Platt *et al.* 1984: 150–1).

An area where the New Englishes differ very much from those of the Inner Circle is that of greeting and leavetaking. In the New Englishes, these are often direct translations from the indigenous language. Some examples of greetings are:

Lankan Eng.	So how? (translation from Sinhala)
Nigerian Eng.	You're enjoying? (translation from Yoruba)
Singaporean/ Malaysian Eng.	Have you eaten already?
West African Eng.	How? How now?
East African Eng.	Are you all right?

and of leavetakings:

Lankan Eng.	I'll go and come.
Singaporean/ Malaysian Eng.	Walk slowly ho!

STANDARD LANGUAGE IDEOLOGY

Standard language and language standards

Standard language and language standards are topics which excite an immense amount of controversy and contention both inside and outside the linguistics profession. **Standard language** is the term used for that variety of a language which is considered to be the norm. It is the variety held up as the optimum for educational purposes and used as a yardstick against which other varieties of the language are measured. Being a **prestige variety**, a standard language is spoken by a minority of people within a society, typically those occupying positions of power.

Language standards are the reverse side of the standard language coin. These are the prescriptive language rules which together constitute the standard and to which all members of a language community are exposed and urged to conform during education, regardless of the local variety. Because a living language is by definition dynamic, these rules are subject to change over time. During its earlier and transitional stages, language change is regarded as error by promoters of standard language ideology (lay as well as professional). It is the subject of much criticism from self-appointed guardians of 'correct' usage, who tend to hark back to a mythical linguistic 'Golden Age', often that of their own childhood.

Because language standards seem not to function in the interests of certain groups, especially speakers of New Englishes, Parakrama argues that standards should be made more inclusive:

> Language standards are rarely contested, even by those who are engaged in radical and far-reaching social critique. Yet, standards discriminate against those who don't conform, and language standardisation has systematically worked against the underclass as well as women and minorities [. . .] The existence of standards, however objectionable, cannot be denied, so the only viable option, politically at any rate, is to work towards broadening the standard to include the greatest variety possible, particularly the 'uneducated' arenas of usage which have so far been considered inappropriate, mistaken, even pathological.
>
> (Parakrama 1995, back cover)

Hudson (1996: 32) describes standard languages as 'quite abnormal' in their development: 'Whereas one thinks of normal language development as taking place in a rather haphazard way, largely below the threshold of consciousness of the speakers, standard languages are the result of a direct and deliberate intervention by society.' Following Haugen (1966) he summarises this process of intervention as going through four stages, selection, codification, elaboration of function, and acceptance.

Selection

This is the most critical stage in the standardising process. It refers to the way in which one variety rather than any other is chosen as the one which will be developed as the standard language. Often, this is an existing variety which already has political and/or economic currency. Standard English, for instance, is based on the variety of English which was preferred by the educated in London after the court moved there from

Winchester following the Norman Conquest. On the other hand, the process could involve the selection of features from several varieties or even, as in the case of Classical Hebrew in Israel, of a language variety that has no native speakers. Selection is, of course, a social and political process, since it is invariably led by those in power and subsequently reinforces and further promotes their interests over those of speakers of other (by definition 'non-standard') varieties.

Codification
Once selection has taken place, the variety chosen to represent the standard has to be 'fixed' in grammar books and dictionaries in order that those people who wish to use the language 'correctly' have access to its standard forms.

Elaboration of function
To fulfil its role, the standard variety has to be capable of performing a wide range of institutional and literary functions particularly, though not exclusively, in government, law, education, science and literature. At this stage, then, new lexical items are added and new conventions developed to fill any gaps.

Acceptance
Clearly, unless the relevant population accept the selected variety as their standard and, most probably, their national language, then all will have been in vain. In practice, though, since those who make the selection tend to be, or to represent, those who have the right of veto, acceptance is unlikely to be an issue. Those who already lacked political and economic power will continue to do so, with their inferior status in society now being symbolised by their use of an 'inferior' language variety: a social, regional or ethnic dialect. For the time being, the standard variety, as Hudson (1996: 33) says, 'serves as a strong unifying force for the state, as a symbol of its independence of other states . . . and as a marker of its difference from other states'. On the other hand, it is quite possible that in times to come, there will be challenges to the 'accepted' variety from those both within and outside its users. This is currently the situation with English, as the next two sections will demonstrate.

What is Standard English?
Standard English is by no means an easy language variety to identify. In the case of languages such as French and Italian, for which academies prescribe the forms that may and may not be codified in their grammars and dictionaries, the standard is evident. Even those people who do not themselves wish to promote it are able, year on year, to ascertain exactly what it is. All is less certain with Standard English, not only in terms of its world-wide use (which is the subject of the following section) but also in its Inner Circle contexts.

The following are some of the main definitions of Standard English which have been proposed in recent years. The first two refer only to British English whereas the remaining four appear to include all Inner Circle Englishes.

❏ The dialect of educated people throughout the British Isles. It is the dialect normally used in writing, for teaching in schools and universities, and heard on radio and television (Hughes and Trudgill 1979).

❏   Standard English can be characterized by saying that it is that set of grammatical and lexical forms which is typically used in speech and writing by educated native speakers. It . . . includes the use of colloquial and slang vocabulary as well as swear-words and taboo expressions (Trudgill 1984).

❏   (The term) 'Standard English' is potentially misleading for at least two reasons. First, in order to be self-explanatory, it really ought to be called 'the grammar and the core vocabulary of educated usage in English'. That would make plain the fact that it is not the whole of English, and above all, it is not pronunciation that can in any way be labelled 'Standard', but only one part of English: its grammar and vocabulary (Strevens 1985).

❏   The variety of the English language which is normally employed in writing and normally spoken by 'educated' speakers of the language. It is also, of course, the variety of the language that students of English as a Foreign or Second Language (EFL/ESL) are taught when receiving formal instruction. The term *Standard English* refers to grammar and vocabulary (***dialect***) but not to pronunciation (***accent***) (Trudgill and Hannah 1994).

❏   Since the 1980s, the notion of 'standard' has come to the fore in public debate about the English language . . . We may define the Standard English of an English-speaking country as a minority variety (identified chiefly by its vocabulary, grammar and orthography) which carries most prestige and is most widely understood (Crystal 1995).

These definitions bear certain similarities. For instance, there is a fair degree of consensus that accent is not involved in Standard English, that it is primarily a case of grammar and vocabulary, and that it is the variety promoted through the education system. Nevertheless, this does not help us to any great extent if we want to know what it all means in practice. Possibly the best attempt to provide such information is contained in an article by Trudgill, the originator of three of the above definitions. In 'Standard English: what it isn't' (1999), Trudgill demonstrates what may be the only feasible way of defining a 'non-academy' standard language such as English. That is, by what it is not:

❏   It is not a language: it is only one variety of a given English.

❏   It is not an accent: in Britain it is spoken by 12–15% of the population, of whom 9–12% speak it with a regional accent.

❏   It is not a **style**: it can be spoken in formal, neutral and informal styles, respectively:

>   Father was exceedingly fatigued subsequent to his extensive peregrinations.
>   Dad was very tired after his lengthy journey.
>   The old man was bloody knackered after his long trip.

❏   It is not a **register**: given that a register is largely a matter of lexis in relation to subject matter (e.g. the register of medicine, of cricket, or of knitting), there is no necessary connection between register and Standard English. Trudgill (1999: 122) provides this example: 'There was two eskers what we saw in them U-shaped valleys' to demonstrate 'a non-standard English sentence couched in the technical register of physical geography'.

❏ It is not a set of prescriptive rules: it can tolerate certain features which, because many of their rules are grounded in Latin, prescriptive grammarians do not allow. Trudgill (1999: 125) provides these examples: sentence-final prepositions as in 'I've bought a new car which I'm very pleased with', and constructions such as 'It's me', 'He is taller than me'.

Trudgill concludes that Standard English is a dialect that differs from the other dialects of English in that it has greater prestige, does not have an associated accent, and does not form part of a geographical continuum. In other words, it is purely a **social dialect**. He goes on to point out that while Standard English has many features in common with the other dialects of the country in question, there are certain differences and that these differences do not necessarily indicate the linguistic superiority of the standard forms.

Non-standard Englishes

It is not unusual for all the regional native speaker dialects of English to be lumped together with all the New Englishes (in both standard and non-standard versions) under the label **non-standard**, with the implication that all are sub-standard and hence incorrect. Somewhat surprisingly, even educated Australian English belonged until recently to this category, only joining the ranks of Standard English in the 1970s. Up to then, Australian English was evaluated in terms of its closeness to Standard British English (known locally as the 'colonial cringe'), with any distinctively Australian forms being regarded as 'bad' English. The first dictionary of Australian English to be edited within Australia's shores rather than in Britain was only published in 1976. Since then, educated Australians have developed a new confidence in their own identity which has translated linguistically into the celebration of their own ways of speaking and a new reluctance to hark back to their British roots and ape Standard British English.

If it was so difficult for a standard native-speaker variety of English to gain acceptance, it is no surprise, then, that non-standard native varieties and both standard and non-standard non-native varieties have not so far met with similar success. In the case of the non-standard native varieties, lack of acceptance appears to have connections with attitudes towards race in the US and class in the UK. In her discussion of Standard American and British English, Milroy argues that people find it easier to identify the non-standard than the standard, and goes on to propose that:

> in a sense, the standard [American English] of popular perception is what is left behind when all the non-standard varieties spoken by disparaged persons such as Valley Girls, Hillbillies, Southerners, New Yorkers, African Americans, Asians, Mexican Americans, Cubans and Puerto Ricans are set aside. In Britain, where consciousness of the special status of RP as a class accent is acute, spoken standard English might similarly be described as what is left after we remove from the linguistic bran-tub Estuary English, Brummie, Cockney, Geordie, Scouse, various quaint rural dialects, London Jamaican, transatlantic slang and perhaps even conservative RP as spoken by older members of the upper classes.
>
> (L. Milroy 1999: 174)

The New Englishes in both their standard and non-standard manifestations tend to be regarded in much the same way as the non-standard varieties of Inner Circle Englishes. In other words, those which have undergone standardisation processes and codified their own standard, for example, Standard Singaporean English, Standard Indian English, are nevertheless considered 'non-standard' by outsiders and it is not uncommon even for their own speakers to regard them as second-best in relation to the Standard Englishes of the Inner Circle.

In several parts of the world including a number of African-English-speaking countries, standardisation processes are currently underway, and it will be some time before local standards can be codified in home-grown grammars and dictionaries. Even when this has been achieved, however, these standard Englishes are unlikely to attract the same prestige as their counterparts in Britain, North America and even, nowadays, Australia. This is because of attitudes held towards these varieties by many members of the Inner Circle, both the general population and a substantial number of linguists. That is, the New Englishes are widely regarded as examples of a process known as **fossilisation**. In other words, the learning of English is said to have ceased (or 'fossilised') some way short of target-like competence, with the target being assumed to be either Standard British or Standard American English. Of course, from a sociolinguistic perspective, however, the idea that the New Englishes should have as their target the standard Englishes of the inner circle is of dubious validity.

THE INTERNATIONALISATION OF ENGLISH   A6

> Not only has 'English' become international in the last half century, but scholarship about English has also become international: the ownership of an interest in English has become international. We are no longer a language community which is associated with a national community or even with a family of nations such as the Commonwealth aspired to be. We are an international community.
>
> (Brumfit 1995: 16)

This quotation from Brumfit neatly encapsulates the changes that took place in the second half of the twentieth century, and that are beginning to impact on the way English is taught and spoken around the world at the start of the twenty-first. In A6, we will consider first, why it is that English has assumed the role of the world's major international language and second, the most serious issue which has to be addressed in the light of this role: the need to ensure mutual intelligibility across international varieties of English.

Why is English the international language?

Despite the fact that most of England's former colonies had become independent states by the mid-twentieth century, they retained the English language to serve various internal functions (see A1). So by virtue of its colonial past, English was already well-placed to become one of the world's main languages of international business and trade. But in the postcolonial period, English has spread well beyond its use as a second or additional language in the countries of the Outer Circle, to be adopted as an international *lingua franca* by many countries in the Expanding Circle for which it performs no official internal functions (see A1 and A3 for figures). Crystal (1995) accounts for the present-day international status of English as the result of two factors, the first being its colonial past, which we have already noted. The second reason, and the one which has ensured the continuing influence of English throughout the twentieth century and beyond, is the economic power of the US:

> The present-day world status of English is primarily the result of two factors: the expansion of British colonial power, which peaked towards the end of the 19th century, and the emergence of the United States as the leading economic power of the 20th century. It is the latter factor which continues to explain the position of the English language today.
>
> (Crystal 1995: 106)

Before we go on to consider the reasons why English remains the world's first international language into the twenty-first century, however, it is important to acknowledge that this is not universally considered to be a beneficial state of affairs. Since the publication of his 1992 book, *Linguistic Imperialism*, Robert Phillipson has continued to argue against the desirability of the spread of English, especially where this spread has the potential to jeopardise the learning of other languages and the very existence of smaller languages (see strand 8 on the latter subject). Others have argued along similar lines. For example, following the events of 11 September 2001, Hilary Footitt, Chair of the University Council of Modern Languages, wrote as follows:

> One of the cultural shocks of September 11 is, overwhelmingly, that English is simply not enough. We cannot understand the world in English, much less search out intelligence, build ever larger coalitions of friends, and heal some of the longstanding wounds of the past. We need to be aware as never before of foreign languages and of the ways in which languages identify and represent their cultures.
>
> (*Guardian Education*, 23 October 2001, p. 15)

This is in direct contrast to the optimistic views regularly expressed by those who, like Telma Gimenez, regard the spread of an international language as wholly positive:

> [H]aving a common language helps us to see ourselves as human beings who live on the same planet, and to that extent can be said to form one community. The value of knowing English lies not only in the ability to access material things, but also in the possibility it offers for creating acceptance of, and respect for, the World's

diversity. English allows us to advance toward global exchange and solidarity among the institutions of civil society, extending bonds between citizens far and wide across the globe. For this reason, considering English as an international language can also bring a sense of possibility in terms of strengthening what might be called 'planetary citizenship' . . .

(ELT Journal 55/3, July 2001, p. 297)

Nevertheless, for the time being English as an International Language – or English as a Lingua Franca (or ELF) – as it is increasingly being called for communication involving no native speakers, is a fact of life. The implications of this situation for L2 English are at last beginning to be addressed, with even the British press finally acknowledging that the English of its non-native speakers may be gaining acceptance in its own right, instead of being considered 'erroneous' wherever it differs from native varieties of English. The *Observer* newspaper, for example, in an article entitled 'Foreign tongues spread the English word', made the following point: 'The accented English of fluent foreigners such as Latino singer Ricky Martin or actress Juliette Binoche is usurping British and American English as the dominant form of the language' (29 October 2000, p. 1). The writer rather spoils his case by going on to report that the Education and Employment Secretary 'will tell a meeting of business leaders on Tuesday to capitalise on their advantage as native speakers', and even that 'the drive to make English the global *lingua franca* comes directly from Tony Blair [the British Prime Minister]' and is known as the 'Blair initiative'. To the extent that English is the 'global *lingua franca*' it is, of course, neither to the advantage of its native speakers nor controlled by them. These are both issues to which we will return.

For the moment, though, let us consider the reasons why those for whom English is not their mother tongue should wish to learn it. Crystal (1997) lists the following reasons. Which, in your view, are most relevant to those who need or want to be able to communicate *internationally* in the English language?

1 Historical reasons
Because of the legacy of British or American imperialism, the country's main institutions may carry out their proceedings in English. These include the governing body (e.g. parliament), government agencies, the civil service (at least at senior levels), the law courts, national religious bodies, the schools, and higher educational institutions, along with their related publications (textbooks, proceedings, records, etc.). This is the case at least to some extent in all the Outer Circle territories.

2 Internal political reasons
Whether a country has imperial antecedents or not, English may have a role in providing a neutral means of communication between its different ethnic groups as it does, for example, in India. A distinctive local variety of English may also become a

symbol of national unity or emerging nationhood. The use of English in newspapers, on radio, or on television, adds a further dimension.

3   External economic reasons
The USA's dominant economic position acts as a magnet for international business and trade, and organisations wishing to develop international markets are thus under considerable pressure to work with English. The tourist and advertising industries are particularly English-dependent, but any multinational business will wish to establish offices in the major English-speaking countries.

4   Practical reasons
English is the language of international air traffic control, and is currently developing its role in international maritime, policing and emergency services. It is the chief language of international business and academic conferences, and the leading language of international tourism.

5   Intellectual reasons
Most of the scientific, technological, and academic information in the world is expressed in English, and over 80 per cent of all the information stored in electronic retrieval systems is in English. Closely related to this is the concern to have access to the philosophical, cultural, religious and literary history of Western Europe, either directly or through the medium of an English translation. In most parts of the world, the only way most people have access to such authors as Goethe or Dante is through English.

6   Entertainment reasons
English is the main language of popular music, and permeates popular culture and its associated advertising. It is also the main language of satellite broadcasting, home computers and video games, as well as of such international illegal activities as pornography and drugs.

To these points made by Crystal (1997) could be added personal advantage/ prestige since, in many cultures, the ability to speak English is perceived as conferring higher status on the speaker.

The conflict between mutual intelligibility and group identity
If English is to fulfil its role as the world's international *lingua franca*, it goes without saying that it must be capable of achieving **mutual intelligibility** among speakers and writers from all first language backgrounds who wish to communicate in English. The main obstacle to such mutual intelligibility is identity. For, as Crystal (1997: 116) points out, 'the need for intelligibility and the need for identity often pull people – and countries – in opposing directions'.

In essence, the problem is this. With the increase in the number of first language (L1) groups who speak English as an International Language, the range of differences among their Englishes has also inevitably increased. These differences are particularly evident in the spoken language, and more so in terms of pronunciation than at the other linguistic levels, since it is on pronunciation that first language transfer has its greatest influence.

The demands of mutual intelligibility point to a need to decrease accent differences among speakers from different L1 backgrounds. This, however, does not necessarily involve encouraging L2 learners to imitate a native-speaker accent. Indeed, such attempts have invariably failed. Accents are closely bound up with feelings of personal and group **identity**, which means that people tend to resist such attempts, whether consciously or subconsciously. Either they wish to preserve their mother-tongue accent in their L2 English or, more probably, they simply do not wish to identify, through mimicking an L1 English accent, with native speakers of the language. And in the case of EIL, there is strong justification for not conforming to the accent (or even the lexicogrammar) of a native-speaker group: the fact that the EIL community is by definition international rather than associated with any one national speech community. In C6 we will look at some possible approaches to preserving intelligibility in EIL pronunciation and lexicogrammar which do not entail universal approximation to native speaker varieties.

You might consider the roles of intelligibility and identity in your own language learning experience, as follows: **Activity**

If you speak English as a second or subsequent language:

❏   Have you ever given thought to retaining your L1 identity in English?
❏   Is it important to you to retain your L1 identity in English?
❏   Are you more concerned to be intelligible to native speakers of English or to non-native speakers of English, or do you not distinguish between the two groups of listener?
❏   Do you believe it is appropriate to retain your L1 accent in your English or that you should attempt to sound 'native-like'?
❏   Do you believe it is possible to retain your L1 accent in English and still be intelligible to native-speakers?/to non-native speakers?

If you speak English as a first language and another language/other languages as second/subsequent languages:

❏   Have you ever given thought to retaining your L1 identity in the other language(s) you speak?
❏   Is it important to you to retain your L1 identity in the other language(s) you speak?
❏   Do you believe it is appropriate to retain your L1 English accent in your other language(s) or that you should attempt to sound like native speakers of the language(s)?
❏   Do you believe it is possible to retain your L1 accent in your other language(s) and still be intelligible to native speakers of that language? Have you had any personal experiences that support your view?

For both groups:

What is your reaction to the following distinction which Prodromou makes between the learning/speaking of English and that of other modern foreign languages such as Spanish? Do you agree or not? Why/why not? If you do agree, what do you see as the most important implications for the speaking of English?

> Most people quite simply do not learn English to speak to native-speakers. On the other hand, people learn Spanish, as I am doing at present, because they are interested in Hispanic culture for some reason (work or pleasure) and will therefore want a spoken and written model which will further this aim. There is a world of difference between English and, in fact, all other living languages at present.
>
> (Prodromou 1997: 19)

A7   THE ROLE OF ENGLISH IN ASIA AND EUROPE

Asia and Europe: similarities and differences

In A7, attention is focused on two large regions in which English is spoken as an L2: Asia and Europe. In Expanding Circle Europe, while change is taking place fast, developments are several paces behind those of the Asian Outer Circle. At the start of the twenty-first century, Euro-English is only just emerging as a distinctive variety or group of varieties with its own identity which, like the Asian Englishes, rejects the concept of having to respect British English or American English norms (see D7). What has become clear is that English is evolving as a European *lingua franca* not only in restricted fields such as business and commerce, but also in a wide range of other contexts of communication including its increasing use as a language of socialisation. The progress of the codified Asian Englishes thus indicates the likely future developmental stages of Euro-English.

A second similarity between Asian and Euro-Englishes is that both, by definition, are developing their varieties of English within contexts of bi- or multi-lingualism. This has implications both for the ways in which English is used by its majority (bilingual) speakers, and for the ways in which it is taught and tested (see C7 on Indian English).

A third similarity is one that Asian and European Englishes share with all non-native Englishes whether institutionalised or not. That is, they are 'linguistic orphans in search of their parents' (Kachru 1992: 66). Kachru is referring here to the still widespread – if slowly diminishing – belief (among both native speakers and non-native speakers of English) that non-native speaker varieties are deficient and unacceptable by virtue of the local characteristics they have acquired in the process of being transplanted. Such attitudes in turn deter speakers of non-native speaker varieties from identifying with and promoting their own local model. This issue will be taken up again in the readings in D7.

English as an Asian language

Asian Englishes can be categorised both regionally and functionally. Regionally, they are typically divided into three groupings (although the Southeast and East Asian varieties are sometimes grouped together):

Table A7.1   Asian Englishes by region

South Asian varieties	Southeast Asian and Pacific varieties	East Asian varieties
Bangladesh	Brunei	China
Bhutan	Cambodia	Hong Kong
India	Fiji	Japan
Maldives	Indonesia	Korea
Nepal	Laos	Taiwan
Pakistan	Malaysia	
Sri Lanka	Myanmar	
	Philippines	
	Singapore	
	Thailand	

Functionally Asian Englishes are divided into two categories, depending on whether they are institutionalised varieties of the Outer Circle or non-institutionalised varieties of the Expanding Circle:

Table A7.2   Asian Englishes by use

Institutionalised varieties (Outer Circle)	Non-institutionalised varieties (Expanding Circle)
Bangladesh	Cambodia
Bhutan	China
Brunei	Indonesia
Fiji	Japan
Hong Kong	Korea
India	Laos
Malaysia	Maldives
Nepal	Myanmar
Pakistan	Taiwan
Philippines	Thailand
Singapore	Vietnam
Sri Lanka	

Of the above territories, numbers of L2 English speakers with reasonable competence range from India (37 million), the Philippines (almost 37 million), and Pakistan (approximately 16 million) to Sri Lanka and Hong Kong each with around 2 million, Singapore with just over one million, Brunei with only 104,000 and Bhutan with only 60,000 (figures quoted by Crystal 1997: 57–9). However, the figures disguise the fact that in some of these areas, the L2 variety of English is spoken by a very large percentage of the total population. For example, over a third of Singaporeans speak English, but this amounts only to a little over a million of the population of around three million. Again, just under two million Hong Kongese speak an L2 variety of English, but they constitute almost a third of the total Hong Kong population. On the other hand, a mere 4 per cent of Indians speak L2 English, but because the total population is almost one billion, the number of L2 English speakers is vast.

The South Asian Englishes (with the exception of the Maldives) belong to the Outer Circle. Indian, Lankan, Pakistani and Bangladeshi Englishes are often characterised collectively as the South Asian English group (see Crystal 1997: 133), and within this group, Indian and Lankan Englishes are the most developed and well-documented. At the other extreme, little information is available about the Englishes of Bhutan, the Maldives and Nepal.

These countries have much in common in terms of their history and culture, and in the way the English language is sustained within each one by similar groups of élites to perform similar roles (Kandiah 1991). On the other hand, there are differences. In postcolonial Bangladesh, for example, there has been relatively little interest in English beyond the utilitarian: that of widening access by bringing non-English speakers to a level of competence that will enable them to participate in those 'modern' spheres of activity traditionally dominated by the English language and its users. The same was true of Pakistan until recently, when the nation became interested in developing its own distinct variety of English. At present, though, the indications are that Pakistani-English is developing exonormatively (i.e. according to external norms), with British English as its reference point (Kandiah 1991).

On the other hand, while spoken by a smaller percentage of the population, English in India operates well beyond the confines of the practical uses for which it is learnt in Pakistan and Bangladesh. This is to a great extent a function of the unifying role it plays as a neutral language of communication across a people of diverse mother tongues and, as a result, the way in which it has become bound up with Indian national consciousness and identity. Today Indian English performs a wide range of public and personal functions in a variety which has evolved its own phonological, syntactic, lexical and discoursal features rather than continuing to defer to those of its British past (see C7).

Like Indian English, Lankan English, too, has acquired a wide range of local functions both public and personal, though for political reasons it has so far not played the same neutral role in communication across speakers of different mother tongues in Sri Lanka as it has in India. Recently the government has been promoting English as a link language between warring Sinhalese and Tamils, though this policy may not succeed because of differences in orientation towards the learning and use of English across the two ethnic groups (Canagarajah 1999: 82).

Brunei, in common with most of the other Outer Circle territories, is linguistically diverse. Malay is the main language group, with Bahasa Melayu being the official
language and Brunei Malay the most widely used. English is the most important non-
native language as a result of colonial links with Britain, and plays an important role
in education (where a bilingual system is in place), law and the media. Attitudes
to English in the region are positive, with a study carried out in 1993 (Jones 1997)
reporting that Bruneians want to study and be proficient in both Malay and English.
Code switching between Malay and English has become common among educated
Bruneians. It appears possible that in future, there will be a further shift towards English,
with Bruneian Malays, like Malays in Singapore, using English in their homes, and
accompanied by the emergence of a more clearly identifiable variety of Brunei English.

Of Fiji's population of 791,000, just over 20 per cent, or 160,000 (Crystal 1997:
57) speak English as an L2. English is the national language of the territory, and is
used in education, government and business. As in several other Outer Circle countries, it also serves as the language of communication among Fiji's different ethnic
groups. From the limited data so far available, it nevertheless seems that Fiji English
has already become a distinctive local variety characterised by a number of features
which differ from L1 Englishes (see Siegel 1991).

Moving on to Malaysia, as Pennycook (1994: 217) tells us, 'The fortunes of
English in Malaysia have waxed and waned and waxed again, and it never seems far
from the centre of debate.' There are in fact eighty languages spoken in Malaysia, with
Malay (Bahasa Malaysia) the national language and primary *lingua franca* across
ethnic groups, English the second most important language, and Chinese, Tamil and
other Indian languages used among ethnic communities – the latter two largely in
family, social and religious domains. It is as a result of the success of nationalism and
confidence in the stability of Bahasa Malaysia as the country's national language that
English can once again be promoted in the Malaysian education system. However,
because of the previous decline in English use, there is wide range of proficiency among
speakers. The most competent are the English-medium-educated Malaysian élite,
and it is this group who will establish norms for Malaysian English and determine the
target model for acquisition. Because these English speakers use English within a complex linguistic repertoire in which they engage in frequent code switching between
English and Malay, there is considerable scope for borrowing from Malay into
Malaysian English as the variety evolves.

The English of the Philippines is possibly the most comprehensively researched
of all Southeast Asian varieties of English including Singaporean (see Tay 1991). English
is the second language of the Philippines, where a bilingual education policy – English
and Filipino (based on Tagalog) – was adopted in 1972 and is now in place at all school
levels, although Filipino remains the national *lingua franca* while English serves as the
language of wider cross-cultural communication. A distinctive Philippine variety of
English has nevertheless been documented since the late 1960s, when idiosyncratic
pronunciation and grammar features began to be considered legitimate varietal characteristics rather than errors. There are considerable differences between the Philippine English of older and younger generations, along with variation in use among
proficient English users ranging from informal (with patterned code mixing known

as 'Mix-mix') to establish familiarity and rapport, to standard Philippine English for careful speech and writing (see Tay 1991).

Thus, English is already well-ensconced in Asia, if more deeply in some of its regions than others. The greatest need now is for more research into these Englishes.

The changing role of English in Europe

Despite the linguistic richness of the European Union (EU), and the eleven languages given official status (Danish, Dutch, English, Finnish, French, German, Greek, Italian, Portuguese, Spanish and Swedish), three languages dominate – English, French and German. Europe has become, in Graddol's (1997: 14) words, 'a single multilingual area, rather like India, where languages are hierarchically related in status. As in India, there may be many who are monolingual in a regional language, but those who speak one of the "big" languages will have better access to material success.' By the end of the twentieth century, however, a single one of the three 'big' languages, English, had become the 'biggest', the *de facto* European *lingua franca*. And for the time being at least, it seems, those who speak English will have the best access to such material success, hence, in part, the current popularity of learning English among Europe's young that Cheshire (2002) documents.

Some scholars, most vociferously Phillipson (1992, 2003), but including Cheshire herself, believe it is critical for all Europeans to learn each other's languages rather than for everyone to learn English. Nevertheless, Cheshire (2002) notes that European English appears to be developing the scope to 'express "emotional" aspects of young people's social identities' by means of phenomena like code switching and code mixing (e.g. the use of half-German half-English hybrid compounds such as *Telefon junkie* and *Drogenfreak* in German youth magazines).

House (2001), whose position is for the most part diametrically opposed to that of the 'Phillipson camp', finds the EU's language policy hypocritical and ineffective. Rather than having several working languages and making heavy use of a translation machinery, she argues, the EU should opt officially for English as its *lingua franca* or, as she puts it, the 'language for communication'. On the other hand, House does not appear to consider the possibility that English can express the 'social identities' of its European non-native speakers. Instead, she believes that individual speakers' mother tongues will remain their 'language for identification' (House 2001: 2–3).

The positioning of English (or **Euro-English** as it is increasingly being labelled) as Europe's primary *lingua franca* is so recent that it is too soon to be able to say with any certainty whether it will remain so, how it will develop, and whether it will expand to become fully capable of expressing social identity as well as performing a more transactional role in politics, business and the like. The linguistic outcome of European political and economic developments is predicted by some scholars to be a nativised hybrid variety of English, in effect, a European English which contains a number of grammatical, lexical, phonological and discoursal features found in individual mainland European languages along with some items common to many of these languages but not to standard British (or American) English.

Berns (1995: 6–7), for example, characterises the **nativisation** process that English in Europe is undergoing as follows: 'In the course of using English to carry out its three roles [native, foreign and international language], Europeans make adaptations and introduce innovations that effectively de-Americanize and de-Anglicize English.' She talks specifically of a 'European English-using speech community' who use English for intra-European communication, and for whom

> the label *European English* identifies those uses of English that are not British (and not American or Canadian or Australian or any other native variety) but are distinctly European and distinguish European English speakers from speakers of other [English] varieties.

In her view, it is possible that British English will eventually be considered merely as one of a number of European varieties of English alongside nativised varieties such as French English, Dutch English, Danish English and the like.

European English speakers are, nevertheless, as Berns (1995: 10) concludes, 'in the midst of an exciting, challenging, and creative social and linguistic phase of their history' in which 'they have the potential to have significant influence on the spread of English'. The situation is, as she puts it, one of 'sociolinguistic history-in-the-making' and one which will therefore need to be reviewed regularly as empirical evidence becomes increasingly available.

THE FUTURE OF WORLD ENGLISHES   A8

In A8, we consider the implications of English having become the language of 'others' along with the possibility that, within this century, it may lose its position as principal world language to one or more of the languages of these 'others'. In B8, the first of these two themes is developed in a debate as to whether English, if it does remain the major world language, will ultimately fragment into a large number of mutually unintelligible varieties (in effect, languages), or will converge so that differences across groups of speakers are largely eliminated. In C8, the first theme is explored in terms of the extent to which English may either become a killer of other languages or evolve as a common language within a framework of world bilingualism. The strand ends with an extract in D8 from Graddol's meticulous study of English in its world context, *The Future of English?* which takes up many of these issues and leads us into the question mark of the unknown.

English as the language of 'others'

I place 'others' in quotation marks to indicate that the term is, of course, culturally loaded and that my usage is ironic here. If English is already numerically the language of these 'others' and, as the century proceeds, is to become more overtly so, then the centre of gravity of the language is almost certain to shift in the direction of the 'others'. In the years to come we are very likely to witness increasing claims by them for English language rights of the sort that were discussed particularly in A4, A6

and A7. In the words of Widdowson, there is likely to be a paradigm shift from one
of language **distribution** to one of language **spread**:

> I would argue that English as an international language is not *distributed*, as a set of
> established encoded forms, unchanged into different domains of use, but it is *spread*
> as a virtual language [. . .] When we talk about the spread of English, then, it is not
> that the conventionally coded forms and meanings are transmitted into different envi-
> ronments and different surroundings, and taken up and used by different groups of
> people. It is not a matter of the actual language being distributed but of the virtual
> language being spread and in the process being variously actualized. The distribution
> of the actual language implies adoption and conformity. The spread of virtual lan-
> guage implies adaptation and nonconformity. The two processes are quite different.
>
> (Widdowson 1997: 139–40)

In this new paradigm in which English spreads and adapts according to the linguistic
and cultural preferences of its users in the outer and expanding circles, many NS assumptions will no longer hold. In A6 I discussed an article that was published in the *Observer*
newspaper in October 2000, in which the fact that English was the global *lingua franca*
was celebrated as a British advantage. This advantage, however, disappears once other
(non-native speaker) varieties of English are accepted internationally.

The main point is that if English is genuinely to become the language of 'others',
then these 'others' have to be accorded – or perhaps more likely, accord themselves –
at least the same English language rights as those claimed by mother-tongue speakers.
And this includes the right to innovate without every difference from a standard native
speaker variety of English automatically being labelled 'wrong'. This is by definition
what it means for a language to be international – that it spreads and becomes a global
lingua franca for the benefit of all, rather than being distributed to facilitate communication with the natives. It remains to be seen whether such a paradigm shift does in
fact take place.

The language(s) of 'others' as world language(s)

The other potential shift in the linguistic centre of gravity is that English could lose
its international role altogether or, at best, come to share it with a number of equals.
Although this would not happen purely or even mainly as a result of native-speaker
resistance to the spread of non-native speaker Englishes and the consequent abandoning of English by large numbers of non-native speakers, the latter could undoubtedly
play a part. Because the alternatives to English as a world language are covered in
some detail in the Graddol extract in D8, we will consider it only briefly here, by
looking at two main factors: first the difficulties inherent in the English language, and
second the arguments in favour of Spanish as the principal world language.

A piece in the *EL Gazette* in October 2001 (p. 3) under the heading 'It's now official:
English is hard' announced: 'you can now motivate your students by telling them that
English is the hardest European language to learn'. It went on to report a research
study carried out at the University of Dundee, Scotland, which compared the literacy
levels of British primary school children with those from fourteen European countries (Finland, Greece, Italy, Spain, Portugal, France, Belgium, Germany, Austria, Norway,

Iceland, Sweden, the Netherlands and Denmark). Children with one year's schooling had been presented with lists of common words in the mother tongue. It was found that all but the native English speakers were able to read 90 per cent of the words correctly, while the British children could only manage 30 per cent. The researchers concluded that the gap between the English-speaking children and those from the other fourteen countries was the result of difficulties intrinsic to the English language.

Rather than 'motivate' learners, however, such difficulties could, if widely publicised, discourage them from attempting to learn the language at all. The difficulties divide into three main categories: orthographic, phonological and grammatical. **Spelling difficulties** are of various kinds although all relate to the fact that English orthography can often not be predicted from the way in which a word is pronounced. There are, for example, several ways in RP of pronouncing the sequences 'ea' (e.g. as in 'bead', 'head', 'bear', 'fear', pearl), and 'ough' (e.g. as in 'cough', 'bough', 'tough', 'dough', 'through', 'thorough'). A large number of words contain silent letters, such as those which begin with a silent 'p' or 'k' ('psychology', 'pneumonia', 'pseud', 'knife', 'know', etc.), another group which end with silent 'b' ('comb', 'thumb', 'limb', 'climb', etc.), and a third with a silent medial letter (e.g. 'whistle', 'castle', 'fasten', 'muscle'). Other problems are doubled consonants (e.g. 'committee', 'accommodation', 'occasional', 'parallel'), and the spelling of unstressed vowels (e.g. the underlined vowels in 'wom<u>a</u>n', '<u>pe</u>rsuade', 'c<u>o</u>ndition', 's<u>u</u>ccess', 'infi<u>ni</u>ty', all of which are pronounced as schwa in RP and many other, but not all, native accents).

As regards pronunciation, difficulties relate particularly to English vowels. Not only does English have more vowel phonemes than many other languages (twenty in RP as compared with, for instance, five in Spanish and Italian), but it has a particularly large number of diphthongs (eight in RP) and makes extensive use of the central vowel, schwa, in unstressed syllables regardless of the spelling – as was demonstrated in the previous paragraph. In addition, many varieties of English including RP and GA make copious use of weak forms in connected speech. That is, schwa replaces the vowel quality in words such as prepositions ('to', 'of', 'from', etc.), pronouns ('her', 'them', etc.), auxiliaries ('was', 'are', 'has', etc.), articles ('a', 'the') and the like. There are also several other features of connected speech such as elision (loss of sounds), assimilation (modifications to sounds), and liaison (linking of sounds across words). All these aspects of English pronunciation conspire to make it more difficult both to produce and to understand than the pronunciation of many other languages.

Grammatically, difficulties relate very particularly to verb forms and functions. First, English has a large number of tenses all of which have both simple and continuous aspect (present, past, perfect, past perfect, future, future perfect) and none of which have a straightforward link with time reference. Second, there are many **modal verbs** ('may', 'will', 'can', 'should', 'ought to', etc.) each with its own problems of form and function. Third, one of the most problematic areas for learners of English is that of **multiword** (or **phrasal**) **verbs** such as 'get' ('get up', 'get down', 'get on', 'get off', 'get over', 'get through', etc.) and 'take' ('take up', 'take on', 'take in', 'take off', 'take out', etc.). Each has several meanings both literal and metaphorical, along with complicated rules as to whether the verb and particle can or must be separated for an object, depending on whether the verb is classed as adverbial or prepositional.

Because of these difficulties, it would not be surprising if there was eventually a move to abandon English in favour of an international language with fewer complicating linguistic factors along with less of a colonialist discourse attached to it. Spanish appears to be a major contender, with its simpler pronunciation, spelling and verb systems, and its increasing influence in both the EU and America. According to a recent article in *The Times Higher Education Supplement* (14 December 2001 p. 23), 'Spanish is spoken by 400 million people around the world and is the second international language of business as its importance in the United States grows.'

In Europe, there is a massive increase in demand for Spanish, with the number of people travelling to Spain and sitting Spanish-language examinations rising by 15 per cent a year, according to Spain's equivalent of the British Council, the Instituto Cervantes. Even the Spanish government has begun to take the Spanish language industry seriously and is funding promotion activities through its overseas trade board. Meanwhile, in the US it is predicted that there will be 51 million native speakers of Spanish by the year 2010, making this the second largest L1 group after English, and comprising almost a fifth of the total population. Already non-Hispanic whites are in a minority in California and there are also particularly large numbers of Hispanics in Arizona and Texas. However, it is not only a case of numerical increase: the US Hispanic community appears also to be experiencing 'a resurgence of cultural pride and confidence' (*Guardian*, 8 March 2001 p. 12), while politicians are beginning to pay far greater attention to the Hispanic community's needs than they have done hitherto, and Latinos such as the Puerto Rican Ricky Martin and Jennifer Lopez are, respectively, topping world pop music charts and winning important film awards. Given the role of the US in promoting and retaining English as the world's international language, it is not unthinkable that the higher profile of Spanish in the US could play a major part in procuring this linguistic pole position for Spanish – despite the best efforts of the English Only Movement (see C1).

Further evidence that English may eventually give way to another language (or languages) as the world's *lingua franca* is provided by the Internet. According to Crystal

> When the internet started it was of course 100 per cent English because of where it came from, but since the late 1980s that status has started to fall away. By 1995 it was down to about 80 per cent presence of English on the internet, and the current figures for 2001 are that it is hovering somewhere between 60 per cent and 70 per cent, with a significant drop likely over the next four or five years.
>
> (in Elmes 2001: 114)

On the other hand, Crystal continues, 'There are at least 1,500 languages present on the internet now and that figure is likely to increase.' Nevertheless, he predicts that English will remain the dominant presence.

Graddol, on the other hand, considers the role of English on the Internet to be 'only a very passing phase'. In his view, although the Internet has been an important factor in the spread of English around the world, 'the biggest story is not the use of English on the Internet but the use of languages other than English' because it is 'a technology that is very supportive of multilingualism' (in Elmes 2001: 114–15). In an address to the British Association of Applied Linguistics in 2000, Graddol discussed how the predominance of English on the Internet was being lost. In particular, he pointed to the fact that on the one hand many multilingual sites are emerging within Europe, while on the other hand, sites which are not visible to American web users are developing outside Europe. In Japan, for example, only 15 per cent of users apparently wish to search (or 'surf') the Internet in English. Whereas Crystal predicts that English will remain the principal player on the Internet for years to come, Graddol's (1997: 51) view is that as computer use spreads around the world, its English-medium content may fall to as little as 40 per cent. Clearly English-medium Internet use has passed its peak, though the implications for both the spread and type of English used in other forms of communication are as yet far from clear.

SECTION B

DEVELOPMENT
IMPLICATIONS AND ISSUES

THE LEGACY OF COLONIALISM

If you are to gain a full picture of the development of World Englishes, then the historical facts outlined in Section A cannot be divorced from the social and political contexts in which events took place. Nor can these 'facts' be taken at face value, but instead need to be problematised. For colonialism was neither a natural nor a neutral process, but one involving large-scale coercion and displacement, and one which inevitably impacted in major ways on the lives of those whose lands were colonised. Its effects have, in certain respects, lasted well into postcolonial times and may continue to affect people's lives far into the future. One result of colonialism is thought to be the endangering of many indigenous languages, a theme which will be taken up in B8. Here in B1, we will consider two other important and related effects of colonialism during the colonial and postcolonial periods: the denigrating of colonised peoples and their loss of identity (though the latter, of course, also has very close links with language loss).

The devaluing of local language and culture

One major legacy of the two diasporas of English is the assumption of the inferiority of the indigenous language, culture and even character of the colonised, alongside the assumption of the superiority of the colonisers and their language. During the colonial period, this took an extreme form, and it is not uncommon in the literature to find references to the native populations of colonised lands as 'savages', to their languages as 'primitive' and to their cultures as 'barbaric'. The following three quotations illustrate this point:

> A knowledge of the English tongue and its authors, therefore, appears to hold a place of the first importance in a plan for the intellectual and moral elevation of the Hindoos. The English language will not only prove a more correct medium of giving public instruction to the students, but it will facilitate their progress in useful knowledge. All the Indian languages have been for so many ages the vehicle of every thing in their superstition which is morally debasing or corrupting to the mind, and so much is the grossly impure structure of heathenism wrought into the native languages, that the bare study of them often proves injurious to the mind of the European
>
> (London Missionary Society 1826, quoted in Bailey 1991: 135–6)

> Fearful indeed is the impress of degradation which is stamped on the language of the savage, more fearful perhaps even than that which is stamped upon his form. When wholly letting go the truth, when long and greatly sinning against light and conscience, a people has thus gone the downward way, has been scattered off by some violent catastrophe from those regions of the world which are the seats of advance and progress, and driven to its remote isles and further corners, then as one nobler thought, one spiritual idea after another has perished from it, the words also that expressed these have perished too. As one habit of civilization has been let go after another, the words which those habits demanded have dropped as well, first out of use, and then out of memory, and thus after a while have been wholly lost.
>
> (Trench 1891, quoted in Bailey 1991: 278)

Probably everyone would agree that an Englishman would be right in considering his way of looking at the world and at life better than that of the Maori or Hottentot, and no one will object in the abstract to England doing her best to impose her better and higher views on those savages.

(Hobson 1902, quoted in Pennycook 1998: 52)

However, as the following example shows, the same sort of ethos still underlies much of what is written in apparently 'neutral' language today:

To understand the momentous nature of the first English voyages to America, we have to appreciate the forlorn position of these weary travellers in a strange landscape without a single reference point. We have to imagine a world in which all languages were foreign, all communications difficult, and even hazardous [. . .] Just as the Saxon English, confronted by the Norse languages, adapted their speech, so the settlers of Roanoke, Jamestown, and Plymouth, confronted by the need to communicate with Indians who could not speak a word of English, also adapted theirs.

(McCrum *et al.* 1992: 121)

Such disparagement of the non-Anglo (and, especially, non-white) 'other' slips in, it seems, even when writers appear to be attempting to produce an unbiased record of events. Note the words used here to describe the colonisers and their situation ('momentous nature', 'forlorn position', 'weary travellers', 'confronted by the need to communicate', 'adapted [their speech]'). Compare these with the references to the indigenous population and their situation ('strange landscape', 'all languages . . . foreign', 'communications difficult, and even hazardous', 'Indians who could not speak a word of English').

The same phenomenon can be seen at work in the regular references in McCrum *et al.* (1992), Crystal (1997) and many other accounts, to the 'discovery' of lands, as though these territories had not been populated and often home to large numbers of human beings before the arrival of the colonisers. Again, the innocuous word **settlers** is frequently used to describe people who were, in essence, invaders and annexers of lands belonging to others. And even when colonised peoples have made efforts to learn English, the phenomenon reappears in the way their use of English has been criticised – and still is today – sometimes in highly emotive language, because it differs from L1 use. The Japanese Yoko Ono, for example, was criticised in the *Guardian* of 7 January 1998 for 'her mauling of the English language', and again in the *Evening Standard* of 17 May 2001 for having 'the voice to be used against peculiarly spirited inmates in a Khmer Rouge death camp'.

Even this represents a major advance, however, since it is only in very recent times that L2 varieties of English have been accorded any sort of recognition whatsoever. Some former British colonies have embarked on the massive task of describing, standardising and codifying their local English. Nevertheless, this is only the beginning, as they are likely to meet resistance when they attempt to promote their Englishes as 'legitimate' standard varieties internationally. For the prevailing attitude of L1 speakers as well as that of a sizeable majority of L2 speakers is still that 'good English' is synonymous with that of educated native speakers born and bred in the United Kingdom or North America. This is an issue which we will examine more closely later on in the book, particularly in strands 3 and 6.

It is not surprising that, after centuries in which non-Anglo languages and cultures and local L2 varieties of English have been undermined in this way, a lack of confidence pervades many L2 speakers' attitudes towards their use of English, even though they now constitute the majority of the world's English speakers. As Medgyes (1994: 40), a fluent bilingual speaker and teacher of English from Hungary, laments: 'we [non-native teachers of English] suffer from an *inferiority complex* caused by a glaring defect in our knowledge of English. We are in constant distress as we realize how little we know about the language we are supposed to teach.' (See also 'linguistic insecurity' in the Glossarial index.)

Activity

❑ To what extent do you believe that the attitudes towards certain non-English languages and cultures expressed by the nineteenth- and early twentieth-century writers above still exist at the start of the twenty-first century? What evidence is there for your answer?

❑ In your view, do non-native speakers of English suffer from an 'inferiority complex' over their use of English? Should they do so? Why/Why not?

❑ What is your response to the following quotation?

> In the days of empire, the natives were the indigenous populations and the term itself implied uncivilized, primitive, barbaric, even cannibalistic . . . With the spread of English around the globe, 'native' – in relation to English – has acquired newer, positive connotations. 'Native speakers' of English are assumed to be advanced (technologically), civilized, and educated. But as 'NSs' lose their linguistic advantage, with English being spoken as an International Language no less – and often a good deal more – effectively by 'NNSs' . . . ; and as bilingualism and multilingualism become the accepted world norm, and monolingualism the exception . . . , perhaps the word 'native' will return to its pejorative usage. Only this time, the opposite group will be on the receiving end.
>
> (Jenkins 2000: 229)

The loss of ethnic identity

A second major legacy of colonialism is the way in which it has led, either directly or indirectly, to the destruction of the ethnic identities of many whose lands were colonised. This is, in part, the consequence of the loss of indigenous languages, since identity and language are often closely interrelated. It also bears strong links with the undermining of the language and culture of colonised peoples that was discussed in the previous section. The situation, nevertheless, is not entirely hopeless. For as the following extract on the crisis among Native American communities demonstrates, it is possible to revive indigenous languages, or **heritage languages** as they are more commonly called today.

If a Child Learns Only the Non-Indian Way
of Life, You Have Lost Your Child

We turn now to the "identity crisis" under way in indigenous communities today –
a crisis suggested by the words of the Navajo elder that head this section. If it is indeed
the stories, songs and daily interactions in the Native language that convey and transmit
sense of place and sense of self, what happens when the language falls out of use?

This is the situation Native American communities now face. Of 175 indigenous
languages still spoken in the United States, perhaps twenty are being transmitted to
children. Languages in the U.S. Southwest are among the most vital – especially Navajo,
Tohono, 'O'odham, Havasupai, Hopi and Hualapai – with a significant though
declining number of child speakers. But by far the largest numbers of indigenous
languages are spoken only by the middle-aged or grandparent generations.

Contemporary Native writers such as Ortiz, Momaday, Tapahonso, and others
demonstrate that indigenous traditions *can* be represented in English. But Native
speakers, particularly those immersed in the oral literature of their people, are quick
to say, "Yes, but the text is not the same. There is something missing." In some cases,
it is easy to point to words that lack even an approximate English equivalent.
The 'O'odham *himdag*, for example, is often translated as "culture." But 'O'odham
speakers say this is only a distant approximation; speakers understand this word to
have various levels of complexity. As a consequence, they have taken up the practice
of using the 'O'odham word when speaking about it in English.

This example highlights the fact that human cultures are not interchangeable; the
loss of even one language and the cultural knowledge it encodes diminishes us all.
Recognizing this, many tribes are actively engaged in language restoration efforts. In
California, where fifty indigenous languages are spoken – none as a mother tongue
by children – a bold language revitalization movement is under way. "No one feels
this impending loss more strongly than the Native Californians themselves," linguist
Leanne Hinton [. . .] maintains. "Many are making enormous efforts to keep the
language and cultural practices alive . . . even as they participate in the cultures and
intercultures more recently derived from Europe and elsewhere" [. . .].

One such effort is the California Master-Apprentice Language Learning
Program, in which Native speakers and younger apprentices live and work together
over months or years, doing everyday things but communicating through the heritage
language. Speakers from ten language groups have thus far been trained, and several
apprentices have achieved conversational proficiency. In Hawaii, language immersion
programs have successfully revived Hawaiian in dozens of homes. Language immersion programs also have been instituted on the Navajo Nation, among the Mohawks
in New York, Ontario, and Quebec, and in numerous other indigenous communities
throughout the United States.

The development of indigenous literacies has accompanied many of these efforts.
As in many tribes, among the Hualapai of northwestern Arizona the development of
a practical writing system grew out of local initiatives in bilingual education. There is
now a significant body of Hualapai literature, including a grammar and dictionary,
children's and adolescents' storybooks, poetry, teachers' guides, and anthologies of

traditional stories and songs. All of this has raised support for larger, community-wide language maintenance efforts, including tribal sanctions for conducting tribal business in English, and the involvement of children, parents, and grandparents in language revitalization projects.

Literacy in indigenous languages, however, remains primarily restricted to schools, buttressing rather than replacing home- and community-based language transmission. Yet literacy is a powerful symbol of indigenous identity; it valorizes the community and publicly demonstrates the ways in which it is using its language in active and creative ways. By providing new forms for the preservation and transmission of traditional knowledge, indigenous literacy tangibly connects the language with the culture and history of its speakers. Finally, as the Hualapai example shows, indigenous literacy can stimulate other, more diffuse forces for language and culture maintenance. In all of these ways, literacy in indigenous languages is an asset and ally in the struggle to resist linguistic assimilation.

But the fact remains that there is an ever-decreasing pool of Native language speakers. This situation is a direct consequence of the history of colonialism and language repression that indigenous people have, for centuries, endured. Nonetheless, as Darrell Kipp of the Piegan Language Institute pointed out at a recent meeting of indigenous language activists, without their tribal languages, many indigenous communities "will cease to be." The loss of language, he states, "is like throwing away your universe."

(McCarty and Zepeda 1999: 207–8)

It is not only language, but also **place**, which provides people with a sense of identity. This is a song written in 1995 by Dan Hanna, a Havasupai medicine man, describing his native land:

> *The land we were given*
> *the land we were given*
> *It is right here*
> *It is right here*
> *Red Rock*
> *Red Rock . . .*
> *Down at the source*
> *A spring will always be there*
> *It is ours*
> *It is ours*
> *Since a long time ago*
> *Since a long time ago . . .*
> (McCarty and Zepeda 1999: 205)

McCarty and Zepeda point out that

What is interesting . . . is the fact that, in many cases, the places identified in the texts have been appropriated by others, disfigured, and even destroyed. Red Rock – the site to which Dan Hanna refers – is not included within the modern Havasupai reservation and is planned as the location of a uranium mine. Yet Hanna repeats, 'It is ours, it is ours, since a long time ago, it is ours'.

The authors conclude

> It is the stories, the poetry, the prayers, and the songs that continue to fix these places in collective memory, recalling their images, commanding respect, and helping those for whom the narratives are intended to define who they are. Landscape or place sense is no more, or no less, important than language in this process. It is within the places in the stories that the "sense of ourselves" resides.
>
> (McCarty and Zepeda 1999: 205–6)

✪ **Activity**

❑ To what extent do you believe it is possible for groups of people to retain their ethnic identity when (a) they are removed from their ethnic homeland and/or (b) they lose the use of their mother tongue?

❑ How strong a role do you think the written language plays in forming and retaining a sense of ethnic group identity? Does there in fact have to be a written language at all, or is oral communication sufficient? And what about the role of literature: how strong a part does it play in identity formation; and can it continue to promote ethnic identity if it is transmitted only orally or in translation?

❑ In the concluding comments to his edited volume, *Handbook of Language and Ethnic Identity*, Fishman (1999: 448–9) quotes a number of scholars who argue that those who feel more secure about their own identity are more tolerant of other ethnic groups and, at the same time, better placed to be an effective member of a cosmopolitan grouping. He finishes his discussion by quoting Haarman (1997) on **European identity** as follows:

> European identity includes cosmopolitan elements, but cosmopolitanism cannot serve as a simplistic substitute for traditional national identity . . . The recipe for a member of a national community to become a self-confident European lies not in the denial or neglect of his national collective identity . . . Somebody who considers him- or herself to be a cosmopolitan at the cost of national identity will hardly be in a position to appreciate the national components in other people's identity, and this can only weaken cooperation among Europeans.
>
> (Haarman 1997: 286)

Do you agree that it is essential to retain one's own national identity in order to become a 'self-confident' member of a larger grouping such as Europe?

CHARACTERISTICS OF PIDGINS AND CREOLES **B2**

This unit first takes you through the main formal features of pidgins and creole lexis, pronunciation and grammar, and then moves on to look at samples of texts serving a range of functions.

Lexis, pronunciation and grammar

Lexis

Generally, pidgin lexis is drawn from the dominant language, usually a European language such as English, French, Portuguese or Dutch (known as the **lexifier language**), while pidgin grammar is that of the indigenous African or Asian languages. Pidgin lexis is systematic and, like any language, has rules of use, although in the earlier stages of evolution, these rules are simpler. In particular:

❑ Concepts tend to be encoded in lengthier ways. For example, in Tok Pisin, an English-based pidgin in Papua New Guinea, the word 'bilong' (from 'belong') means 'of', so that 'papa bilong mi' means 'my father', and 'haus bilong yu' means 'your house'.

❑ There is extensive use of **reduplication**. This is partly to intensify meaning (e.g. 'tok' means 'talk', whereas 'toktok' means chatter, and 'look' means 'look', whereas 'looklook' means 'stare'), and partly to avoid confusions which could result from phonological similarity (e.g. in some Pacific pidgins, 'sip' means 'ship' whereas 'sipsip' means 'sheep', 'pis' means 'peace' whereas 'pispis' means 'urinate', and in some Atlantic pidgins, 'was' means 'watch' whereas 'waswas' means 'wash'; see Todd (1990: 53) for more examples).

Pronunciation

Pidgins have fewer sounds than those of the corresponding standard language, even at creole stages in their evolution. For example, Tok Pisin has only five vowel sounds [a] [e] [i] [o] [u] and most Caribbean creole speakers twelve, whereas American English (General American) has seventeen and British English (Received Pronunciation) has twenty. This means that in Tok Pisin there is, for example, only one sound /ɪ/ for the two British and American English sounds /ɪ/ as in the word 'dip' and /iː/ as in the word 'deep', and one sound /ɔː/ for the British English sounds /ɜː/ as in 'work' and /ɔː/ as in 'walk'.

Moving to consonants, one feature of most pidgins and creoles is the **simplification** of consonant clusters so that, for instance, 'friend' becomes 'fren', 'cold' becomes 'col' and 'salt' becomes 'sol'. Another feature is **conflation**: most Caribbean creole speakers conflate the sounds /t/ with /θ/, /d/ with /ð/, and /tʃ/ with /ʃ/, while Tok Pisin speakers also conflate a number of other consonant sounds including /f/ and /p/, and /s/, /ʃ/ and /tʃ/. The result of this reduced phoneme inventory, even allowing for the effects of reduplication described in the section on lexis, is a much larger number of **homophones** (two words pronounced identically, e.g. 'pear' and 'pair') than exist in British or American English.

Grammar

Some of the main grammatical characteristics of pidgins and creoles are:

❑ They have few **inflections** in their nouns, pronouns, verbs and adjectives, especially in pidgin phases. For example, nouns are not marked for number or gender and verbs have no tense markers. Pronouns are not distinguished for case, so that most pidgins use 'me' to indicate both 'I' and 'me'. However, Tok Pisin, like many other Melanesian languages, distinguishes between inclusive 'we', 'yumi' referring to the addressee and speaker, and non-inclusive 'we', 'mepela' (literally 'me and fellow') referring to the speaker and others, but not the addressee. The suffix '-fela' or '-pela' is also added to attributive adjectives describing people and things, e.g. 'naispela haus' ('nice house') and 'gutpela meri' ('good woman', 'meri' deriving from 'Mary').

❏ **Negation** is formed with a simple negative particle, often 'no' for English-based pidgins and 'pa' for French-based. For example, Krio from Sierra Leone uses 'no', as in 'I no tu had', while the French-based Seychelles Creole uses 'pa' as in 'I pa tro difisil'.

❏ In pidgin phases, **clause structure** is uncomplicated so that, for example, there are no embedded clauses such as relative clauses.

As pidgins develop into creoles, four main types of change take place:

❏ People begin to speak them much faster, so that they start employing processes of **assimilation** and **reduction**: Tok Pisin 'man bilong mi' (my husband) becomes 'mamblomi'.

❏ Their vocabularies expand:
  ❏ New shorter words are formed alongside phrases: 'paitman' develops along-side 'man bilong pait' (fighter). Eventually the longer expression dies out.
  ❏ The capacity for word-building develops, e.g. the suffix '-im' is added to adjectives to form verbs as in 'bik' (big, large), 'bikim' (to enlarge), 'brait' (wide), 'braitim' (to widen).
  ❏ Technical words are borrowed from Standard English.

❏ They develop a tense system in their verbs, e.g. 'bin' is used to mark past tense and 'bi' (from 'baimbai') to mark future tense.

❏ They develop greater sentence complexity, for example their speakers are able to form relative clauses (Aitchison 1991: 190–1, and see also Sebba 1997: 107–33).

Social functions

Extended pidgins and creoles perform a very wide range of **social functions** that go well beyond the original purpose of pidgins to serve as basic contact languages. They are used, for instance, in literature, both oral and written, in education, in the mass media, in advertising and in the Bible. The important point to note about the scope of pidgins and creoles is that they are, or can easily become, capable of expressing all the needs of their speakers.

Activity

Below there are samples of Tok Pisin translations of an excerpt from Shakespeare's *Julius Caesar*, the Lord's Prayer from the Gospel of St Matthew in the Bible, and an advert for Colgate toothpaste. The translation of Mark Antony's famous speech from *Julius Caesar* was, in fact, undertaken by a European, Murphy, in 1943 for the specific purpose of demonstrating that pidgins are not inadequate languages. In each case, see how much of the pidgin text you are able to understand before turning to the English versions that follow the Tok Pisin group.

The Tok Pisin versions

1 The Lord's Prayer in the *Tok Pisin Nupela Testamen* translation, 1969
Fader bilong mifelo, yu stop long heven – Ol i santuim nem bilong yu – Kingdom
bilong yu i kam – Ol i hirim tok bilong yu long graund olsem long heven. Tude
givim mifelo kaikai bilong de – Forgivim rong bilong mifelo – olsem mifelo forgivim rong – ol i mekim long mifelo. Yu no bringun mifelo long traiim – tekewe
samting no gud long mifelo. Amen.

(From Mühlhäusler 1997: 329)

2 Excerpt from *Julius Caesar*
Pren, man bilong Rom, Wantok, harim nau. Mi kam tasol long plantim Kaesar. Mi
noken beiten longen. Sopos sampela wok bilong wampela man i stret; sampela
i no stret; na man i dai; ol i wailis long wok i no stret tasol. Gutpela wok bilongen
i slip; i lus nating long giraun wantaim long Kalopa. Fesin biling yumi man. Maski
Kaesar tu, gutpela wok i slip.

(From Mühlhäusler 1997: 325)

3 Colgate toothpaste advertisement
Colgate i save strongim tit bilong yu
Lukaut: planti switpela kaikai na loli
i savi bagarapim tit hariap

(from Aitchison 1996: 142, reproduced from Wantok,
Tok Pisin newspaper, 1980)

The British English versions

1 Our Father in heaven,
may your name be held holy,
your Kingdom come,
your will be done,
on earth as in heaven.
Give us today our daily bread.
And forgive us our debts,
as we have forgiven those who are in debt to us.
And do not put us to the test,
but save us from the evil one.
(*The Jerusalem Bible*, Matthew 6, 9–13)

> Friends, Romans, Countrymen, lend me your ears;
> I come to bury Caesar, not to praise him.
> The evil that men do lives after them;
> The good is oft interred with their bones;
> So let it be with Caesar.
> (*Julius Caesar* Act 1, Scene 2)

> *Colgate strengthens your teeth.*
> *Take care. Lots of sugary foods and sweets*
> *rot your teeth fast.*
> (Note: 'bagarapim' = the verb 'to destroy', from English 'bugger up',
> and 'hariap' = the adverb 'fast', from English 'hurry up')

We finish this section with an example of contemporary Tok Pisin, a news item which appeared in the Papua New Guinean newspaper, *Wantok*, in April 1994:

Ol meri gat bikpela wari yet

> Helt na envairomen em ol bikpela samting ol meri long kantri tude i gat bikpela wari long en.
>
> Bikos dispela tupela samting i save kamap strong long sindaun na laip bilong famili na komyuniti insait long ol ples na kantri.
>
> Long dispela wik, moa long 40 meri bilong Milen Be provins i bung long wanpela woksop long Alotau bilong toktok long hevi bilong helt na envairomen long ol liklik ailan na provins.
>
> Bung i bin stat long Mande na bai pinis long Fraide, Epril 22. Ol opisa bilong Melanesin Envairomen Faundesen wantaim nesenel na provinsal helt opis i stap tu bilong givim toktok insait long dispela worksop.

Before you go on to compare the original with the verbatim and British English versions which follow, see how much of the text you can already understand, and make a note of any features of lexis, grammar and (by implication) pronunciation that fit into the categories described in the first part of this unit:

All women got big-fellow worry yet

Health and environment him all big-fellow something all woman along country today he got big-fellow worry along him.

Because this-fellow two-fellow something he know come-up strong along sit-down and life belong family and community inside along all place and country.

Along this-fellow week, more along 40 woman belong Milne Bay Province he meet along one-fellow workshop along Alotau belong talk-talk along heavy belong health and environment along all little island and province.

Meeting he been start along Monday and bye(-and-bye) finish along Friday April 22

All officer belong Melanesian Environment Foundation one-time national and provincial health office he stop too belong give-him talk-talk inside along this-fellow workshop.

Women still have big worries

Health and environment are two of the major things which women in the country today have big concerns about.

Because these two things often have a strong effect on the situation and life of families and communities within villages and in the country.

This week, more than 40 women from Milne Bay Province are meeting in a workshop at Alotau in order to talk about the difficulties of health and environment in the small islands and provinces. The meeting began on Monday and will finish on Friday April 22.

The officers of the Melanesian Environment Foundation together with the national and provincial health office are there too in order to give talks in the workshop.

(Text and translations from Sebba 1997: 20–1)

THE *ENGLISH TODAY* DEBATE

With an ever-growing number of people speaking English in an increasing number of regions of the world, it is not surprising that the language is diversifying and 'English' becoming 'Englishes'. Local conditions, including the influence of the languages of indigenous peoples and, for ESL and EFL speakers, that of the other languages they speak, are inevitably affecting the English that is evolving in different contexts around the world. Even within the ENL group, there are cross-cultural differences especially in accent, but also in vocabulary and, to a lesser extent, grammar. Nevertheless, the standard varieties of English in the countries of the Inner Circle are regarded as 'legitimate' world norms, even if some ENL speakers regard their own country's standard forms as superior to those of the other ENL countries.

The situation is rather different for speakers of English in the Outer and Expanding Circles. World English scholars argue that the institutionalised varieties of English of countries like India in the Outer Circle should, in their standard (acrolect) forms, be accepted as being comparable with the standard Englishes of the Inner Circle countries, and so just as valid as local teaching models. On the other hand, many others consider differences from British or American standards not to be local innovations but errors and, as such, evidence of the substandard nature of these varieties. They regard English spoken in the Outer Circle as **interlanguage** (in effect, learner language which has not reached the target) containing incorrect forms that have 'fossilised' (i.e. learning has ceased short of nativelike competence – see B7). The situation is even more controversial in relation to English speakers in the Expanding Circle, and their position is not helped by the fact that those who argue for the recognition of ESL varieties are slow to extend the argument to the Expanding Circle. Because of the major changes currently taking place in the latter circle, it forms the topic of the entire strand 6, while much of what follows here in B3 is concerned mainly, though not exclusively, with Outer Circle Englishes.

Non-native Englishes as 'deficit'

The controversy over the legitimacy of non-native varieties of English is crystallised in a debate which took place in the pages of the journal *English Today* in the early 1990s. In 1990, the journal published an article by Quirk, 'Language varieties and standard language'. In essence, Quirk's position was that non-native Englishes are inadequately learnt versions of 'correct' native English forms and therefore not valid as teaching models. Kachru's strongly-worded response, 'Liberation linguistics and the Quirk concern' followed in 1991. Read through these points taken from Quirk's article and decide how far you agree or disagree with him:

 Activity

❏ The native/non-native distinction is a valid one because research by Coppieters (1987) shows that native and non-native speakers have different intuitions about a language. For example, they differ in their judgements of the grammatical correctness of sentences. This research finding implies 'the need for non-native teachers to be in constant touch with the native language' (pp. 6–7). It also implies that natives and non-natives 'have radically different internalizations' of the language, so that it will be unwise to attempt to institutionalise non-native varieties.

❏ Learners of English outside Britain come to the language with little or no prior knowledge, and need to learn Standard English in order to 'increase their freedom and their career prospects' (note that this is the argument used by Honey

1997 in his book *Language is Power*). The teacher's 'duty' therefore is not to question notions of correct and incorrect use, but to teach Standard English (p. 7).

❑ There are no institutionalised varieties of English. In countries where these are claimed to exist, those in authority

> tend to protest that the so-called national variety of English is an attempt to justify inability to acquire what they persist in seeing as 'real' English. [...] No-one should underestimate the problem of teaching English in such countries as India and Nigeria, where the English of the teachers themselves inevitably bears the stamp of locally acquired deviation from the standard language ("You are knowing my father, isn't it".) The temptation is great to accept the situation and even to justify it in euphemistically sociolinguistic terms.
>
> (pp. 8–9)

❑ The teaching of English in the countries of the Expanding Circle should not involve any conflict over standards and where it does, is a reflection of 'half-baked quackery' and is mainly perpetuated by minimally trained teachers and 'academic linguists with little experience of foreign language teaching'. Just because, for example, the use of the phrase 'several informations' is intelligible, this is no reason to ignore the incorrect use of an uncountable noun (p. 9).

❑ Quirk concludes

> If I were a foreign student paying good money in Tokyo or Madrid to be taught English, I would feel cheated by such tolerant pluralism. My goal would be to acquire English precisely because of its power as an instrument of international communication. I would be annoyed at the equivocation over English since it seemed to be unparalleled in the teaching of French, German, Russian, or Chinese.

He recommends that while 'it is not easy to eradicate once-fashionable educational theories . . . the effort is worthwhile for those of us who believe that the world needs an international language and that English is the best candidate at present on offer' (p. 10).

Non-native Englishes as 'difference'

 Activity   Now read through some of the points Kachru makes in criticising what he describes as Quirk's **deficit linguistics** position:

❑   The solution of "constant touch with the native language" does not apply to the institutionalized varieties for more than one reason: first, the practical reason that it is simply not possible for a teacher to be in constant touch with the *native* language given the number of teachers involved, the lack of resources and the overwhelming *non-native* input; second, the functional reason that the users of institutionalized varieties are expected to conform to local norms and speech strategies since English is used for interaction primarily in intranational contexts . . . The natives may have "radically different **internalizations**" [intuitions about grammaticality] regarding their L1 but that point is not vital for a rejection of institutionalization. In fact, the arguments for recognizing institutionalization are that non-native users of English have internalizations which are linked to their own multilinguistic, sociolinguistic and sociocultural contexts.

(p. 5)

❏ Quirk seems to perceive the spread of English primarily from the perspective of monolingual societies, and from uncomplicated language policy contexts. The concerns he expresses are far from the realities of multilingual societies, and negate the linguistic, sociolinguistic, educational and pragmatic realities of such societies.

(p. 6)

❏ Kachru goes on to argue (p. 10) that Quirk's approach is based on at least four false assumptions (see Kachru 1992: 357–9, where these are presented as 'Six fallacies about the users and uses of English'):

1 that in the outer and Expanding circles . . . English is essentially learnt to interact with the native speakers of the language . . . The reality is that in its localized varieties, English has become the main vehicle for interaction among its non-native users, with distinct linguistic and cultural backgrounds – Indians interacting with Nigerians, Japanese, Sri Lankans, Germans with Singaporeans and so on. The culture-bound localized strategies of, for example, politeness, persuasion and phatic communion transcreated in English are more effective and culturally significant than are the 'native' strategies for interaction.

2 that English is essentially learnt as a tool to understand and teach the American or British cultural values, or what is generally termed the Judeo-Christian traditions . . . In culturally and linguistically pluralistic regions of the Outer Circle, English is an important tool to impart local traditions and cultural values.

3 that the international non-native varieties of English are essentially "interlanguages" striving to achieve "native-like" character . . . In reality, the situation is . . . that such institutionalized varieties are varieties of English in their own right rather than stages on the way to more native-like English.

4 that the native speakers of English as teachers, academic administrators and material developers are seriously involved in the global teaching of English, in policy formulation and in determining channels for the spread of language . . . In proposing language policies for English in the global context . . . there is a need for a "paradigm shift" . . . reconsidering the traditional sacred cows of English . . . I am thinking of concepts such as the "speech community" of English, "ideal speaker-hearer" of English and the "native speaker of English". In the context of world Englishes, what we actually see is that diversification is a marker of various types of sociolinguistic "messages" . . .

❏ Kachru concludes that what Quirk describes in terms of 'deficit' is in the global context a matter of 'difference which is based on vital sociolinguistic realities of identity, creativity and linguistic and cultural contact'.

❏ Whose arguments do you find more convincing, Quirk's or Kachru's?

❑ How can we decide whether a non-standard English usage is an 'error' or an 'innovation'? Does it depend entirely on whether the speaker is native or non-native or are there other criteria such as frequency of use, number of users and so on?

❑ What is your response to these comments made by Bamgboṣe and de Klerk?

> The main question with innovations is the need to decide when an observed feature of language use is indeed an innovation and when it is simply an error. An innovation is seen as an acceptable variant, while an error is simply a mistake, or uneducated usage. If innovations are seen as errors, a non-native variety can never receive any recognition
>
> (Bamgboṣe 1998: 22)

> When does a substratal [indigenous] feature assert itself sufficiently to overcome the fear that if deviations are allowed, the rules will be abandoned and chaos will ensue? Is it when speakers use it often enough to silence or exhaust the prescriptors?
>
> (de Klerk 1999: 315)

❑ What do you see as the advantages and the disadvantages of a **pluricentric approach** to English, in which there are several global centres, native and non-native, each with their own standard variety of English? For example, how far is the way this enables a variety of English to express the culture of its speakers outweighed by problems such as the threat of fragmentation of English into mutually unintelligible languages? And if you think this is a realistic fear, what measures could be taken to prevent it from materialising?

❑ Kachru appears to take offence at Quirk's rejection of the distinction between speakers of English in the Outer Circle and those in the Expanding Circle, and the fact that he settles instead for a simple dichotomy between native and non-native speakers of English. In your view, are speakers of L2 Englishes in the Outer Circle 'privileged' over those in the Expanding Circle when it comes to English language rights?

B4 **THE LEGITIMATE AND ILLEGITIMATE OFFSPRING OF ENGLISH**

The naming of the New Englishes

B4 takes its title from that of an article by the World Englishes scholar Mufwene. In the article, he argues that the way in which New Englishes are named 'has to do more with who have appropriated and speak them than with how they developed and how different they are structurally from each other, hence with how mutually intelligible they are' (Mufwene 1997: 182).

In particular, Mufwene attacks the view of many western linguists that the 'legitimate offspring' of the English language are those varieties spoken by descendants of European speakers of English while its 'illegitimate offspring' are the varieties spoken by those who are not. In other words, the Englishes of the Inner Circle have the right to be named 'English', while those outside this charmed circle forfeit that right. The most extreme group of 'illegitimate offspring', according to this view, argues Mufwene, is that of the English-based pidgins and creoles. These are often classified as separate languages or even, in the case of pidgins, considered not to be entitled to the name 'language' at all. Also disenfranchised are the indigenised New Englishes of the Outer Circle. Despite the fact that they are used for a wide range of daily purposes in many countries of the Outer Circle and have developed their own varietal characteristics (i.e. have become **nativised**), the New Englishes are to this day called 'non-native' Englishes by western linguists.

Mufwene goes on to argue that this classification of Englishes into 'legitimate' and 'illegitimate' is based on a mistaken belief about language contact. According to this belief, a **mother language** gives birth to **daughter languages** without the intervention of any other languages prior to the production of the 'offspring', that is, without any language contact. Mufwene points out that **language contact** was in fact a feature of the development of the 'legitimate' Englishes, but that this is generally overlooked. For example, Irish and Scots-Irish Englishes were influenced by contact with Gaelic. However, because the latter Englishes are spoken almost entirely by communities of native speakers, they are not termed creoles, even in their most non-standard forms, despite the contact involved in their development.

Mufwene provides examples of a range of Englishes past and present, to demonstrate his point that the sharing of an identifiable ancestor does not at all guarantee the intelligibility of a variety: 'if mutual intelligibility were such a critical criterion over sharing an identifiable ancestor, there would be more reasons for treating Modern English varieties and creoles as dialects of the same language than for lumping the former together with Old English while excluding creoles' (Mufwene 1997: 190). In the next section, some of the examples used by Mufwene to support his argument are reproduced, along with further examples from other sources.

A range of Englishes

As you read through the following extracts, assess how easy it is to make sense of each one and, if you can, identify the time and place in which each one is/was written or spoken. Finally, before you consult the key and discussion which follow the extracts, decide which you consider to be 'legitimate' and which 'illegitimate' Englishes. You will need to think here about the criteria on which to base your decisions, e.g. degree of (evident) contact with other languages, intelligibility and suchlike. Activity

Extract 1

Nu scylun hergan hefænricæs Uard,
Metudæs mæcti end His modgidanc,
uerc Uuldurfadur, sue He uundra gihuæs,
eci Dryctin, or astelidæ.
He ærist scop ælda barnum
heben til hrofe, haleg Scepen.
Tha middungeard moncynnæs Uard,
eci Dryctin, æfter tiadæ
firum foldu, Frea allmectig.

Gaelic

Extract 2

O dronke man, disfigured is thy face,
Sour is thy breeth, foul artow to embrace,
And thurgh they dronke nose semeth the soun
As though thou seydest ay 'Sampsoun, Sampsoun';
And yet, god wot, Sampsoun drank never no wyn,
Thou fallest, as it were a stiked swyn.

Old English

Extract 3

Creole

JR	You trow way . . . trow way wha? En one day, I gone down deh, en talk bout shrimp bin a bite! I bin ondat flat, en I had me line, I done ketch couple a whiting . . . I say, I ga put up da drop net . . . when I look up, duh look from yah to your car deh, I see sompin on da damn side da shoulder comin, like a damn log. I watch um, en when I see him gone down . . .
EL	Hm hm!
JR	En dat tide bin a comin in . . . en dat sucker swim close, closer en closer, den
	I look en I see dat alligator open e damn mouth!

Extract 4

Well, I seen the time you'd buy a farm for . . . five or six hundred . . . Seen farms selling and I young lad.

But when the house is quiet and us alone you never heard such talk that's going on there

He fell and him crossing the bridge.

Hiberno-English (Irish)

Extract 5

. . . Went down there and he's a-holding three dogs in one hand and the coon in the other hand. And they's all a-trying to bite the coon and the coon a-trying to bite Jack and the dogs, and Jack pulled out a sack and it wasn't a dang thing but an old pillow case that Maggie had used, his wife, it was about wore out . . .

Appalachian (Elizabethan) English

Extract 6

Owar ya? Ts goota meecha mai 'tee.
Naluk. Djarem membah dabrah nai dul? Tintin zluk infu rit'h. Kanyah elpim?

Dabrah nai dul? Oi, oi! Slaika toljah. Datrai b'gib dabrah nai dul ta'Walker. Ewuz anaisgi. Buttiz'h felaz tukahr presh usdjuel. Enefda Arumbayas ket chimdai lavis gutsfa gahtah'z. Nomess in'h!

Arumbaya fictional!

Extract 7

When it was early in the morning of the next day, I had not palm-wine to drink at all, and throughout that day I felt not so happy as before; I was seriously sat down in my parlour, but when it was the third day that I had no palm-wine at all, all my friends did not come to my house again, they left me there alone, because there was no palm-wine for them to drink.

Yaruba-sping Nigerian.

Intelligible.

Extract 8

> In the upgrowth o a leid ti haill matuirity o lettirs, the staiblishin o an exponent prose is aften deimit a determant stage. A leid may hae a weil-founnit tradeition o hameilt sang, leirit indyte, an ein nerratif prose; but wantan a registir conding for academic screivins, hit maun bide be a'hauf-leid' . . .

Scotish

Extract 9

> A no wahn a ting tu du wid yu bika yu kom . . . lang taym an yu no kom luk for Titi. Hu iz dis, Pap?

Miskito Indians Nicaragua

Key

Extract 1

This is Cædmon's Hymn, an early Old English religious poem composed by the poet Cædmon, and dating from 657 to 680. The above version of the text is in a Northumbrian dialect. It has been translated as follows:

> Now must we praise the Guardian of heaven,
> The power and conception of the Lord,
> And all His works, as He, eternal Lord,
> Father of glory, started every wonder.
> First He created heaven as a roof,
> The holy Maker, for the sons of men.
> Then the eternal Keeper of mankind
> Furnished the earth below, the land for men,
> Almighty God and everlasting Lord.
>   (Hamer, R. ed. 1970, *A Choice of Anglo-Saxon Verse*,
>   London: Faber and Faber: 122–3)

Extract 2

This extract is by the Middle English author, Geoffrey Chaucer. It comes from the 'Pardoner's Tale', one of Chaucer's *Canterbury Tales* (*c.*1386–1400), and tells the story of a fraudulent preacher who preaches against avarice, a sin which he himself commits. The section of the tale provided in Extract 2 comes from part of the Pardoner's sermon in which he rails against drunkenness (lines 223–8). The language is clearly considerably closer to modern English than is the Old English example which precedes it, but not necessarily any closer than some of the contemporary New English extracts, such as the one which follows it.

Extract 3

This conversation comes from Mufwene's field records (1997: 191) gathered in the 1980s. The language exemplified is the Creole, Gullah, spoken along the US coast from Florida to South Carolina and the Sea Islands.

Extract 4

This set of extracts is also taken from Mufwene's article (though the original sources are Odlin 1992 and Filppula 1991). They all exemplify spoken Hiberno-English, that is, Irish English. Only the third one may need translating: 'He fell while crossing the bridge'.

Extract 5

This is an example of Appalachian speech from West Virginia in the US. It is from a study carried out by the sociolinguist Walt Wolfram (cited in Crystal 1995: 315). Appalachian speech is considered to represent a very conservative dialect of American English and therefore to be closer than others to the speech of the original Elizabethan settlers. Despite certain features that are not used in modern English dialects, e.g. the a-prefix with -ing forms, you should find the extract intelligible.

Extract 6

This is another of the examples cited by Mufwene (1997: 193). Once you work out the 'system', you should be able to understand it without translation. If you have not yet managed to do so, read through the translation, return to the original, and all should become clear:

> How are you? It's good to meet you, matey.
>
> Now look. Do you remember the brown idol? Tintin's looking for it. Can you help him?
>
> The brown idol? – It's like I told you. The tribe gave the brown idol to Walker. He was a nice guy. But his fellows took our precious jewel. And if the Arumbayas catch him, they'll have his garters. No messing!

The extract is from 'The Arumbaya language according to Leslie Lonsdale-Cooper and Michael Turner, the translators of Hergé's *The Adventures of Tintin: The Broken Ear* (1975)'. It is, then, fictional and, as Mufwene points out, 'perhaps the only development which one may consider unnatural in settings where English has been appropriated by a foreign group'. He comments that his eight-year-old daughter could not interpret it because she could not recognise any English words which, in turn, is because the creators of the language have 'segmented the phonetic strings in ways that violate English word boundaries'. Mufwene adds that there are no pidgin or creole languages which restructure English in this way.

Extract 7

This sample (cited in Platt *et al.* 1984: 179) remains in the realms of literature. This time, it comes from the Nigerian author, Amos Tutuola's work, *The Palm-Wine*

Drunkard. Tutuola's English is influenced by his mother tongue, Yoruba (an indigenous Nigerian language), and this comes across in his writing. While exhibiting features not found in the English of native speakers (e.g. 'all my friends did not come . . .'), Tutuola's English should be perfectly intelligible to those who speak other varieties.

Extract 8

These are the opening lines of a journal article on Scots, published in the journal *English World-Wide* in 1981 (cited in Crystal 1995: 333), and originally presented at the symposium *Our ain lied?* (Our own language?). This is one of the few extracts for which you will probably need a translation. This is how Crystal translates it:

> In the development of a language to full maturity of literature, the establishment of an expository prose is often judged a crucial stage. A language may have a well-founded tradition of domestic song, learned poetry, and even narrative prose; but lacking a register suitable for academic writers, it must remain a 'half-language'.

Extract 9

This extract exemplifies the variety of English spoken by the Miskito Indians on the Miskito coast of Nicaragua. According to McCrum *et al.* (1992: 219–20), from whom the extract is taken, the Miskito Indians 'use a variety of English that has evolved from a unique collision of languages: the speech of seventeenth- and eighteenth-century British settlers, their African slaves, the Indians themselves, and later the Spanish-speakers who seized the area at the end of the nineteenth century'. Miskito was isolated from mainstream English for almost 200 years and, as a result, evolved differently from the latter, although it also has features in common both with more standard varieties and with West African pidgins. The extract is translated by McCrum *et al.* as: 'I want nothing to do with you because you have not come for a long time to see Titi. Who is this?'

Activity

❏   Try to pick out any features of lexis, grammar, pronunciation or discourse style which characterise the variety in each extract.

❏   Which extracts did you originally decide represented 'legitimate' and which 'illegitimate' varieties of English? What were your criteria? Did your decision depend to some extent on whether you thought the sample was spoken or written (or a literary representation of speech or writing)? To what extent did your decision depend on the degree of standardness? Having read the Key, have you changed your mind in any respect? If so, why?

❏   Kachru (1997: 228) distinguishes between *innovation, deviation* and *mistake*. An **innovation** is concerned with creativity which, as Kachru points out, the gatekeepers of English in the UK have not generally accepted from speakers of English in the other Inner Circle countries, let alone in the countries of the Outer Circle. A **deviation** involves a comparison with another variety, normally one from the Inner Circle, while a **mistake** (or 'error') relates to acquisitional deficiency.

To what extent would you describe the characteristic features you were able to identify as representing innovations, deviations, or mistakes in the varieties of English concerned?

STANDARDS ACROSS SPACE

Standard English across regions

In both parts of B5 we will be focusing primarily on English spoken in Britain, North America and Australia, and looking in particular at vocabulary and grammar. In the first part we will be concerned with the similarities and differences across the Englishes designated 'standard' in each of these three regions, while in the second, attention will shift to the similarities and differences across varieties of English within two of the regions, Britain and North America.

Although the differences across the standard native-speaker varieties of English are far outweighed by the similarities, each of these three standard Englishes has certain features which characterise it as specifically British, American or Australian. The most noticeable level of divergence is that of vocabulary, with lexical differences between British and American Englishes far exceeding those between Britain and Australia. In the case of British and **North American English**, thousands of words either do not exist at all in one or other variety, or have completely or partially different meanings. The main reasons for this are to some extent obvious. First, the early settlers needed to name those items for which they did not already have names. They did this by extending the meaning of existing English words, creating new words, or borrowing items from the indigenous population, the **Native Americans**. Examples of words with extended meaning are 'corn' (referring to grain in Britain, maize in North America) and 'robin' (a small red-breasted warbler in Britain, a large red-breasted thrush in North America). An example of a new creation is 'butte' (an isolated hill with a flat top). Examples of borrowing are 'moccasin', 'squash' and 'toboggan' (see McCrum *et al.* 1992). Second, developments taking place since North American English separated from British English have led to further divergences between the two varieties. This is particularly true of vocabulary resulting from technological innovation, such as car-related words. For example, North American English has 'windshield', 'hood' and 'trunk' for the items which in British English are designated 'windscreen', 'bonnet' and 'boot'.

Trudgill and Hannah (2002: 85–8) divide **English English** (their preferred term for **Standard British English** from England) and US English differences into four main categories:

 Activity

1 *Same word, different meaning*
2 *Same word, additional meaning in one variety*
3 *Same word, difference in style, connotation, frequency of use*
4 *Same concept or item, different word*

The following is a selection of items from Trudgill and Hannah's lists. Can you place them in the correct categories and explain the difference in British/American use? (NB one word fits two categories.) Think about the sorts of communication problems that might arise as a result of these differences. Which category, in your view, has the greatest potential to cause miscommunication between speakers of English from the UK and the US?

faucet   smart   autumn   regular
bathroom   pants   sophomore   to fancy
a queue   pavement   homely   school
quite   (as in *quite good*)   (key opposite)

Category 1 probably has the greatest potential to cause miscommunication. This is because the difference in meaning may never be appreciated and clarified, and so the miscommunication is more likely to remain unresolved.

The differences between **Australian English** and British English lexis are relatively few in number except at the level of idiomatic language and slang. One source of Australian lexical innovation was initially borrowings into English from the Australian aboriginal languages. These include words like 'kangaroo' and 'boomerang' which are widely known outside Australia, as well as some which are less well-known, such as 'gibber' (a rock), 'corroboree' (a large gathering), and 'jumbuck' (a sheep). Many are words for the indigenous flora and fauna, e.g. plants such as 'calombo', trees such as 'mallee' and birds such as 'kookaburra'. Oddly, although the number of borrowings from aboriginal languages into Australian English was small, these words are now regarded as 'quintessentially Australian' (Elmes 2001: 66).

Other Australian English lexical innovations are intra-English in origin, the result of adaptations in form or range of meaning of words already in existence in English English. For example:

Australian English	*English English*
barrack for	support
footpath	pavement
parka	anorak
sedan	estate car
station	stock farm
stroller	push-chair
bludger	loafer, sponger
singlet	vest
station wagon	saloon car
paddock	field

B

Key:

Category 1: same word, different meaning

Word	EngEng meaning	USEng meaning
homely	down to earth, domestic	ugly (of people)
pants	underpants	trousers
pavement	footpath, sidewalk	road surface

Category 2a: additional meaning in USEng

Word	Meaning in common	Additional meaning in USEng
bathroom	room with bath or shower and sink	room with toilet only
regular	consistent, habitual	average (as in size), normal
school	institution of education at elementary level	all institutions of education including universities

Category 2b: additional meaning in EngEng

Word	Meaning in common	Additional meaning in EngEng
smart	intelligent	well-groomed

Category 3: same word, difference in style, connotation, frequency of use

Word	EngEng usage	USEng usage
autumn	common; all styles	uncommon; poetic or formal ('fall' used instead)
to fancy (to like, want)	common, informal	uncommon
quite	negative or neutral	positive

Category 4: same concept or item, different word

USEng only	Corresponds to EngEng
faucet	tap
sophomore	second year student

EngEng only	Corresponds to USEng
queue	line
pavement	sidewalk

Figure B5.1 British English/American English lexical differences

By far the majority of lexical differences across varieties of English are in their colloquial usage, especially in often ephemeral slang words and phrases. The following are examples of Australian English slang items which are not used in English English (from Elmes 2001 and Trudgill and Hannah 2002):

a dag (an affectionate term meaning an eccentric person)
a drongo (a fool)

a galah (a fool)
a chine (a mate)
an offsider (a partner or companion)
a sort (an attractive person)
a sheila (a girl)
tucker (food)
splosh; boodle (money)
spiflicated; rotten; full as a boot (drunk)
crook (ill, angry)
to spit the dummy (to lose your temper)
to bot (to cadge, borrow)
to gammon (to fool someone into thinking something)
to front up (to arrive, present oneself somewhere)
to fine up (to improve – used of weather)
to retrench (to sack, make redundant)
to shout (to buy something for someone, e.g. a round of drinks)
shooting a fairy (farting)
she'll be apples (everything is going to be OK)

Activity   Are you familiar with equivalent slang words and expressions in other (Inner or Outer Circle) varieties of English? For example, British English has words such as 'rat-arsed' and 'legless' for the adjective 'drunk', and 'to con' for 'to fool someone into thinking something'. If you are using this book in a class where students come from a range of English-speaking backgrounds, select a number of categories (e.g. drink, money, weather, etc.) and compare slang words and expressions across Englishes for lexical items within these categories. How do you account for any cross-cultural similarities and/or differences that emerge?

Another feature of Australian lexis is the love of abbreviations. There is a tendency among all speakers of English to shorten words, a process known as **clipping**, to the extent that the original word may no longer be known to most speakers, e.g. 'pants' is an abbreviation of 'pantaloons', and 'bus' of 'omnibus' (see Gramley 2001: 94). However, it seems that Australians engage in clipping more frequently than do speakers of other Englishes. In Australian English, again more so than in other Englishes, the clipped word may then be given a diminutive suffix, especially '-ie' or '-y' but also '-o'. For example, the word 'barbecue' becomes 'barbie'; the word 'Australian' becomes 'Aussy', and the word 'afternoon' becomes 'arvo'.

Turning to grammar, the grammatical differences between English English and Australian English are relatively few in number at the level of educated speech and writing and, as Trudgill and Hannah (2002: 18) point out, it is often impossible to tell, unless there is distinctive use of vocabulary, whether a text was written by an Australian or British writer.

The grammatical differences between English English and US English, however, are far more wide-ranging. It is only possible to single out some of the main categories of difference here (see Trudgill and Hannah 2002: 55–79 for details).

Verbs

❏ Morphology: differences in past and participle endings, e.g. EngEng 'dived', 'sneaked', 'got'; USEng 'dove', snuk', 'gotten'.
❏ Auxiliaries: use of epistemic 'must': EngEng uses 'can't' in the negative, e.g. 'He can't be in – his car has gone', whereas USEng uses (uncontracted) 'must not' (not to be confused with 'mustn't' meaning 'not be allowed').

Nouns

❏ Greater use of certain noun endings in USEng, e.g. '-ee' ('retiree', 'draftee'), '-ster' (teamster, gamester).
❏ Difference in derivational ending. e.g. EngEng 'candidature', 'centenary', USEng 'candidacy', 'centennial'.
❏ Greater tendency to use verbs as nouns in USEng, e.g. 'to run down', 'to be shut in', 'to try out' become 'the rundown', 'a shut-in' ('an invalid'), 'a try-out' ('an audition').

Adjectives and adverbs

❏ The comparative adjective 'different' is followed by 'than' in USEng and by 'from' (or more recently, 'to') in EngEng. For example, 'This one is different than/from (to) the last one'.
❏ The adverbs 'yet' and 'already' cannot occur with the simple past tense in EngEng, whereas they can do so in USEng. In such cases, EngEng uses the present perfect tense: USEng ' I didn't buy one yet', 'Did you read it already?', EngEng 'I haven't bought one yet', 'Have you read it already?'

Prepositions

❏ A few prepositions differ in form in the two varieties, e.g. EngEng 'behind', USEng 'in back of' ('I put it behind/in back of the shed').
❏ Differences in prepositions in specific contexts, particularly in expressions of time, e.g. EngEng 'I haven't seen him for ages/weeks', USEng 'I haven't seen him in ages/weeks'.
❏ Clock time: EngEng 'twenty to three', 'five past eight', USEng 'twenty of/till three', 'five after eight'.
❏ Different uses of 'in' and 'on': EngEng 'to live in a street', 'to be in a sale', USEng 'to be on a street', 'to be on sale' (whereas in EngEng, 'on sale' means 'for sale').

If you are familiar with both British English and either New Zealand English or South African English, which grammatical features would you single out as differing most from English English? In your view, do any of these differences have the same degree of potential for miscommunication as lexical differences do? Have you had any personal experience of miscommunication arising from grammatical differences in your own and an interlocutor's English?

 Activity

Standard English and dialect

The differences between standard and non-standard Inner Circle Englishes receive much comment, with the non-standard Englishes (or 'dialects') being stigmatised in so far as they diverge from the variety regarded as the standard. Despite this, and the extent of the stigmatising which continues in Britain to this day, Trudgill and Chambers regard the grammatical and lexical differences in the regional and social varieties of English spoken by its native speakers as trivial:

> The vast majority of native speakers around the world differ linguistically from one another relatively little, with more differentiation in their phonetics and phonology than at other linguistic levels. Most English people, for example, betray their geographical origins much more through their accents than through their vocabulary or grammar. This vast majority speaks mainstream varieties of English, standard or non-standard, which resemble one another quite closely, and which are all reasonably readily mutually intelligible. Differences between these mainstream varieties may be regionally and socially very diagnostic, but they are generally linguistically rather trivial, and where not trivial, quite regular and predictable. Grammatically, in particular, these varieties are very close to standard English.
>
> (Trudgill and Chambers 1991: 2)

The linguist Stubbs provides evidence of the truth of Trudgill and Chambers's claim by showing how working class speech in many regions of Britain differs morpho-syntactically from Standard British English in only a few ways. These are among the examples he cites:

1 Multiple negation:
   I didn't do nothing.
2 Ain't as a negative form of be or auxiliary verb have:
   I ain't doing it.
   I ain't got one.
3 Never used to refer to a single occasion in the past:
   I never done it (SE: I didn't do it).
4 Extension of third person -s to first and second person verb forms:
   I wants, you wants, he wants.
5 Regularisation of be:
   We was, you was, they was.
6 Regularisation of some irregular verbs:
   I draw, I drawed, I have drawed.
   I go, I went, I have went.
   I come, I come, I have come.
7 Optional -ly on adverbs:
   He writes real quick.
8 Unmarked plurality on nouns of measurement after numerals:
   twenty year, ten pound.
9 Different forms of the relative pronoun:
   The man as/what lives here.

10 Regularisation of reflexive pronouns:
    myself, yourself, hisself, herself; ourselves, yourselves, theirselves.
11 Distinction between main and auxiliary verb do:
    You done it, did you? (SE: You did it, did you?).

(Mitchell 1993, selected from Stubbs 1986)

Note that if a speaker uses certain of the above features even once – a double negative, for example – he or she will be 'diagnosed' as a speaker of a non-standard English. On the other hand, other features, such as the *-ly* ending on adverbs (no.7) seem to be slowly dying out of common usage, perhaps by analogy with forms such as 'fast' and 'hard' which do not take the *-ly*, or because of complications with adverb forms of adjectives such as 'friendly' which already end in *-ly*. Presumably when sufficient numbers of educated speakers of English have dropped the *-ly* adverb ending, it will no longer be considered a dialect marker. Do you envisage this happening in the reasonably short term to any other items on Stubbs' list? If so, do you think that the change will be restricted to the spoken language or that it will ultimately work its way into the written standard?

★ Activity

Despite claims that standardness is not an issue in the US to the same extent as it is in Britain (see, for example, Baron 2000: 134–5), the evidence provided by Lippi-Green (1997) and others suggests otherwise. The difference is that attitudes towards standardness are connected in the US with race rather than class, with the dialects spoken by speakers of Hispanic English and Black English (AAVE) being the most highly stigmatised. The following extract in which members of the studio audience and telephone callers participate in a screening of the Oprah Winfrey show demonstrates this point:

1	*2nd caller*:	Hi, Oprah?
	Winfrey:	Yes
	2nd caller:	I guess what I'd like to say is that what makes me feel that blacks tend to be ignorant is that they fail to see that the word is spelled A-S-K, not A-X. And when they say aksed, it gives the sentence an entirely different meaning. And this is what I feel holds blacks back.
	Winfrey:	Why does it give it a different meaning if you know that's what they're saying?
	2nd caller:	But you don't always know that's what they are saying.

<table>
<tr><td>2</td><td>9th audience member:</td><td>The problem seems to be that everybody tries to push something down your throat by arrogance. That's not the way to get something done. You could speak your own language, you could have your own way, but don't force someone else to have to suffer and listen to it.</td></tr>
<tr><td></td><td>Winfrey:</td><td>You say what?</td></tr>
<tr><td></td><td>10th audience member:</td><td>Well I'm an accountant and –</td></tr>
<tr><td></td><td>Winfrey:</td><td>Well, wait, wait, let me get back to you. What is causing you to suffer?</td></tr>
<tr><td></td><td>9th audience member:</td><td>Well I think there is a certain way of speaking that has been considered the acceptable way of speaking. And because of that this is the type of language you speak when you're out in the world. If you want to speak Spanish at home that's fine. If you want to speak black with your friends that's fine. But don't insult someone else's ears by making them listen to it.</td></tr>
</table>

(quoted in Milroy and Milroy 1999: 152–3)

Activity If you were Oprah Winfrey, how would you have responded to the second caller and ninth audience member?

According to Wolfram and Schilling-Estes (1998: 149), 'despite ever-increasing inter-communication among different dialect areas, the dialect lines which were laid down when the first English speakers began arriving in the US remain relatively intact'. They go on to say that the North–South distinction is particularly strong and may even be growing stronger, especially in terms of pronunciation, although the Midland and West continue to be less dialectally distinctive than the North and South.

As with the British English dialects, it is only possible to summarise some of the main socially diagnostic grammatical structures. These are all taken from Wolfram and Schilling-Estes (1998: 331–44):

The verb phrase

1 Irregular verbs

The majority of vernaculars in the North and South exhibit the following features:

- ❑ past as participle form e.g. 'I <u>had went</u> down there';
- ❑ participle as past form e.g. 'He <u>seen</u> something out there';
- ❑ bare root as past form e.g. 'She <u>come</u> to my house yesterday'.

Some rural vernaculars in the South may also exhibit this pattern:

- ❑ different irregular form: e.g. 'Something just <u>riz</u> up right in front of me'.

2 *Completive* **done**
In Southern Anglo and African American vernaculars (AAVE), the form 'done' may mark a completed action or event in a different way from a simple past tense form, e.g. 'I <u>done</u> forgot what you wanted'.

3 *Habitual* **be**
In AAVE as well as in some rural Anglo varieties, the form 'be' in sentences such as 'She usually <u>be</u> home in the evening'.

4 *A-prefixing*
In vernacular Appalachian English and some other rural dialects, an a-prefix may occur on *-ing* forms functioning as verbs or adverbs, e.g. 'She was <u>a</u>-coming home', 'He starts <u>a</u>-laughing'. This form cannot occur with *-ing* forms which function as nouns or adjectives, and is also restricted phonologically in that it can only occur on forms whose first syllable is accented. It is also preferred on items which begin with a consonant sound.

5 *Double modals*
In some Southern states such as the Carolinas, these combinations of two modal verbs are widespread and apparently not particularly stigmatised. e.g. 'I <u>might could</u> go there', 'You <u>might oughta</u> take it'.

Adverbs

-ly *absence*
In Southern-based dialects, especially Upper Southern varieties such as Appalachian and Ozark English, the *-ly* adverb ending is being lost, e.g. 'They answered <u>wrong</u>', 'She enjoyed life <u>awful</u> well', 'I come from Virginia <u>original</u>'.

Negation

1 *Multiple negation*
Almost all vernacular varieties of American English participate in multiple negation of Type 1; most Southern and restricted Northern vernaculars participate in Type 2; most Southern vernaculars participate in Type 3; and restricted Southern and AAVE varieties participate in Type 4:

> Type 1: marking of the negative on the auxiliary verb and the indefinite following the verb, e.g. 'The man <u>wasn't</u> saying <u>nothing</u>'.
> Type 2: negative marking of an indefinite before the verb phrase and of the auxiliary verb, e.g. '<u>Nobody</u> <u>didn't</u> like the mess'.
> Type 3: inversion of the negativised auxiliary verb and the pre-verbal indefinite, e.g. '<u>Didn't</u> <u>nobody</u> like the mess?'
> Type 4: multiple negative marking across different clauses, e.g. 'There <u>wasn't</u> much that I <u>couldn't</u> do' (meaning 'There wasn't much that I could do').

2 ain't

This item may be used instead of certain standard forms including forms of *be + not*, e.g. 'She <u>ain't</u> here now'; forms of *have + not* e.g. 'I <u>ain't</u> seen her in a long time'; and *did + not* e.g. 'I <u>ain't</u> go to school yesterday'.

Pronouns

The following types of pronominal difference are found in most vernacular dialects of American English:

❏ regularisation of reflexive forms by analogy with other possessive prounouns, e.g. 'He hit <u>hisself</u> on the head', 'They shaved <u>theirselves</u>'.
❏ Extension of object forms to coordinate subjects, e.g. '<u>Me and him</u> will do it'.
❏ Adoption of a second person plural form: (a) <u>Y'all</u> won the game (Southern); (b) <u>Youse</u> won the game (Northern); (c) <u>You'uns</u> won the game (specific regions such as Western Pennsylvania, Southern Appalachia).
❏ Extension of object forms to demonstratives, e.g. '<u>Them</u> books are on the shelf' (note: this is also a common feature of non-standard BrEng).
❏ A special personal dative use of the object pronoun form, e.g. 'I got <u>me</u> a new car', 'We had <u>us</u> a little old dog' is also a common feature of non-standard BrEng.

Activity ✪   What is your reaction to these two quotations?

> Why should we consider some, usually poorly educated, subculture's notion of the relationship between sound and meaning? And how could a grammar – any grammar – possibly describe that relationship?
>   As for "I be," "you be", "he be." etc., which should give us all the heebie-jeebies, these may indeed be comprehensible, but they go against all accepted classical and modern grammars, and are the product not of a language with roots in history but of ignorance of how language works.
>
> (US journalist John Simon speaking of AAVE, quoted in Pinker 1994: 385)

> If you allow standards to slip to the stage where good English is no better than bad English, where people turn up filthy at school . . . all these things tend to cause people to have no standards at all, and once you lose standards then there's no imperative to stay out of crime.
>
> (Norman Tebbit, a (British) Conservative MP speaking on BBC Radio 4 in 1985; quoted in Cameron 1995: 94)

B6   **NATIVE AND NON-NATIVE SPEAKERS OF ENGLISH**

A number of scholars have begun to argue that when English is used for international communication, that is, among speakers from a wide range of international settings, then it cannot have 'non-native speakers'. In other words, while the native speaker/ non-native speaker distinction holds good for EFL and for other modern foreign languages, since these are largely learnt as L2s for use in interaction with their L1 speakers, EIL is used mainly among L2 speakers of English, often with no NS present at all.

Is nativeness a viable concept for EIL?

So what are the arguments against the use of the terms 'native' and 'non-native' speaker of English? The following have been suggested. Do you agree with them? If not, what are your reasons? Which of them do you regard as most relevant to EIL rather than ESL?

 Activity

❏ The term 'native speaker' fails to recognise that some varieties of English in the Outer Circle, e.g. in Singapore, are spoken not only for official purposes but also in the home.

❏ It ignores the fact that English is often one of several languages available in the repertoires of the multilingual populations of countries such as India, and that it is often difficult to decide which language is a speaker's first, second, third and so on.

❏ It perpetuates the view that monolingualism is the world's norm when, in fact, the majority of people are bi- or multilingual.

❏ It implies that the English of the ethnic Anglo speaker is a reference point against which all other varieties of English should be measured.

❏ It is offensive to label as 'non-native' those who have learnt English and achieved bilingual status as fluent, proficient (but probably not *ambi*lingual) users.

❏ The perpetuation of the native/non-native distinction causes negative perceptions of and among 'non-native' speakers in general and teachers and researchers in particular. It leads to their being refused places on ELT teacher training courses, and to limited publication of their work in prestigious ELT and applied linguistics journals.

❏ Perhaps most seriously, it encourages a very simplistic view of what constitutes error in English language use, and leads to deficiencies in the testing of English internationally, because users of English, regardless of their own variety of the language, are being measured against an irrelevant and unrealistic 'native' standard.

On the other hand, some do not agree that the concept of 'native speaker' of English as an International Language is untenable. Andreasson (1994) draws what is, for all those who support the native/non-native distinction, the logical conclusion:

> In the Expanding Circle . . . the ideal goal is to imitate the native speaker of the standard language as closely as possible. Speaking English is simply not related to cultural identity. It is rather an exponent of one's academic and language-learning abilities. It would, therefore, be far from a compliment to tell a Spanish person that his or her variety is Spanish English. It would imply that his or her acquisition of the language left something to be desired.
>
> (Andreasson 1994: 402)

Activity ⭐ Andreasson's claim raises a number of questions, which are listed below. What is your reaction to them? Are there any other questions that you would wish to raise in response to her claim?

1   Who is 'the native speaker of the standard language'? Defining 'native speaker', as you will have realised, is far from unproblematic. Does it apply, for example, to English speakers in Singapore who learn and speak English at home? Does it apply to the millions of people around the world who grow up as bilinguals or multilinguals, with English being just one of the languages within their linguistic repertoires?
2   Does one's use of English really exemplify no more than one's 'academic and language-learning abilities'?
3   Is it a fact that 'speaking English is simply not related to cultural identity'?
4   Does it seem reasonable that mother-tongue speakers of English should (generally) be comfortable with the idea that their accents reveal their geographical origins, while non-mother-tongue speakers should equate regional accents with poor acquisition of English and regard them as an embarrassment?
5   Compare Andreasson's view with that of an Austrian teacher of English in an Austrian university. Whose view do you have greater sympathy with?

> I've been here [name of institution] very, very long and this has been a tradition that you're supposed to approximate the native speaker, and unless you approximate the native British speaker you are sort of regarded as inferior . . . I don't see why a good EFL teacher, Austrian English teacher, shouldn't have a trace of an accent of his local variety of English. We're talking about international English . . . and we're still keeping to this idea that the Austrian teacher . . . you must sound more British than the British.
> (quoted in Jenkins 2000: 30)

What are the alternatives?

If we abandon the use of the terms 'native' and 'non-native' in relation to EIL, what are the alternatives?

Rampton (1990: 98–9; Leung, Harris and Rampton 1997) proposes the use of the term 'expert' to describe all accomplished users of English, arguing that **expertise** has the following advantages over nativeness:

1   Although they often do, experts do not have to feel close to what they know a lot about. Expertise is different from identification.
2   Expertise is learned, not fixed or innate.
3   Expertise is relative. One person's expert is another person's fool.
4   Expertise is partial. People can be expert in several fields, but they are never omniscient.
5   To achieve expertise, one goes through processes of certification, in which one is judged by other people. Their standards of assessment can be reviewed and disputed. There is also a healthy tradition of challenging 'experts'.

On the other hand, use of the term 'expert' for fluent speakers of English implies the use of 'non-expert' to describe less fluent speakers. This, it could be argued, imposes something of the value judgement of the term 'non-native'. For this and other reasons, I prefer to reconceptualise the issue by turning the traditional terminology upside down and propose the following system:

1   for speakers of English who speak no other language, **Monolingual English Speaker (MES)**;
2   for proficient speakers of English and at least one other language, regardless of the order in which they learnt the languages, **Bilingual English Speaker (BES)**;
3   for those who are not bilingual in English but are nevertheless able to speak it at a level of reasonable competence, **Non-Bilingual English Speaker (NBES)**.

These are what I see as the two main advantages of my reconceptualisation (for fuller details, see Jenkins 1996, 2000: 8–10):

1   MES as an epithet is considerably less favourable than BES given that it signals the greater linguistic competence of the BES and the lesser of the MES. Thus, this system of labelling reflects the fact that monolingualism is not the preferable condition – and neither is it the world norm.
2   BES removes the artificial distinction – in an international context – between speakers of L1 and L2 varieties of English. This should, in turn, eventually lead to the end of discrimination against teachers of English on the grounds that they are not so-called 'native speakers' (see C7 for more on this issue and, in particular, the advantages of being a bilingual teacher of English).

On the other hand, this system is not without its disadvantages. In particular, there is the problem of what counts as 'bilingual' competence, and where to draw the line between non-bilingual and bilingual competence (and, of course, who should be responsible for drawing it). At the time of writing, these problems are far from being resolved.

Activity

❑   What do you consider to be the pros and cons of each of these attempts to replace the terms 'native' and 'non-native' speaker? Do you agree with the advantages and disadvantages already mentioned? Can you think of others? Which of the two approaches do you prefer overall, and why or, alternatively, can you devise another solution?
❑   If you were made responsible for deciding how to distinguish between Jenkins's BES/NBES competence or Rampton's expert and, by implication, non-expert speaker of English, what would your criteria be?
❑   McKay (2002: 27) is in favour of using the term 'bilingual user of English' to describe a wide range of proficiency because of the difficulty in drawing a line between more and less proficient speakers. Do you think this is a viable alternative?

EN ROUTE TO NEW STANDARD ENGLISHES

In B7 we will be looking at Asian Englishes in terms of the stages in the codification process (see A7) and the problems they are encountering on the way to achieving fully standardised and codified status.

As D'souza (1999: 271) has pointed out, codification is 'the crux of the matter'. Without codification, the Outer and Expanding Circle Englishes will continue to lack prestige not only in the eyes of speakers of 'accepted' (i.e. Inner Circle) standard varieties, but also among their own speakers. In order for local classroom models in Asia (and Europe) to be considered acceptable internationally as alternatives to British and American models, it must be possible to find their grammatical, lexical, phonological and discoursal characteristics in widely respected works of reference such as grammars and dictionaries. Even then, it will be difficult, yet vital, to ensure that learners of world Englishes are not 'victims of a system that has one *de jure* model but a somewhat different *de facto* one' (D'souza 1999: 272), that is, that they are not taught local norms which remain unacceptable to Inner Circle gatekeepers. In this respect, selection is critical, and one of the main tasks for the codifiers of world Englishes in the twenty-first century will be to distinguish between items for local informal use and those which have the 'right' to international status.

Codifying Asian Englishes

One of the greatest obstacles to the codifying of Asian Englishes in recent years has been the claim of a large number of Second Language Acquisition (SLA) scholars in the Inner Circle that these **indigenised varieties of English (IVEs)** along with the African IVEs of the Outer Circle are 'interlanguages', that is, 'learner' languages characterised by 'errors', rather than legitimate L2 varieties of English containing forms which happen to differ from forms used in L1 English varieties. Because this issue is still not resolved, because it has been so hotly debated, and because it has been represented on the IVE 'side' largely by speakers of Asian IVEs, we will look at what has been said before moving on to consider codification itself.

Sridhar and Sridhar (1992: 97) discuss the 'IVE = Interlanguage' claim in terms of the 'Dangers of an uncritical application of the current SLA paradigm'. They argue that SLA researchers have neglected the IVEs as a result of certain assumptions which underpin their perspective on SLA, chiefly:

1 that the goal of SLA is (or ought to be) native-like competence;
2 that the (native speaker) input available to learners is sufficient to allow acquisition of full active competence;
3 that the SLA process can be studied without reference to the functions which the L2 will serve for the learner in his/her community;
4 that the 'role' of the learner's L1 should be evaluated only in terms of its contribution in 'interfering' with and (less often) facilitating the acquisition of L2 structures, with no interest in its contribution to the communicative function involved;
5 that the ideal motivation for success in SLA is 'integrative', i.e. 'one that involves admiration for the native speakers of the language and a desire to become a member of their culture'.

(adapted from Sridhar and Sridhar 1992: 93–4)

However, as Sridhar and Sridhar point out, IVE settings have a very different character from those typical of most SLA research. First, the communicative target is no longer native speakers but other non-native speakers. This, in turn, renders the native-speaker norm against which non-native speaker performance is measured in a traditional SLA paradigm irrelevant. Instead, the optimum model of instruction and reference point for performance evaluation derives from IVE norms. Second, the input available to learners is an IVE, not a native variety of English. In fact most learners of IVEs have no contact with native-speaker English and often the latter is barely understandable to them. Third, learners of IVEs go on to use their English in multilingual settings in a distribution comparable to that of the High variety in a diglossic situation (**diglossia** being the use of a 'high' variety for some functions and a 'low' variety for others). Thus their English does not serve all the functions that it does in the case of monolingual native English speakers, and nor should it be expected to. Fourth, the motivation of most IVE learners is instrumental rather than integrative. That is, it is learnt as a result of the desire to achieve some functional goal (e.g. to pass an exam, to participate in a particular field of employment, whether local or international) rather than to identify with the target-language culture. According to a traditional SLA perspective, this should mean a low level of success in acquiring the L2, and yet the opposite is often the case.

Interlanguage (a term coined by Selinker 1972) is defined during the language learning phase by its instability, in that a learner's interlanguage (IL) passes through a range of intermediate systems between the native and target languages before reaching a point where it stabilises. Because it rarely stabilises with a competence identical to that of a native speaker of the language, IL is said to 'fossilise' at the point of stability (Selinker 1972), with fossilisation clearly implying deficit rather than difference. IL is thus one of two things: unstable learner language or fossilised learner language. Since most IVEs are stable (to the extent that any *bona fide* language is stable), the only way SLA can apply the concept 'interlanguage' to IVEs is to claim that competence 'in whole groups of individuals' can become fossilised 'resulting in the emergence of a new dialect ([such as] Indian English), where fossilized IL competences may be the normal situation' (Selinker 1972). In other words, entire communities' varieties of English are being characterised as 'fossilised IL competences'.

This view of the IVEs is unsatisfactory on account of both the unprincipled way in which it assigns the term 'fossilised', and the failure to take account of the bi- or multilingual context in which IVEs are acquired and used, including the fact that the goal of SLA is by definition bilingualism (see C7 for discussion of the latter issue). As regards the first point, Y. Kachru argues:

> The question of why a stable system should be characterized as an IL is not answered. It is also not clear what the difference is between 'stable' and 'fossilized': that which is fossilized is surely unchanging and therefore stable! Additionally, if 'an entirely fossilized IL competence' refers to a community . . . it is difficult to see why it is an IL and why it is 'fossilized'. Presumably American English developed as an IL among a large portion of the immigrant population from the non-English-speaking parts of Europe. Does this mean that American English represents an 'entirely fossilized IL'?
>
> (Y. Kachru 1993: 266)

On the second point, Canagarajah has this to say:

> Often the speaker's L1 is considered to be the culprit in creating fossilized items. Furthermore, code-mixed versions of bilingual communication can be stigmatized as fossilized forms that prevent progression towards native-speaker competence. This means that the unilateral movement towards native norms, and the uniform criteria adopted to judge the success of acquisition, ignore the positive contributions of L1 in the construction of unique communicative modes and English grammars for periphery speakers.
>
> (Canagarajah 1999: 128)

Brutt-Griffler (2002) adds to the debate by arguing that the source of the problem is SLA scholars' exclusive focus on individual acquisition of English and hence their ignoring of its acquisition by bilingual speech communities.

The IL debate remains unresolved. Nevertheless, the IVEs, particularly those of several Asian Outer Circle countries, are increasingly being recognised as fully-fledged language varieties, if not yet by the majority of SLA researchers. But even where the derogatory interlanguage label has been removed, there is still the problem of deciding on what is to be included in the standard version of a variety, a decision involving factors and challenges which codifiers of the traditional (Inner Circle) varieties have not hitherto had to face. In particular, codifiers of Asian Englishes are having to establish a novel set of criteria as the basis on which they make their selection, since the native-speaker English standard varieties of the US and UK are of minimal relevance in the standard *Asian English* selection process. Instead, local educated varieties are (or should be) the focus of attention. However, in these countries there are often a number of educated varieties each influenced by the mother tongue of its speakers, which means that difficult and sometimes controversial decisions are having to be taken. And these decisions cannot even be tackled yet in a few Asian countries such as Hong Kong (see C7), because of the remaining strength of attachment to native-speaker English norms. The issue of the choice of standard in Asia, as Pakir (1997: 175) argues, 'can only be resolved when the myth of the Native Speaker Interlocutor has been laid to rest'.

A second major challenge facing Asian-English codifiers is the resolution of the conflict between centrifugal forces pulling them inwards towards local needs and centripetal forces pushing them outwards towards international intelligibility and acceptability. A codified Asian English will need to combine local features that signal its difference from other Englishes and perform the functions required by its *intranational* community, with modifications which render it intelligible and acceptable to English speakers (primarily non-native speakers, but not forgetting the native-speaker minority) *internationally*. This is a mammoth task, one far more complex than that of Inner Circle codifiers, who up to now have worked on the assumption that whatever they deem standard at the national level will also be intelligible and acceptable internationally. Intranational needs involve, for example, the acceptance of local (Asian) innovations in English including the standardising in the English lexicon of non-English words for which there is no precise English equivalent. For instance, the Tagalog adjective 'malambing' translates very roughly as 'demonstrative' or 'loving', but there are occasions when neither translation expresses exactly what a Filipino-English speaker wants to say (Bautista 1998). There is, then, a strong case for including such lexical gaps in a dictionary of Philippine English. Similarly, given that almost all Asian-English speakers are bi- or multilingual (apart from a small minority of Singaporeans who speak only English) it seems reasonable to include code switching and code mixing devices in dictionaries and grammars of Asian Englishes. However, extensive inclusion of these along with local words to cover L2 lexical gaps will mean that codified Asian Englishes risk some loss of international intelligibility and acceptability unless speakers are given very clear guidance as to which items are for local use only.

The most comprehensive attempt at codifying Asian Englishes to date is the **Macquarie Regional Asian English dictionary**, now being co-published with Grolier Publishers as the *Grolier International Dictionary: World English in an Asian Context* (Bolton 2000: 278), which documents the Englishes of Southeast and South Asia. Its aim is to meet the needs of English speakers in the region by providing up-to-date coverage of items with international currency along with local words which 'though part and parcel of everyday English in the region, have never appeared in a dictionary before' (Butler 1997: 97). In this way the dictionary recognises that Asian-English speakers need English for both international communication and communication at home.

❑ As regards local words, the Macquarie dictionary acknowledges that the Englishes
   of the Asian region are not monolithic, but 'function in their totality, combining a standard dialect in formal and informal register, with a nonstandard and colloquial form' (Butler 1997: 99) – just like the Inner Circle Englishes, in fact. The dictionary does not try to cover all these dialects, but for each Asian variety presents the standard form mainly in its formal style, while including some informal items. All items are selected from a corpus of English in Asia, **ASIACORP**, which is being collected from texts (e.g. newspapers, fiction and non-fiction) produced in the respective variety of English and intended for local rather than international use. These are some of the items included in the dictionary. If you are not familiar with the Englishes of Southeast Asia, can you understand any of them?
   1   academician
   2   actsy
   3   adobo
   4   aggrupation
   5   aircon
❑ One of the most difficult decisions for the dictionary compilers has been to decide whether items are standard informal (and thus candidates for inclusion) or non-standard colloquial (and therefore to be excluded). The following are citations of localisms taken from the corpus material under the heading 'Social organisation'. Some were accepted by the consultants for Singaporean, Malaysian and Philippine Englishes while others were discarded, mainly on the basis of the consultants' intuitions as to the boundary between standard informal and non-standard colloquial. Which do you think they accepted and discarded?

Singaporean/Malaysian English

community centre
One of the better seafood places in Sandakan is a restaurant, behind the Community Centre and the long distance Mini bus terminal.

kongsi
She could not find domestic work and had to rely on the benevolence of her kongsi, or sorority.

mui tsai
By the post war period, girls from as young as four or five years, pledged as mui tsai or bond servants by their parents or guardians were almost certainly no longer being brought in from China.

Philippine English

dalaga
It is generally understood that the more difficult it is to invite a dalaga to a feast, the higher she is in the estimation of the community. A feast is considered particularly successful if one or more well-known dalagas are persuaded to attend.

(Butler 1997: 109)

Activity Now look at the Key. If you are an Asian-English speaker, do you agree with the consultants' decisions?

Key

1 *noun* an academic
2 *adjective* conceited, proud [ACT + -SY]
3 *noun* a Philippine dish of pork or chicken stew cooked in soy sauce, vinegar and garlic. [Spanish: pickle, sauce]
4 *noun* a group, especially within a political party. [Spanish agrupación]
5 *noun* 1. airconditioning. – *adjective* 2. airconditioned

(Butler 1997: 96–7)

community centre: not selected
kongsi: selected
mui tsai: not selected
dalaga: not selected

The Macquarie Asian English Dictionary clearly represents a critical phase in the evolution of codified Asian Englishes. Relaying a discussion about who the dictionary would be used by and for what purposes, which took place at a conference in Manila in 1996, Bautista (1998: 64) reports the conclusion that 'it would be used both by Filipinos and non-Filipinos – the Filipinos would find evidence that their words have gained legitimacy . . . while the non-Filipinos would use the dictionary to know the meaning of certain local usages'. However, as she points out in relation to Philippine English, but in words which should have resonance for speakers of all Asian

Englishes, 'eventually a full-blown Philippine English Dictionary should be prepared by Filipinos themselves'.

POSSIBLE FUTURE SCENARIOS

Convergence or divergence

The 'English language family' at the start of the twenty-first century is described by Mesthrie (2002: 112–13) as comprising the following nine members:

1   Colonial standards in the UK, the USA, Australia, New Zealand, Canada and South Africa, the territories having a large settlement of 'traditional' English speakers.
2   Regional dialects, involving identifiable subvarieties within the above territories, e.g. the broad division between north and south linguistically in England.
3   Social dialects, which involve particular varieties characteristic of social groups within a territory, e.g. Cockney within London, Appalachian English in the USA.
4   Pidgin Englishes.
5   Creole Englishes.
6   ESL (English as a second language): these are forms which have arisen in countries where English was introduced in the colonial era in face-to-face communication or in the education system in a country in which there is, or had once been, a sizeable number of speakers of English. In ESL countries such as Kenya, Sri Lanka and Nigeria English plays a key role internally in education, government and administration.
7   EFL (English as a foreign language): this refers to English as used in countries in which the influence of English has been external, rather than via a large body of 'settlers'. For such countries English plays a role mainly for international rather than intra-national communication (Japan, China and Germany).
8   Immigrant Englishes: in the context of migration to an English-dominant country, second-language varieties of English might retain their distinctiveness or merge with the English of the majority depending on the social conditions. Thus whilst English in Mexico is of the EFL variety, Chicano English of Mexican immigrants shows greater affinity with general US English, though it is still a distinctive variety.
9   Language-shift Englishes: these are varieties that arise when English replaces the erstwhile primary language of a community. Frequently the linguistic properties of ESL become stabilised; so that even though English is an L1 . . . for many groups of native American Indians, the Irish in Ireland and Indian South Africans, the new first language retains a distinctiveness and sense of continuity with the ancestral languages and cultures.

(Mesthrie 2002: 112–13)

All nine members of the English language family have featured in earlier units of this book, and some of the varieties within each member category have been discussed in detail. Note, though, that Mesthrie's numbers 6 and 9 were classified as a single grouping (known variously as 'ESL', Institutionalised/Indigenised Varieties of English (IVEs), Nativised Varieties of English (NVEs), and 'New' Englishes), but with some varieties closer to standardising and being codified than others.

With so many different English language groupings in existence, new varieties within these groupings continuing to emerge, and the numbers of speakers of existing varieties expanding year on year, there is a very real concern as to how long the English languages will retain the potential for mutual intelligibility. Increased diversification may be inevitable. As Crystal argues:

> The growth in diversity is noticeable at both national and international levels. Nationally, urban dialects are adapting to meet the identity needs of immigrant groups, such as the currently evolving Caribbean Scouse in Liverpool [UK]. With over 300 languages now spoken within London, for example, it would be surprising indeed if several did not produce fresh varieties as they interact with English [. . .] The linguistic consequences of immigrant diversity have long been noted in cities in the USA, but are now a major feature of contemporary life in the urban centres of most other countries where English is a mother-tongue, notably Australia. At an international level, the evidence is overwhelming of the emergence of a new generation of nonstandard Englishes as the global reach of English extends. [. . .]
>
> Because no language has ever been spoken by so many people in so many places, it is difficult to predict what will happen to English as a consequence of its global expansion; but increasing variation, extending to the point of mutual unintelligibility, is already apparent in the colloquial speech of local communities [. . .] such as the code-mixed varieties now found all over the world, and identified by such names as Singlish, Taglish, and Chinglish (McArthur 1998). Nor do current models yet allow for what is going to happen to English in communities where new types of social relationship have linguistic consequences – such as the thousands of children being born to parents who have only English as a foreign language in common, and who find themselves growing up with this kind of English as the norm at home. In such cases, non-native English (presumably including features which would be traditionally considered as learner errors) is being learned as a mother-tongue, and new kinds of nonstandard English must surely be the outcome.

(Crystal 2002: 241–2)

Crystal also cites evidence of increasing diversity in lexis, pronunciation and grammar to demonstrate that regional distinctiveness is already increasing steadily, and predicts that the gap between standard and non-standard Englishes will widen further. On the other hand, he points out elsewhere (1997: 134) that talk of the complete fragmentation of English is nothing new. The American Noah Webster predicted as much (in relation to American and British Englishes) in the late eighteenth century, and the British Henry Sweet (in relation to American, British and Australian Englishes) in the late nineteenth. In Crystal's view, however, speakers of World Englishes will use their local English dialects in their own countries, but will speak a new form of English, which he labels **World Standard Spoken English (WSSE)** in international situations (1997: 137). Although it is too early for him to say with certainty how WSSE will evolve, he predicts that American English will be the greatest influence on its development. In other words, Crystal seems to see local Englishes as becoming increasingly divergent while international Englishes increasingly converge to the point of merging into a single world variety based on American English.

Trudgill (1998) approaches the subject from a rather different perspective. In his view English lexis will increasingly converge and pronunciation will increasingly diverge, while the grammatical situation is as yet unclear. He considers the lexical effect to be the result of the '**Americanisation** of the English language – **homogenisation** in the direction of North American usage' (1998: 31). For, despite the fact that some British English words find their way into American usage, 'the general trend does seem to be towards increasingly international use of originally American vocabulary items' (p. 32). Trudgill points out that this trend is easily explained in terms of widespread exposure to the American-English dominated media and film industries around the world: 'We learn new words readily and constantly, and it is a simple matter to pick up new items from what one reads, and from what one hears on radio, on television, and at the cinema' (1998: 32). Words cited by Trudgill as once specifically American but now in general use include 'briefcase', 'dessert', 'junk', 'peanut', 'radio', 'raincoat', 'soft drinks', and 'sweater'.

At the grammatical level, on the other hand, Trudgill does not consider developments to be as clear, partly because grammatical change takes place more slowly and is thus more difficult to document. Among the few items which Trudgill presents as potential candidates for the Americanisation of world English grammar are:

❑ 'hopefully' used in AmEng as a sentence adverbial, as in 'Hopefully it won't rain tomorrow', whereas in standard BrEng it has traditionally functioned as an adverb of manner (e.g. 'She watched the door hopefully').
❑ 'have' used dynamically as in AmEng 'Do you have coffee with your breakfast' compared with standard BrEng where it has traditionally been used statively in such sentences (e.g. 'Have you (got) coffee in the cabinet?').

On the other hand, Trudgill identifies a feature of British English grammar that is filtering through into American use. He labels this item 'pro-predication *do*' and gives the example of 'I don't know if I'm going to the party tonight, but I might do', where American speakers have traditionally omitted the final 'do', but are now beginning to include it. He concludes that as far as grammar is concerned, 'there is no conclusive evidence as to whether convergence/homogenisation or divergence/disintegration' is taking place (Trudgill 1998: 33).

However, the situation appears much clearer in the case of phonology and here, argues Trudgill, the picture which is emerging is one of divergence. For example, **th-fronting**, the substitution of /θ/ and /ð/ with respectively /f/ and /v/ as in 'think' pronounced 'fink' and 'brother' as 'brover', is spreading rapidly in both England and New Zealand but not affecting American English. And some phonological changes are moving in opposite directions. For instance, areas of England and New Zealand which have traditionally been **rhotic** (i.e. pronounced the 'r' which follows vowel sounds as in 'far' and 'part') are steadily becoming non-rhotic, while in North America, areas which have been non-rhotic are becoming rhotic.

Trudgill concludes that 'English looks set to become increasingly homogenised at the level of lexis, although there is still a long way to go, but at the level of phonology, the dominant national native-speaker varieties of the language are slowly diverging from one another. Since there is still relatively little face-to-face contact, for the vast majority of people, between speakers of American English and Australian English, or between New Zealand English and Irish English, we must expect that this trend will continue for the forseeable future' (Trudgill 1998: 35).

Trudgill is concerned here, of course, primarily with the Inner Circle Englishes – the first three members of Mesthrie's 'English language family'. Apart from a reference to the fact that 'English . . . has more non-native than native speakers' (p. 30), he makes no mention of non-Inner Circle Englishes. We could nevertheless infer that if the phonological divergence he predicts is borne out by events, it will affect every English regardless of which type of family member it is. By the same token, if lexical convergence takes place, we could infer that all World Englishes will converge on American English lexis. Or could we? Given the small number of native speakers of English compared to its non-native speakers, the spread (as opposed to concentration) of English around the globe, and the increasing economic power of the east, it seems unlikely that any native-speaker variety will continue for much longer to exercise such influence over the development of World Englishes. As Graddol (1999: 68) argues

> At one time, the most important question regarding global English seemed to be 'will US English or British English' provide the world model? Already that question is looking dated with the emergence of 'New Englishes', and dictionaries and grammars that codify new norms.

If there is to be a world model at the lexical or any other linguistic level, the role, surely, will go to one of the other six family member groupings.

Activity   Which of these alternatives do you consider to be most likely?

- ❏ regional dialects and WSSE with AmEng as the main influence
- ❏ lexical convergence on AmEng and phonological divergence
- ❏ fragmentation of World Englishes into mutually unintelligible varieties
- ❏ convergence of World Englishes on one or more non-native speaker variety
- ❏ another scenario.

SECTION C

EXPLORATION
CURRENT DEBATES IN
WORLD ENGLISHES

C1   POSTCOLONIAL AMERICA AND AFRICA

C1 presents perspectives from two particular sites of English use: first, the 'English Only' movement in the US, with its opposition to any form of institutional bilingualism; and second, English in Africa and the controversy over whether or not its use serves the purposes of the large number of multilingual ethnic Africans.

'English Only' in the US

In the US census of 1990, 62 million of a total population of 251 million, were found to belong to 'visible' ethnolinguistic minority groups:

- ❏ African (31 million)
- ❏ Latin American (22 million)
- ❏ Asian (7 million)
- ❏ Aboriginal, First Nations (2 million).

(Bourhis and Marshall 1999: 245)

By 2001, the white population of **California** had fallen to below half the state's total population of 34 million. Although California represents an extreme example, the trend is being repeated throughout the US, with the largest overall increase being in those from Hispanic backgrounds.

With this dramatic increase in multi-ethnicity, fear of bilingualism is inevitably increasing among the largely monolingual L1 English population. It is against this backdrop that the **English Only movement** is conducted, although it has its roots in the late nineteenth century. Up until that time, although the languages of 'inferior' groups (African and Native American) were disparaged (see B1), multilingualism was tolerated. But at this point, immigrants from Southern Europe began to arrive in the US in substantial numbers. These people were regarded as racially inferior by the northern Europeans who had initially colonised the territory. Theodore Roosevelt's response to the arrival of these immigrants was, as the Milroys point out, 'similar to the rhetoric of the contemporary English Only movement':

> we have room but for one language here and that is the English language, for we intend to see that the crucible turns our people out as Americans, of American nationality, and not as dwellers in a polyglot boarding house.

(quoted in Milroy and Milroy 1999: 157)

As a means of safeguarding their position, the US government began reversing the policy of allowing education for immigrants to take place in their native languages.

By the early 1920s, nearly three-quarters of the US states were insisting on English as the only language of instruction, a policy which was often executed inhumanely. For example, Native Indian children could be kidnapped from their reservations and families, and forced to live in boarding schools in order to learn the English language and the culture of its mother-tongue speakers. These children, as McCarty and Zepeda (1999: 203) point out, 'faced a system of militaristic discipline, manual labor, instruction in a trade, and abusive treatment for "reverting" to the mother tongue. Many children fled these conditions only to be rounded up by Indian agents (called "school police" in Navajo) and returned to school'.

Tolerance for other languages increased in general through the twentieth century. In 1968, the Bilingual Education Act officially recognised the need for education to be available in immigrants' native languages, albeit as a means of enabling immigrants to progress to English only education rather than to maintain L1 proficiency. However, from the late 1960s, when large numbers of people began to arrive in America from developing countries in Africa, the Caribbean, Latin America and Asia, the xenophobia that followed led directly to the establishing of the English Only movement. In California, the motivation to end bilingual education was especially strong. In 1998, The English Language Education for Children in Public Schools Initiative (more commonly known as Proposition 227) was passed, requiring all children for whom English is not their L1 to be placed in **immersion** programmes for a year and then to be transferred to mainstream education. Given that the language of the environment is English and the aim to subtract rather than add a language (i.e. **subtractive** rather than **additive bilingualism**), it would be more appropriate to describe these programmes as 'submersion' (Richard Watts, personal communication). Despite an abundance of research into Second Language Acquisition demonstrating the effectiveness of bilingual education as compared with that of immersion, school officials worked hard to justify the switch in policy. For example, the Superintendent of Schools in Oceanside, California, Ken Noonan, wrote a paper titled 'Why we were wrong about bilingual education' in the *Washington Post*, concluding:

> Now I am convinced that English immersion does work, and that it should begin on a student's first day of school . . . Now I believe that using all of the resources of public education to move these students into the English-speaking mainstream early and quickly is far more important than my former romantic notions that preserving the child's home language should be the ultimate goal of our schools.

Compare this official's firm conviction in the superiority of monolingual English-only education (and the underlying ethos that other languages are inferior), with the accounts of some of those bilingual students who actually experienced it. The following is a sample of the 250 language biographies collected from Asian American college students by Hinton over a number of years at the University of California at Berkeley:

 Activity

> 1 At the age of ten, my family on my mother's side immigrated to America and this is where I learned my second language. Going to school made me feel deaf, mute, and blind. I could understand nothing that was going on around me.

> 2 . . . . I didn't have any friends at all because nobody spoke Chinese. How I longed to go back to Taiwan and to see familiar faces and to hear my native language being spoken . . .

> 3 . . . It was two heartless comments from a group of small boys in my "white" neighborhood for me to want to deny my language let along my culture, as well. How was I to react to a racist comment of "Ching chong chooey go back home to where you belong. You can't even speak English right." Sixteen small words which possessed so much strength and contained so much power caused a small naïve child to lose her heritage – to lose what made her.

4 . . . I know that I have been extremely fortunate to have been able to learn English so easily, but I have paid a dear price in exchange. I began my English education with the basics, starting in first grade. As a result, I had to end my Chinese education at that time. I have forsaken my own language in order to become "American." I no longer read or write Chinese. I am ashamed and feel as if I am a statistic adding a burden and lowering the status quo of the Asian community as an illiterate of the Chinese language.

5 . . . When some of my classmates began to ridicule and throw racist remarks at Chinese people, I began to distance myself away from Chinese culture. I felt ashamed when my parents spoke to me in Cantonese at a supermarket. I got into heated arguments about why only English should be spoken at home. . . . I continuously tried to fit in, even if it meant abandoning culture and identity. I was probably most hostile to my background during those years in junior high.

6 The loss of one's cultural language symbolized the loss of one's cultural identity. Many Asian Americans pride themselves for successfully turning their kids into "complete" Americans who speak English in flawless American accent. In my perspective, this actually is something that they should be ashamed of. Without doubt, fitting oneself into the mainstream is important; yet retaining one's cultural language is not at all trivial. To me, I will try my best to excel both in English and my mother tongue, Cantonese.

(Hinton 1999: 21–30)

Activity

❏ Bearing in mind the experiences quoted above along with any relevant language learning experiences of your own, draw up a list of arguments that could be used to oppose the English Only movement. You might like to consult a book on Second Language Acquisition (e.g. Lightbown and Spada 1999), to read for yourself some of the research findings which demonstrate how L2 learners draw on their knowledge of the L1 in order to tackle the complexities of the L2.

❏ If you have access to people who have learnt English by immersion, prepare a questionnaire to find out about their experiences and their reflections on them. You might want to include questions on some of the issues which Hinton's subjects raise, such as:
  ❏ their parents' attitudes
  ❏ their feelings/experiences in the classroom
  ❏ any experiences of racism
  ❏ their rejection (or not) of their L1
  ❏ any effect on their L1 (degree of L1 attrition)
  ❏ any effect on their communication with older generations
  ❏ effects on their identity
  ❏ their attitude towards bilingualism.

❏ If you learnt English by immersion yourself, reflect on the experience and discuss it. With hindsight, to what extent do you think you benefited or otherwise?

English in Africa

African English is normally taken to refer to the English spoken in sub-Saharan Africa by the indigenous population. As discussed in A1, the history of English in Africa is complex and has led to the evolution of three distinct strands: West African, East African and South African English. There is a debate over whether they should employ their own local (**endonormative**) standards or continue to look outside to Britain for (**exonormative**) standards. There is as yet little agreement on which items constitute features of the various new African Englishes, and which are simply examples of 'learnerese' – incorrectly learnt English containing errors (see, for example, de Klerk 1999 and Titlestad 1998).

A still more fundamental issue is that of whether the use of English in fact serves the interests of the indigenous peoples of Africa. In his influential book, *Linguistic Imperialism*, Phillipson (1992: 49) argues that 'the dominance of English is asserted and maintained by the establishment and continuous reconstitution of structural and cultural inequalities between English and other languages'. He believes that the spread of English serves to promote the interests of the British and American 'Centre' at the expense of the countries of the 'Periphery'.

The rest of this section presents the reaction of a Nigerian linguist, Bisong (1995), to the **linguistic imperialism** claim, followed by a number of counter arguments, including Phillipson's own response. Although focused on Nigeria, Bisong believes his arguments have wider relevance, providing insights into the role of English in other African contexts. This debate is thus a critical one for the future of English as a world language.

Bisong asks and answers three questions:

1   Has English succeeded in displacing or replacing other languages in **Nigeria**?

> Although English is the official language of Nigeria, it has not succeeded in displacing or replacing any of the indigenous languages. It performs a useful function in a multilingual society and will continue to do so, since no nation can escape its history. But attitudes to the language have changed since colonial times. It is no longer perceived as the Imperial tongue that must be mastered at all costs. Reasons for learning English now are more pragmatic in nature, and run counter to Phillipson's argument that those who acquire the language in a situation where it plays a dominant role are victims of linguistic imperialism. I would want to maintain that Nigerians are sophisticated enough to know what is in their interest, and that their interest includes the ability to operate with two or more linguistic codes in a multilingual situation. Phillipson's argument shows a failure to appreciate fully the complexities of this situation.
>
> (Bisong 1995: 131)

2   Has the dominance of English caused Nigerian culture to be undervalued and marginalized?

> Because Nigeria is a multicultural society, the Euro-Christian culture embodied in the English language is only one of a number of cultures that function to shape the consciousness of Nigerian people. To maintain that one of the foreign cultures must play a dominant role since the language that embodies it is widely used is again to fail to come to grips with the reality of the situation.
>
> (Bisong 1995: 131)

3   Why did writers like Chinua Achebe, Wole Soyinka, and Ngũgĩ wa Thiong'o, all of them literate and fluent in their mother tongues, write in English?

> It would be naïve to assume that creative writers like Achebe, Soyinka, and Ngũgĩ chose to write in English because they were victims of Centre linguistic and cultural imperialism. Because of the peculiar history of countries in the Periphery, English has become *one* of the languages available for use by the creative writer. This sociolinguistic reality has to be accepted for what it is. Arguments that carry the implication that the users of this language do not know what is in their interest should not be seen simply as patronizing. They reveal a monolingual failure to grasp the complex nature of a multilingual and multicultural society.
>
> (Bisong 1995: 131)

Activity   Phillipson (1996) responded to Bisong by taking up four central issues. Consider his counter-arguments to Bisong's claims and decide where you position yourself in this debate.

1   African multilingualism and stigmatisation: Phillipson cites evidence showing the degree to which African languages are marginalised in favour of English.
2   the Centre and Periphery: he points out that his 1992 book 'does not attribute responsibility for what happens exclusively to people in the Centre', but that local governments such as that of the newly independent Nigeria, have also played a part in promoting English over local languages' in order to 'deemphasize "ethnicity" and build up a sense of nationhood' (Phillipson 1996: 161–2). He also points out that his approach is not monolingual as he does not recommend replacing English with a single (indigenous) African language in each country.
3   literature: he points out that 90 per cent of the African population do not speak English, and therefore do not have access to literature in English. Phillipson (1996: 164) argues here that writing in English in Africa is a form of elitism and that choosing to write in an African language is 'a political choice to reach a particular community and assist it to resist a repressive government'.
4   language choice at school: he maintains that parents select English-medium schools because of 'the appalling neglect of state schools' which 'generally use the dominant local language as a medium and are starved of funds by politicians who send their children to private English-medium schools' (Phillipson 1996: 165). He then counters Bisong's claim that three or four hours of exposure to English at school cannot threaten competence in the mother tongue, with the argument that

> if success in education through the medium of English is the primary route to the upper sections of the education system and positions in the modern sector of the economy, and if the rich wealth of Nigerian oral culture has little place in this scheme of things, then the three or four hours are presumably the most important ones of the day. Parents are doubtless acutely conscious of this.
>
> (Phillipson 1996: 166)

Which camp are you in: Bisong's or Phillipson's, and why?

Bisong claims that 'no nation can escape its history'. You might choose to disagree with him, as the Sri Lankan scholar, Canagarajah, does implicitly in his book, *Resisting Linguistic Imperialism in English Teaching*. Canagarajah argues, as the title of his book suggests, for a policy of resistance to colonialism as manifested in the present-day teaching of (British) English in Sri Lanka. On the other hand, if you tend to agree with Bisong, then it is important to be clear about which 'history' cannot be escaped. For, as Omoniyi points out, before the era of colonialism, African kingdoms like Zulu, Shona, Yoruba, Berber, Hausa, Igbo and so on, were in fact monolingual ethnic states. It was only when the African continent was arbitrarily divided up in the nineteenth century that their structure was no longer ethnically determined, so that they were transformed into the multi-ethnic, multilingual African societies of the present day (Omoniyi 1999: 373). At the other extreme, however, there are, today, children of élite families in Nigeria who are being brought up as monolingual speakers of English.

❏ Obeng and Adegbija (1999: 365) argue that

> infighting and sociopolitical rancor among major language groups have stifled the emergence of bona fide national languages that could be symbols of identity in most African countries. In Nigeria, for instance, although the constitution recognizes Hausa, Yoruba, and Igbo as coofficial with English, it is very obvious that the English language performs most official and quasi-national roles. However, being bereft of any Nigerian cultural or ethnic flavoring has made it difficult for English to effectively perform the role of a national language.

And they ask: 'If you were asked to advise a sub-Saharan African government on the selection of a national language, would you recommend an African language of wider communication or a European language?' How would you answer this, and to what extent does their argument contradict that of Bisong?

❏ Bisong cites the authors Achebe, Soyinka and Ngũgĩ in support of his claim. While he is right in respect of Achebe and Soyinka, the same cannot be said of Ngũgĩ, who has written about his own experience of colonialism and, in particular, his enforced learning of English in Kenya with disgust. If you want to pursue this point now, look ahead to the extract from Ngũgĩ in D4. Having read it, how would you respond to Bisong's claim about this author?

CREOLE DEVELOPMENTS IN THE UK AND US

C2

In B2 the examples were taken mainly from the Pacific pidgin, Tok Pisin. In C2, the focus is on two varieties of English which originated in the Atlantic, in the creoles of West Africa and the Caribbean: London Jamaican and Ebonics.

London Jamaican

In recent years, interest has grown in the **patois** of British blacks whose origins are in the Caribbean. This speech style, heard particularly (though not exclusively) in the London area, is known as **London Jamaican**. It is spoken mainly by adolescents, most of whom were born in Britain and, as such, seems in some respects to reflect the process of recreolisation, i.e. where a creole that has moved further along the creole continuum in the direction of the standard language, shifts back towards earlier creole forms (see Romaine 1988: 188–203, Sebba 1997: 43–4, Todd 1990: 61–5). London Jamaican, although essentially a language variety of British Blacks, is also spoken by whites and Asians who have networks of black friends. (See Rampton 1995 on the use of minority language varieties by members of ethnic outgroups, or 'language crossing'.)

The most comprehensive account of London Jamaican is that of Sebba (1993). He examines in detail the features of **Jamaican Creole** in Britain and shows how the speech code switches between London Jamaican and **London English (Cockney)**. In this section, many of the details are taken from a master's dissertation by Graham (2000), which contributes to this work. Graham was convinced that the patois of the black youth living in her part of Brixton (South London) differed in striking ways from the London English of the local white youth, and that these black adolescents were engaging in acts of identity by looking to their Jamaican roots for some aspects of their speech style. She set out to find out precisely which features of Jamaican Creole they did and did not adopt.

Jamaican Creole grammatical features in the data:

- ❑ interchangeable use of pronouns, e.g. 'mi' and 'I' both used for 'I' and 'me'; 'im', 'i' both used for 'he', 'she', 'it', 'him', 'her', 'its', 'his', 'hers', 'its';
- ❑ use of present tense for both present and past, e.g. 'an I se' meaning 'and I said';
- ❑ elimination of tense suffixes '-s', '-ed', '-t' and participle endings '-ing';
- ❑ -ed, -en, -t, e.g. 'yu bret stink' for 'your breath stinks';
- ❑ negation with 'no', often with phonological changes, as in 'no bret stink' for standard English 'my breath doesn't stink'.

Jamaican Creole phonological features in the data

- ❑ substitution of /θ/ and /ð/ with /t/ and /d/ e.g. 'bret' for 'breath' and 'dis' for 'this' (whereas speakers of London English substitute these sounds with /f/ and /v/);
- ❑ labialisation when the sound /b/ is followed by certain vowels, e.g. 'boys' is pronounced 'bwoys';
- ❑ dropping of word-final consonants, e.g. 'bulleh' for 'bullet';
- ❑ realisation of the vowel sounds /ɒ/ and /ɔː/ as /aː/ so that 'cloth' becomes 'klaat';
- ❑ lack of weak vowels especially schwa, so that, e.g. the word 'rapper' is pronounced /rapa/ rather than /rapə/ and the article 'the' is regularly pronounced /da/ and /di/.

Jamaican Creole lexical features of London Jamaican

- ❑ Examples which Graham quotes from Hewitt (1986: 129–30) include 'mash-up' ('destroy'), 'picky-picky' ('frizzy', of hair), and 'duppy' ('ghost'). However, she repeats Hewitt's (1986) caution that words of Jamaican Creole origin may also be used by speakers from other groups including whites and non-Caribbean blacks.

❑ Examples in Graham's own data include the taboo Jamaican Creole words 'bombklaat' ('toilet paper') and 'blodklaat' ('sanitary towel').

Features of the London Jamaican data which are also markers of London English but do not occur in Jamaican Creole are as follows:

❑ the glottal stop (represented by ʔ), e.g. 'ghetto' pronounced /gheʔo/ and 'gotta' as /goʔa/;
❑ the vocalisation of dark 'l' (the RP 'l' sound when it does not occur before a vowel) e.g. 'tell' as 'tew', whereas in Jamaican Creole, this 'l' is pronounced as clear 'l' (the RP 'l' sound when it occurs before a vowel);
❑ the substitution of /θ/ and /ð/ with /f/ and /v/ alongside /t/ and /d/.

Other features of Jamaican Creole (from Sebba 1997) are:

❑ lack of inversion in question forms, as in 'im did phone you?';
❑ absence of the copula, as in 'dis party well rude';
❑ the addition of the sound /h/ to the beginnings of words which start with vowel sounds, e.g. 'accent' pronounced 'haccent';
❑ use of the suffix 'dem' added to a noun to indicate plurality, e.g. 'man-dem' meaning 'men', or a large quantity as in 'kaan-dem' ('a lot of corn').

Although the parents claim to disapprove of their children using patois, they evidently speak it at home themselves. Graham (2000) argues that their own use of this variety in the home seems to have provided a model for their children and this explains why, on reaching adolescence, the children are fully competent in patois. She concludes:

> Barry [one of her subjects] strongly believes that creoles originated from 'secret languages' which were 'sung' by slaves but were incomprehensible to white people. Whether this is true or not, there would seem to be a strong need among Caribbean peoples for languages to call their own; languages which reflect their identities and preserve something of their African languages and cultures; languages which white people do not understand. In choosing to focus on JC [Jamaican Creole] as the model for their 'Patois', 'London Jamaican' or 'Street Talk', young black adolescents are refusing to be 'Standardised' and are refusing to be swallowed up by the more dominant white middle-class culture which surrounds them.
>
> (Graham 2000: 46)

❑ How do you account for the fact that London Jamaican speakers have in their repertoires features of both London English and Jamaican Creole? Can you see any reason for their selection of features in each case? For example, why do they use the London English glottal stop? Why do they not use Jamaican Creole /h/ before a vowel? If they are engaging in acts of identity, how fluid is this identity?

❏ If you have access to adolescent speakers of Black English, ask them questions based on the features set out above. Find out whether they think they use (or do not use):

    ❏ the linguistic items identified above as being exclusive to London Jamaican

    ❏ those items identified as featuring also in London English

    ❏ other features not mentioned.

If possible, record the speakers talking to each other to see how far their intuitions agree with what they do in practice.

❏ If you do not have access to young speakers of Black English, you could devise a similar small-scale research project for another adolescent group that you have identified as speaking a variety of English which differs in interesting ways from that of their local peer group.

Ebonics

On 18 December 1996, the School Board in Oakland, California, passed a resolution regarding its policy in relation to the language skills of African-American pupils. Despite the various attempts that had been made by the Board up until that point, these pupils had continued to exhibit far higher levels of illiteracy than their peer group. The Board decided on a novel approach: to treat African-American pupils in the same way that they had treated Asians and Hispanics. In other words, they proposed teaching them Standard English through their 'mother tongue', African-American Vernacular English (AAVE), also commonly known as **Ebonics** (from 'ebony' and 'phonics'). As the pupils' English skills improved, the teaching of other subjects through the medium of English would then be phased in.

The Oakland Board's resolution included the following claims:

❏ Many African-Americans speak Ebonics.

❏ Ebonics is not a debased dialect or jargon but a valid linguistic system influenced by the West and Niger-Congo languages spoken by their ancestors.

❏ African Language Systems are genetically based.

❏ Ebonics could and should be used as a medium for the children who were being failed by the current education system.

❏ Funds would be set aside for the devising and implementing of a teaching program in Ebonics.

(Todd 1997: 13–14)

Activity

There was an immediate and highly polarised outcry. These are some of the responses (taken from McArthur 1998: 217–19). Decide for yourself whether your sympathies are with the Oakland Board or with its critics:

From the *San Francisco Chronicle*, 21 December 1996

Tatum Willoughby, a fifth-grade student at Prescott Elementary on Campbell Street in West Oakland, used to cry because she had trouble 'speaking the right language,' as she calls it. The bright African American child tried hard to translate the phrases and words she uses at home – black English – into the standard English her teacher said would help her excel. But after months of being taught through a program that recognizes that African American children may come into the classroom using Ebonics . . . Tatum reads her essays with pride. Occasionally, the 10-year-old slips into black English, such as saying 'dis' for 'this.' But she quickly corrects herself. 'Most people won't understand you if you speak (black English),' Tatum said.

(front page: Thaai Walker and Nanette Asimov)

I think it's tragic. Here we have young black kids who are incapable in far too many cases of negotiating even the most basic transactions in our society because of their inability to communicate . . . We're going to legitimize what they're doing. To me it's just ass backwards.

(editorial section: quoted comment by Ward Connerly,
a University of California regent)

If people are not willing to accept ebonics as a second language, then they should at least accept that African American students are not achieving at the level they need to, and we need to do something about that.

(editorial section: quoted comment by Alan Young, director of state and
federal programs, Oakland School Board)

Editor – I am absolutely thrilled at the Oakland school district's choice of ebonics as the language of choice in the classroom. I expect that very shortly we will see New York punks being taught in Brooklonics, Georgia rednecks in Ya'allonics, Valley girls in Bimbonics, chronic nerds in Siliconics and farm boys in Rubiconics. But what most of us need to keep up with the bureaucrats is a thorough understanding of Moronics.

(letter section: Richard Ogar of Berkeley)

Editor – The real goal of those backing this move is multiculturalism, as opposed to the melting pot society which is what made this nation so successful. If the U.S. is to remain a leading economic and social force as we enter the 21st century, we must not allow the PC crowd to have its way in imposing multiculturalism on the nation. The action of the Oakland school board does a tremendous disservice to black students, and I hope it is soundly rebuked by higher authorities, without whose funding it cannot succeed.

(letter section: Jack D. Bernal in San Francisco)

From the *Oakland Tribune*, 21 December 1996

The [board's] report offers sound goals – African-American students will become proficient in reading, speaking and writing standard English. It recommends greater involvement of parents and incentives for teachers who tackle these challenges. The Ebonics approach would presumably make African-American students eligible for state and federal bilingual funds, giving the district more resources to provide additional help for them. District officials deny the approach is a strategy to get more funding. There's nothing wrong with looking for additional ways to help a population that is struggling in the public school system. But making non-standard English a language undermines the very goals the board has embraced. It sends a wrong and confusing message to students. If what they are speaking is a language, what's the urgency of learning another language?

(front page: Brenda Payton)

From the *International Herald Tribune*, 24–25 December 1996

The Reverend Jesse Jackson said Sunday that the school board in Oakland, California, was both foolish and insulting to black students throughout the United States when it declared that many of its black students speak a language distinct from traditional English . . .' I understand the attempt to reach out to these children, but this is an unacceptable surrender, border-lining on disgrace,' he said. 'It's teaching down to our children' . . . Mr Jackson said the Oakland board had become a laughing stock, and he urged its members to reverse their decision.

('Jesse Jackson Ridicules Acceptance of Black English', by Neil A. Lewis)

From the *New York Times*, 26 December 1996

To the Editor: The California State Board of Education endorsed ebonics in 1991, and the State Department of Education has financed research institutes and conferences that have studied the subject exclusively. I spoke at two such conferences this year alone. Oakland's school board is not the first district to apply this policy. Los Angeles and San Diego have used it for years. . . . Those like the Rev. Jesse Jackson, who seek the quick headline will find themselves out of step with the legitimate demands for cutting-edge education.

(letter by John W. Templeton, Executive Editor,
Aspire Books, San Francisco)

From the *New York Times*, 14 January 1997

Hoping to quell the uproar set off by its resolution to treat black English as a second language in its classrooms, the Oakland school board will scratch part of a plan that suggested it would offer instruction in the tongue that some linguists call ebonics, school officials said today. After almost a month of national debate and a weekend of sometimes tense meetings here, the Oakland schools task force that introduced the black English policy . . . produced a new resolution on Sunday that calls only for the recognition of language differences among black students in order to improve their proficiency in English. "The debate is over," the head of the task force, Sylvester Hodges, said. "We are hoping that people will understand that and will join us." . . . The many writers, educators and politicians who have attacked the school board's original plan have tended to agree that the issue is perhaps more about the symbolism than the specifics of what black children in Oakland might be taught.

(Oakland Scratches Plan To Teach Black English, by Tim Golden)

From *The Economist* (UK) 4 January, 1997

The school board thought it might help if the slang these children used at home were recognized as a distinct primary language, separate from English, and if teachers showed respect for this language and used it in the classroom, as a means to bridge the gap between standard English and the speech of the ghetto . . . The quasi-language in question has been christened 'Ebonics', a lumpish blend of 'ebony' and 'phonics'. Supporters of Ebonics say it derives from the structures of Niger-Congo African languages and marks the persistent legacy of slavery. Other linguistic scholars note that some usages have appeared only recently, as the ghettos have become more isolated from mainstream American life.

❏ Todd (1997: 16) says 'the Oakland debate revealed more about the attitudes of the partakers than it did about Ebonics or about educational problems'. What do you think she means? How do you account for the fact that opposition to the resolution was voiced by both members of the black population and members of the conservative white population?

❏ Which side, if either, do you support, and why?

❏ How does the Oakland Board's approach to the education of its blacks fit in with the ethos of the California-wide English Only Movement which you looked at in C1?

❏   Why do you think so much importance, not to mention emotional investment, is attached to the variety of English used for educational purposes? You may like to read the article on pidgin English in Cameroon (in D2) before you think about this issue.

TEACHING AND TESTING WORLD ENGLISHES

The English varieties that are revered, taught and tested in most parts of the world are still those of educated native speakers, particularly British and North American; the methodologies and materials that are promoted are those favoured by the ENL centres – communicative (interactive) approaches with an emphasis on 'learner autonomy' and problem solving, and unilingual (English only) textbooks; the teachers who are most highly sought after are native speakers of English; and the tests which are taken most seriously measure competence in relation to native-speaker norms.

B3 was concerned with the language itself, and the question of which Englishes are suitable to serve as teaching models. In this unit we go on to consider issues concerned with first the teaching and second the testing of English.

Teaching English today

Given the fact that native speakers are widely held to make better teachers of English than non-native speakers, we will start by asking why this should be so. Is it really a question of their being better teachers, or simply one of knowing English (as a Native Language) better? Here are three views.

> The discourse of Applied Linguistics as well as the vast amount of supporting material brought out by the ESL/EFL enterprise have created and perpetuated the image of the native speaker as the unquestionable authority of not just language ability but also of expertise in its teaching. Native speaker status is often seen as the *sine qua non*, automatically bestowing authenticity and credibility on a teacher, as an English Language expert or even a teacher trainer. As an initial gate-keeping shibboleth, nativeness can assume primacy over pedagogic expertise or actual language competence in the ELT enterprise.
>
> (Nayar 1998: 287)

> [T]eachers of English are required to teach not English as a general linguistic phenomenon but English as a subject – a subject which keeps company with others on the curriculum – history, physics, geography and so on. Now nobody, I think, would suppose that somebody who lived through a particular period of history was especially well qualified to teach it as a subject – that the best teachers of the history of the Second World War, for example, are a diminishing group of octogenarian old soldiers who have actually lived the experience. Similarly, it is would surely be odd to argue that the best teachers of the geography of, say, the Austrian Alps are Tyrolean

shepherds because they have a unique intimacy with the landscape . . . Of course these people have a wealth of intimate experience which can be drawn upon as data, and so they can serve as expert *informants* on certain aspects of the subjects concerned. But this does not make them expert *instructors*.

The same kind of argument applies to the subject English. And in our case the subject is English *as a foreign language (EFL)*. It has generally been the case, I think, that teachers of EFL have been considered (or consider themselves) as teachers of English which happens incidentally to be a foreign language. In this definition of the subject, English is paramount and its speakers privileged. But we can also conceive of EFL as the teaching of a foreign language which happens to be English. Now the focus of attention is on the foreignness and not the nativeness of the language, on what makes it foreign, and how, as a foreign language, it might be most effectively taught.

Now when it comes to expertise in the teaching of foreign languages, those in the English speaking world have little to offer. In this respect, the fact that their own language is so dominant does them a disservice. The British are not noted for their ready acquisition of any language other than their own. The record of foreign language instruction in their schools has, generally speaking, been one of dismal failure. And yet there is this pervasive assumption that they are naturally expert in the teaching of a foreign language to other people . . . But why should the British claim any authority to advise on foreign language teaching, in which they have no credible credentials at all? It seems perverse. And yet such authority is claimed. And furthermore, it is conceded. Why?

Because there is this persistent confusion, I suggest, between the phenomenon English as a native language, and the subject English as a foreign language, and the invalid assumption that arises from it that experience in the one readily transfers to an expertise in the other. In other words, that pedagogic competence in EFL follows easily on from a linguistic competence in E – the FL can be added on without too much effort or trouble. Start with native speaker ability, add on a little common sense, or perhaps a brief rudimentary training in technique, get hold of a resource book, and hey presto, you are an EFL teacher, eligible for employment, a genuine article with customer appeal.

(Widdowson 1994: 1.10–1.13)

[T]he non-native teacher has been through the process of learning the same language, often through the same L1 'filter', and she knows what it is like to have made the foreign language, in some sense, her own, to have appropriated it for particular purposes. This is an experience which is shared only between non-native teachers and their students. One could say that native speakers know the destination, but not the terrain that has to be crossed to get there: they themselves have not travelled the same route. Non-native teachers, on the other hand, know the target language as a foreign language. Paradoxically, it is precisely this which is often perceived as a weakness, although it can be understood and drawn upon as an important resource. This shared language learning experience should thus constitute the basis for non-native teachers' confidence, not for their insecurity.

(Seidlhofer 1999: 238)

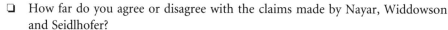

❏ How far do you agree or disagree with the claims made by Nayar, Widdowson and Seidlhofer?

❏ Prepare a short questionnaire to enable you to find out whether people believe native speakers or non-native speakers make better teachers of English, or if they think there is no difference, along with the reasons for their answer. Give the questionnaire to as many people as possible, both native and non-native speakers of English and, if you can, both students of English and non-students. Analyse your results: what is the consensus? If they favour native speaker teachers, do the reasons they give focus entirely on linguistic competence (e.g. accent, knowledge of grammar and idioms) or do they also refer to teaching ability? What do the responses tell you about attitudes to non-native teachers? How much do these attitudes seem to depend on whether or not the respondent is him/herself a native or non-native speaker? Finally, do you detect among your non-native speaker respondents any feeling of **linguistic insecurity** (an acceptance of the negative stereotyping of their English by the dominant native speaker community)?

❏ In your view what qualities make a good teacher of English to speakers of other languages? To what extent (if at all) do you believe that the qualities you mention are different for teachers of second languages *other than* English? How compatible is your checklist of qualities with the common view of native-speaker teachers as being better than non-native speaker teachers? Compare your views with those of others and try to account for any serious differences.

Testing English today

At the end of the day, no matter how much effort is put into making the teaching of English more appropriate to the contexts of teaching, if the examination boards continue to measure students' success in English against native-speaker norms, then little is likely to change. It is well known that tests have a **backwash** effect on classroom teaching: that is, the language and skills that are tested in examinations are the ones that teachers choose to teach and learners desire to learn. Otherwise they have nothing to show for the efforts they have made.

So far, however, there are few signs that the testing of English is embracing non-native speaker variation and innovation. As Peter Lowenberg (2000: 67) points out, little consideration has as yet been given to

> the linguistic norms for English against which proficiency in English is generally assessed, that is, the norms of Standard English. Rather, an implicit, and frequently explicit, assumption has been that the universal target for proficiency in Standard English around the world is the set of norms which are accepted and used by highly educated native speakers of English.

He goes on to demonstrate how many of these NS norms do not reflect the norms of non-native speaker varieties in a large number of world English (Outer Circle) settings such as Bangladesh, Kenya, Nigeria, Sierra Leone, Singapore.

Lowenberg (2000) provides several examples of the sort of English usage which is considered standard in its local context, but which diverges from native speaker use and would therefore be regarded as deviant in international tests of English. For example:

- ❏ The use of 'would' rather than 'will' in Malaysian and Indian English as in 'We accept the verdict of the Kelantan people and we hope they *would* accept the verdict of the rest of the country'.
- ❏ The use of uncountable nouns as countable in a number of countries including the Philippines, Nigeria and Malaysia, as in 'Thank you for upkeeping the *equipments* and facilities provided on this train'.
- ❏ Similarly, (Malaysian) 'West said they used *a digital equipment* that was capable of transmitting both video and still images'.
- ❏ Prepositional collocations such as (Singaporean) 'I live in an apartment *at* Belmont Road'.
- ❏ Use of prepositions considered to be redundant in standard British and American English, such as in the phrase 'discuss *about*' which is attested as standard use in a number of non-native speaker varieties of English such as Nigerian, Malaysian, Zambian, and Singaporean, and also found widely in Expanding Circle Englishes.

World English testing, then, still reflects very strongly the 'deficit linguistics' view that was discussed in B3 and gives a clear impression that what is being tested is not proficiency *per se*, but proximity to native-speaker norms. The difficulty nevertheless remains of establishing precisely which features exemplify difference and which deficiencies. It cannot be assumed that all divergences from native-speaker norms represent developing varietal norms: they could also be either errors (but in relation to the L2 norm) or **nonce** words (words invented for a specific purpose and used only once).

- ❏ As regards the Outer Circle, Lowenberg (2000: 81) describes as 'almost neo-colonial' the 'assumption held by many who design English proficiency tests . . . that the native speakers still should determine the norms for Standard English around the world'. He does, however, think it is reasonable for native speakers to provide the norms in tests for English speakers in the Expanding Circle, in countries such as Japan, Egypt and Spain, where English does not have intranational functions. Do you agree with him on either of these points?
- ❏ If you are able to do so, look at some English language tests that are used on a world-wide basis, e.g. TOEIC, TOEFL, IELTS, any of the University of Cambridge (formerly UCLES) tests and such like. Better still, look at the practice books produced by one of the examination boards, as then you will be able to check the key to find out which answers are considered acceptable. How strictly do the tests conform to native-speaker norms of correctness? Do they make any allowance for non-native speaker variation?
- ❏ If you live in an Outer Circle setting, try to design a short grammar test that takes account of your local norms. If you live in an Expanding Circle setting, try to design a similar test, but this time, one that takes international use of English in purely

non-native speaker interaction into consideration. To what extent do you need to break away from native-speaker English norms in order to do this?

❑ Kachru (1992: 361) considers that the only solution to the current inappropriateness of English language teaching and testing around the world is for a 'paradigm shift' in which, for example, a clear distinction is made between the use of English in monolingual and multilingual societies, there is mutual exposure to the major native and non-native varieties of English, and while one variety may be the focus of teaching, emphasis is given to the 'awareness and functional validity' of the others. Think about the ways in which such a paradigm shift could be implemented. For example, how could awareness of a range of non-native varieties of English be raised in ELT classrooms?

C4   EMERGING SUB-VARIETIES

In this unit, we will look at two sub-varieties of English which are still in the process of emerging: Singlish and Estuary English. They are both associated to some extent with youth, and are both currently considered to be non- (even sub-) standard, as is generally the case with much youth language.

Singlish

Singlish is sometimes called **Colloquial Singapore English (CSE)** in order to differentiate it from **Standard Singapore English**. Currently the issue of whether Singlish should be banned is exercising the minds of educationalists, government officials and journalists alike. Some are concerned that the use of Singlish among the young is likely to affect their literacy. Another fear is that if young people grow up speaking only Singlish, they will not be able to speak an internationally acceptable or understandable form of English, something which many Singaporeans regard as crucial to the continuing success of a country with a population of only three million.

Gupta defines Singlish, or Singapore Colloquial English, as a contact variety rather than a 'semi-institutionalised codemix variety' such as Spanglish or Hindlish. She points out that 'the Sing- of Singlish is Singapore, not a language' and that 'the main difference from StdE [Standard English] is syntactic, and the lexis is dominated by English'. She adds that 'it is Singapore Colloquial English which is the most usual ENL of those who learn English at home' (1999: 62).

Below are some examples of Singlish.

The following utterances were made by a child, Yingchun, recorded by her anxious mother as an example of '"regression" in spoken English after only a month of playing with other Singapore children at a day care centre' (in Pakir 1993: 28):

Yingchun's Singlish	Standard Singapore English
ting	thing
dank-u	thank you
bang! you die already	bang! you're dead
my one, not your one	mine, not yours
you keep this toy and I bring you anudder one	put away the toy while I get another
wearing shoes	putting on shoes
plucking a flower	picking a flower
can you go to sleep with me	put me to bed

Try to describe some of the linguistic features of Singlish based on this evidence.

The second example, from Gupta (1999: 62) also features a child, this time one of almost six years old, who is a native speaker of English. The conversation is between Gupta herself (AG) and the child (R). They are looking at a photograph of a crowd of people in a performance:

R	Then this is the Jesus son.
AG	Jesus's son!
R	No, this is Jesus son.
[1 sec]	
	Hah?
AG	Jesus son?
R	Yah
AG	Jesus didn't have any children.
R	That one – ah – because ah, like us hor, /is/ Jesus daughter and son ah. Acting only lah.

Again, identify features here that appear to you to be Singlish features.

The third example also comes from Pakir (1995: 7). In this school, while Mandarin is the normal language used by the girls for informal interaction, in this particular class they regularly use English even informally, though they code switch to Mandarin for humorous effect. Here, the girls are engaged in group work. The formality level has dropped from the standard spoken English which tends to characterise these students' speech and, as Pakir points out, their language includes a number of colloquial features:

> **S1** On the way to Damascus, saw bright lights, heard Jesus . . .
> Conversation with Jesus, Jesus gives him instructions . . .
> **S3** Got instructions. Can lah.
> **S1** OK, so what . . . Then Saul is blinded, right?
> **S2** He was instructed to go into the city; but he was going into the city anyway!
> **S1** Ya woh.
> **S3** Saul was baffled. Mystified. He heard the sound but did not see anyone.
> **S2** But '. . . did not see anyone' indicates that Saul must have seen something.
> **S3** He saw a bright light!
> **S2** Sorry, I'm sorry. So cheem.
> (cheem = Hokkien meaning 'deep')

Activity   Once again, identify features which seem to you to signal Singlish usage. Then compare your notes with the following account.

Maley (1997: 16–17) sums up the features of Singlish as follows.

Pronunciation

❏ Replacement of final consonants such as t, d, k, g, p, b and l by a glottal stop, as in 'Wan? Or no?' (where ? represents a glottal stop).

❏ This is often associated with a shortening of vowels before stops. For example in 'Wan? a por? cho??' the vowel in 'pork' is indistinguishable from the one in 'want' and 'chop'.

❏ There is a tendency to lengthen final vowels, so that 'stories' becomes 'storeees', 'quality' becomes 'qualiteee', 'shopping' becomes 'shoppeeeng'.

❏ This, too, is associated with two stress features: the tendency to shift stress towards the end of words of compounds, and the tendency to place stress more or less equally on all syllables. For example 'Victoria CONcert Hall' (General English) is regularly pronounced 'Victoria Concert HALL' and words like 'nOminated' (GenE) become 'nominAted'.

Grammar

❏ Omission of the verb 'to be' in contexts where it would be required in GenE. For example: 'I very scared', 'I so blur', 'That boy so havoc, you know'.

❏ The all-purpose substitution of 'to be' as in: 'My father is stay here what'. 'I was study in Primary School'. 'This house was belong his son'.

❏ The use of the all-purpose tag 'is it?' as in 'You teaching NUS [= National University of Singapore], is it?' and the substitution of Chinese-style question forms such as 'right or not?', 'Chicken rice, got or not?', 'Curry gravy, want or not?', 'Come on Sunday, can or not?'

❏ The movement of 'already', 'also', 'only' to the end of the sentence, as in: 'He is resign already', meaning simply 'He has resigned'.

❏ The substitution of 'would' for 'will' and of 'had' for a simple past action. For example: 'I hope the Ministry would take the necessary action'. 'Anyone who had lost their money in the scam is requested to come forward'.

❏ The widespread use of discourse particles such as 'lah', 'a', 'lor', 'what'.

❏ Countability of nouns often varies. For example, we can speak of 'jargons', 'slangs', 'feedbacks', 'staffs', etc.

Lexis

❏ There is a large number of loanwords from the other Singaporean languages, such as 'ang moh' (a Caucasian), 'siau' (crazy), 'ngeow' (difficult to please), 'yaya' (smart ass), 'kiasu' (someone scared of losing out to the competition), 'maakan' (food), 'teruk' (terrible), 'buaya' (womaniser), 'ulu' (country bumpkin), 'rojak' (all mixed together), 'obiang' (vulgar, tasteless dressing or display of wealth), and many more.

❏ There is a tendency to extend the grammatical functions of verbs to adjectives and of nouns to verbs. For example: 'blur' which is a verb in GenE becomes an adjective meaning 'confused', 'don't know the time of day' in Singlish. 'So tiring, lah! I feel so blur, you know.' (Note that 'blur' with this meaning has an entry in the 1999 *Encarta Dictionary*.)

❏ The all-purpose noun 'Thisthing' ('you know what I mean') can also be used as a verb, as in 'You know, he thisthinged his thisthing'.

❏ There is also a whole series of idiomatic forms peculiar to Singlish. For example: 'I feel so frus' (frustrated), 'I just go zap this article' (photocopy) . . . 'Now her boss away, she shake legs only' (idles away her time).

(from Maley 1997: 16–17)

Estuary English

Estuary English (EE) has, in its relatively short life, proved as controversial as Singlish. For example, the UK Education Secretary in 1994 launched a campaign to stop the spread of EE among schoolchildren.

The term 'Estuary English' was originally coined by Rosewarne, a pronunciation specialist, in 1983. This is how he described EE some thirteen years later, in 1996:

> Estuary English, a new accent variety I first described in 1984, is neither Cockney nor RP, but in the middle between these two. "Estuary English . . . is to be found in its purest form along the seaward banks of the Thames, whither it has drifted from the eastern end of the capital" (leader article in the *Independent on Sunday* of 18 June 1995). The heartland still lies by the banks of the Thames and its estuary, but it has spread to other areas, as *The Sunday Times* announced on 14 March 1993 in a front-page headline "Estuary English sweeps Britain". Experts on British English agree that it is currently the strongest influence on the standard spoken form and that it could replace RP as the most influential accent in the British Isles.
>
> (Rosewarne 1996: 15)

Rosewarne (1996: 16–18) then describes the pronunciation features which he has observed among EE speakers, as follows:

Rosewarne

- ❏ The most obvious pronunciation feature – the loss of alveolar contact in final position /t/ – can be heard in the younger members of the British royal family, as in 'There's a lo of i abou', using glottal stops where the /t/s are missing in this utterance.
- ❏ In EE the dark /l/ of RP is realised with a sound which may be transcribed phonemically as /w/. In rapid EE speech *Paul's, pulls, pause* and *paws* are homophones.
- ❏ The final vowel sounds in the words *very funny* in EE are long and are represented by the symbol /i:/. This long vowel sound in EE occurs in other positions where RP would use a shorter phoneme, as in for example, *various*, which sounds something like *vareeous*.
- ❏ The yod (the y sound after the c in 'cure', represented phonemically as /j/) is dropped in EE pronunciation of *assume* and *pursuit*.
- ❏ The sound combinations /tj/ and /dj/ in RP are pronounced /tʃ/ and /dʃ/ in EE, as in the utterance '*it's due on Tuesday*'.
- ❏ EE avoids the syllabic consonants that RP has in, for example, *middle* and *button* /mɪdl/ and /bʌtn/, placing a schwa between the /d/ and /l/ and the /t/ and /n/.
- ❏ Observers generally report that the voice quality of EE speakers is more nasal than RP or Cockney.
- ❏ EE is also slower than these, with fewer words spoken per minute than these other two. The 'deliberateness' that observers comment on in EE speech may be the result of stress patterns used. EE speakers frequently stress prepositions, auxiliary and that-clauses . . . Examples of this are: *Get off <u>at</u> the station / The phone <u>was</u> ringing / I'm interested <u>that</u> you say that.* In polysyllabic words the stress in EE is often placed later than in RP. An example of this is 'temporarily', which receives stress on the first syllable in RP but on the third in EE.

Rosewarne (1996: 20) concludes 'It will be interesting to see the direction of change in the future, whether RP will change so as to absorb EE, or if EE replaces RP as the standard form of British English.'

However, other writers have questioned the existence, status and features of EE. First, Wells:

It is not entirely clear whether EE is to be regarded as a variety (lect, dialect) in its own right, or whether it is simply the formal style/register for which Cockney is the informal one. A decision depends on two empirical issues:

1 Is there a casual style of EE that is unquestionably distinct from Cockney? Tentatively, yes: there may well be speakers who avoid stigmatized h-dropping even in their most casual style (as RP speakers do; NB we are not dealing here with /h/ in unstressed pronouns).

2 Is there a formal style of Cockney that is distinct from EE? Tentatively, yes: Cockney is arguably the speech of the uneducated, who are unable to achieve standard grammar even where it might be called for; while EE speakers are those who can consistently use standard grammar with ease and fluency.

The boundary between EE and RP is also hard to establish. Presumably it rests on the degree of localizability: EE is localizable as belonging to the southeast of England . . . whereas RP is not. Many of Rosewarne's comments surely relate to change over time, rather than to the decline of RP, to localizability or to the Thames estuary area. Things like 'cheers' for 'thank you'/'goodbye' are surely part of contemporary casual RP/StEng . . . Some commentators seem not to appreciate that RP can be spoken in informal situations.

(Wells 1994)

Maidment (1994) claims that Rosewarne's description of EE suffers from naïvety because it fails to take account of the sociolinguistic fact of intraspeaker accent variation. In other words, 'a speaker of a given accent has within his or her competence a range of styles from informal to formal' and will adjust their accent according to contextual factors such as location, addressee and topic of conversation. He goes on, '[I]f this is the case, then the boundary between Cockney and EE becomes extremely fuzzy unless style of speech is controlled for', and concludes:

> All this leads to the possibility that EE is no more than slightly poshed up Cockney or RP which has gone "down market" in appropriate situations and that rather than there being a newly developed accent which we should call EE, all that has happened over recent years is that there has been a redefinition of the appropriateness of differing styles of pronunciation to differing speech situations. For example, the perception may be that it is now more acceptable to use informal style in broadcasting. He also points out that the name EE is inappropriate, as the features claimed to define it are used by speakers in places far away from the Thames Estuary. He suggests that a better name would therefore be "Post-Modern English".

(Maidment 1994)

Finally, Maidment (1994) quotes some of the media reactions to the EE phenomenon:

- ❏ It is not an accent . . . just lazy speaking that grates on the ear and is an extremely bad example to our children.
- ❏ The spread of Estuary English can only be described as horrifying. We are plagued with idiots on radio and television who speak English like the dregs of humanity.
- ❏ God forbid that it becomes standard English. Are standards not meant to be upheld? We must not slip into slovenliness because of a lack of respect for the language. Ours is a lovely language, a rich language, which has a huge vocabulary. We have to safeguard it.
- ❏ It is slobspeak, limp and flaccid: the mouths uttering it deserve to be stuffed with broken glass.

- ❏ The media as well as certain members of the general public in both Singapore and the UK seem to have a very low opinion of, respectively, Singlish and Estuary English. Why do you think this is so?
- ❏ Make a list of some of the most typical features of Singlish or Estuary English (depending on your local context) and interview a range of people in different age groups to elicit their views of these varieties. How do you account for the differences of opinion?

❑ Why do you think it is young people who are currently the main users of both Singlish and EE? Do you anticipate that these varieties will spread to other age groups over time?

❑ Who do you support in the EE debate? In particular, do you consider that the features identified as characteristic of EE are evidence of a new variety of British English or simply of changes to RP as it acquires features from Cockney?

C5   STANDARDS ACROSS CHANNELS

In this unit, we will explore the notion of standard usage across the different **channels** of speech and writing, and the recent third channel of e-discourse.

Speech and writing

When people talk about 'standard English', they generally have the written channel in mind. However, the inappropriacy of evaluating English speech on the basis of writing has become increasingly apparent with the growth in the past decade in the number and size of corpora of authentic speech, such as the British National Corpus, COBUILD, and CANCODE (Cambridge and Nottingham Corpus of Discourse in English).

Baron (2000: 21–2) discusses three different approaches to speech/writing differences, the 'Opposition View', the 'Continuum View' and the 'Cross-Over View'. According to the **Opposition View**, speech and writing have the following dichotomous characteristics:

Writing is	Speech is
objective	interpersonal
a monologue	a dialogue
durable	ephemeral
scannable	only linearly accessible
planned	spontaneous
highly structured	loosely structured
syntactically complex	syntactically simple
concerned with past and future	concerned with the present
formal	informal
expository	narrative
argument-oriented	event-oriented
decontextualised	contextualised
abstract	concrete

The **Continuum View**, on the other hand, looks at speech and writing in real-world contexts and regards them as being located at various points on a continuum, depending on the specific context of use:

Traditional Writing   Face-to-Face Speech

<--->

Word processors   Telephones   Videophones,

Teleconferencing

Figure C5.1 Continuum view of speech and writing

The **Cross-Over View**, meanwhile, takes into account the fact that 'merely because a linguistic message looks as if it is designed to be spoken or written hardly ensures that will be the medium through which everyone experiences it' (Baron 2000: 22). For example, it is common nowadays to find 'talking books' (books that are read aloud on cassettes rather than with our eyes), or for lectures to be posted on websites where students who cannot attend in person are able to read them. Can you think of further examples to demonstrate the Cross-Over View, as well as examples which support or contradict the Opposition View?

Leech *et al.* (1982: 139–40) reconcile the differences in the Opposition and Continuum approaches by talking of '**typical speech**' and '**typical writing**'. They categorise the typical features of the two channels as follows:

Table C5.1 Features of typical speech and writing

	Typical speech	**Typical writing**
1	Inexplicitness	Explicitness
2	Lack of clear sentence boundaries	Clear sentence boundaries
3	Simple structure	More complex structure
4	Repetitiveness	Non-repetitiveness
5	Normal non-fluency	Fluency
6	Monitoring features	No monitoring features
7	Interaction features	No interaction features
8	Features reflecting informality	Features reflecting formality

Source: Leech *et al.* (1982: 139–40)

In the above table, non-fluency (5) refers to features which reflect the fact that speech tends to be unprepared and therefore includes phenomena such as hesitations, false starts, grammatical blends and unfinished sentences. **Monitoring features** (6) and interaction (7) features relate to the dialogic nature of speech. Speakers monitor the effect their speech is having on the addressee(s) with words and phrases such as 'well', 'I mean', 'sort of' and 'you know', and they use **interaction features** to invite participation, particularly by means of second-person pronouns, questions, and imperatives. By characterising typical speech and writing in this way, Leech *et al.* are then able to demonstrate how they operate on a continuum rather than in direct opposition:

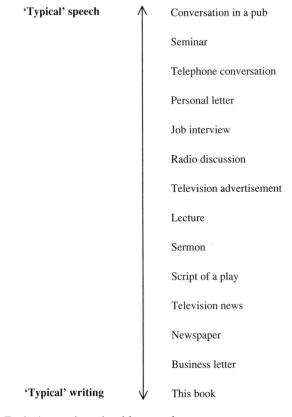

'Typical' speech ↑	Conversation in a pub
	Seminar
	Telephone conversation
	Personal letter
	Job interview
	Radio discussion
	Television advertisement
	Lecture
	Sermon
	Script of a play
	Television news
	Newspaper
	Business letter
'Typical' writing ↓	This book

Figure C5.2 Typical speech and writing continuum

Activity ✪

❏ Do you agree with the order in which Leech *et al.* have placed the speech/writing contexts on their continuum? If not, what changes would you suggest? Do you think any of these result from the fact that their continuum dates from 1982? Why might this be so? And where on the continuum would you place the following: business email, social email, Internet chat room discussion, text message?

❏ Here is a transcribed conversation (from Crystal and Davy 1975, reproduced in Leech *et al.* 1982). Speaker A is describing the family holiday to speaker B. Look back to Leech *et al.*'s lists of features of typical speech and typical writing and see how many of them are exemplified in the transcript. For example, inexplicitness (1) occurs in lines 8/9 ('and all this'), non-fluency (5) occurs in line 4 ('er'), and monitoring (6) in line 1 ('sort of'). Because this is a transcript, there is no punctuation, but vertical lines are used to indicate units of intonation (tone units or 'word groups') and dashes to indicate pauses. The items in brackets are B's responses to A.

C

B	so what how did you map out your day | you had your	1
	breakfast in the kitchen |	2
A	we have our breakfast | (*laughs*) in the kitchen | – and	3
	then we sort of did what we liked | and er got ready to	4
	go out | (m |) we usually went out quite soon after	5
	that | – erm the children were always up | at the crack of	6
	dawn | (m |) with the farmer | – and they went in the	7
	milking sheds | and helped him feed the pigs | and all	8
	this | you know we didn't see the children | – and er	9
	then we used to go out | we – we had super weather | –	10
	absolutely super | – and so we went to a beach | usually	11
	for er but by about four o'clock it we were hot and we	12
	had to come off the beach (m | m |) – so we'd generally	13
	go for a tea somewhere | just in case supper was delayed	14
	you know | (*laughs*) *laughs* and then we'd get back | and	15
	the children would go straight back on to the farm | . . .	16

Now imagine that you are speaker A and that you are describing your farm holiday, not in a conversation, but in a letter. Write the letter retaining as much of the information provided in A's speech as possible. Then compare your written version with the spoken original above and see how many differences there are to illustrate Leech *et al.*'s distinctions between typical speech and typical writing. Are there any other differences which are not covered in their lists of characteristics? And how far can any similarities be accounted for by the fact that conversations and personal letters are fairly close together at the 'Typical speech' end of their continuum?

 Activity

This is Leech *et al.*'s (1982: 141–2) own version of the imaginary letter:

Dear B,

　　　I thought I would write and tell you about our
summer holiday, which we spent on a farm.

　　　Every day, the children were up at the crack
of dawn with the farmer. They went to the milking
sheds with him and helped him feed the pigs, so that we
barely saw them at all.

　　　Then we would have our breakfast in the
kitchen. After breakfast, we usually did what we liked
for a short while, and then went out.

　　　We had absolutely super weather, and so we
usually went to a beach. But by about four o'clock we
were hot and had to come off the beach. Then we'd
generally go and have tea somewhere just in case supper
was delayed. When we got back, the children would go
straight back on the farm . . .

In more recent years, computerised database **corpora** have continued to demonstrate in increasing detail the way in which speech operates according to its own grammatical rules, with writing tending 'to reflect earlier norms while speech commonly embodies innovation' (Baron 2000: 95). The work of Carter and McCarthy for CANCODE, for example, has provided useful evidence of the **grammar of spoken (British) English**. These are some of the phenomena they found in their data. Try to identify the feature of spoken English exemplified in each set of examples before reading on for the technical names and details:

1

    a   Jamie, normally you put him in his cot and he's . . .
    b   That chap over there, he said it was okay . . .
    c   The women in the audience, they all shouted.

2

    a   Cos otherwise they tend to go cold don't they pasta.
    b   They do, I suppose, take up a lot of time, don't they, kids?
    c   It's not actually very good is it that wine?

3

    A   What's the matter?
    B   Got an awful cold.
    A   Just seen Paco.
    B   Did he say anything?
    A   Nothing.
    B   Interesting isn't it?

4

    a   Why I rang you was that I needed to check something.
    b   Where we always go wrong is that we forget it's a one-way street.
    c   What fascinates me with that is the way it's rolled.

Brief notes:

1 Heads (or 'left dislocation')

Heads are nouns or noun phrases which are brought to the front of a clause to identify them for the listener as the most important part of the message. They are then repeated with a pronoun in the clause which follows. In the above examples, the heads are (a) 'Jamie', (b) 'That chap over there', and (c) 'The women in the audience'.

2 Tails (or 'reinforcement')

Tails parallel heads by repeating the subject of the preceding clause in order to amplify and reinforce what has been said. They thus tend to serve an affective function by showing the speaker's attitude towards his or her subject. The tails in the above examples are (a) 'pasta', (b) 'kids' and (c) 'that wine'.

3   Ellipsis

Ellipsis simply means omission. It refers specifically to the omission of items in a grammatical structure which go unnoticed in speech but which would be required in a written text. The items which are omitted are those which are retrievable from either the immediate situation or from the surrounding text (i.e. the 'cotext'). In the example dialogue, the ellipted items are: 'I've (got an awful cold)'; 'I've (just seen Paco)'; 'He said (nothing)'; 'It's (interesting, isn't it?)'.

4   Word order

Word order varies considerably across speech and writing. One area in which this is particularly so is that of reported speech. The examples above all demonstrate **wh-clefting**, which CANCODE has shown to be far more widespread in spoken than in written English. These wh-clauses are brought to the front of the clause often, as with heads, for emphasis, though they can also serve to contradict an anticipated response. The wh-clefts in the above examples are: 'Why I rang you', 'Where we always go wrong', and 'What fascinates me with that'.

Can you think of further examples of the grammar of speech? One fairly recent phenomenon, for instance, is the use of quotative *like* as in ' "I walked in the front door" and it was like "Where the hell have you been?" '. As recently as the year 2000, quotative *like* was used only by younger speakers of English, but over the following two years was adopted by older age groups, demonstrating the relative speed with which speech innovations spread through the speech community.

E-discourse

Look at the following examples of authentic emails (all sent or copied to me) and identify features that are typical of written and spoken English (see above and below), and features which do not occur in either and, instead, seem to be emerging features of e-style:

> 1   change of plan, im going to stay in leeds instead, all trains are booked up for coming back up, and none of my m8s are coming back to london like i thought they would. ive got 4 essays to write and i want to get them done before xmas so i think i will spend this weekend working! plus im going to be coming back on the 12/13th anyway so its hardly anytime anyway. sorry to disapoint, and give my luv to the the wrinklies!
> nick

2   Alessia and Martin,
The book I mentioned at our last meeting is:
Kelly Hall, J. and Eggington, W.G. (eds) (2000) The sociopolitics of
English language teaching. Clevedon: Multilingual Matters.
I spoke to Jenny today and she said that she might have referred this
title already. If you have difficulties in accessing this book in the
near future, let me know.
Constant

3   Dear Jenny,
it's that time of year again. Any chance of meeting up before
christmas. You name some dates as you are probably busier than me, now
that the tasting season is calming down. Looking forward to seeing you.
love Rosemary

4   sorry jenny am just doing the revisions, and your 'proff'-reading is
very useful! I've just been through the bit with the upper-
intermediate etc, and when looking at it now it really sees ok to
me, don't think it'll be all that important after all. sorry about that.
If you get the message and want me to change it after all, then
please, if possible, give me the wording that you want. I don't think
it matters much one way or another.
And on...
B

5   Dear Dr. Jenkins,
Thank you for your quick response. I'm afraid I can't send you my IELTS
certificate right now, because I won't take it until March, 2002. But before that,
I'll send my application form and two references to you as soon as possible.
Will that be OK?
And if there's anything else I should do, please let know.

Thank you very much.

Sincerely,
(first name + family name)

6   Dear Professor Jenkins,
Thank you very much for your kind assistance. The pertinent materials will
be couriered to your office at due course.

Yours sincerely,
(first name + family name)

---

7   Dear Jenny,
I am writing regarding my decision to change courses
from the MA in Applied Language Studies in Education
to Applied Linguistics and ELT.

In the conversation I had this morning with Dermot, he
said that you had authorized the late change and that
I should get in touch with you. I have been unable to
contact you by phone. My phone number at work is
(.... ....) and at home is (.... ....).

I will keep trying to call you this week.
Thank you very much for allowing me to change at such
a late stage.
Kind regards,
(first name + family name)

---

8   It might be worth bearing in mind that (in spite of what Metrical
Phonologists and others might claim) it is not universally accepted that
"knowing the stress pattern" is necessary for recognizing English words.
There's a good (and short) review of the question by James McQueen and Anne
Cutler in W. Hardcastle and J. Laver 'The Handbook of Phonetic Sciences'
(Blackwell, 1997), pp. 579–582. On p. 580 they say ". . . stress information
does not facilitate human word recognition". I find the section on Prosodic
Information in their chapter (Cognitive Processes in Speech Perception) very
useful reading for my final year students.
Peter

Despite the fact that emails seem to make use of conventions drawn from both speech
and writing, there is, as Baron (2000: 193) points out, 'evidence for an increasingly
oral basis to written language' in **e-style**. She outlines the linguistic profile of email
at the end of the 1990s as follows:

❏ *Social dynamics*: Predominantly like writing
  ❏ interlocutors are physically separated
  ❏ physical separation fosters personal disclosure and helps level the conversational playing field
❏ *Format*: (Mixed) writing and speech
  ❏ like writing, email is durable
  ❏ like speech, email is typically unedited
❏ *Grammar*:
  ❏ LEXICON: predominantly like speech
  ❏ heavy use of first- and second-person pronouns
  ❏ SYNTAX: (mixed) writing and speech
  ❏ like writing, email has high type/token ratio, high use of adverbial subordinate clauses, high use of disjunctions
  ❏ like speech, email commonly uses present tense, contractions
❏ *Style*: Predominantly like speech
  ❏ low level of formality
  ❏ expression of emotion not always self-monitored (flaming)

(Baron 2000: 251)

Baron concludes that 'email is largely speech by other means'. Nevertheless, just as with speech and writing, there will always be differences in email style depending on who is emailing whom and on the age, sex and L1 of the emailer. Younger emailers, for example, tend to use fewer apostrophes and contractions and more features of telephone **text messaging**. Five of the above eight messages were from emailers for whom English is not their L1. Although in one case (5), the content of the message clarifies this, I am not convinced that it would otherwise be possible to identify this emailer as an L2 speaker And were you able to identify the four who did not reveal themselves in this way? Perhaps, as Baron argues, 'email is beginning to develop a group of "native users" who are learning email as a primary and distinct avenue for creating many types of messages, rather than transferring to email prior assumptions from face-to-face speech or traditional writing' (p. 258). If this is so, it may be that differences across the native and non-native Englishes are being lost in the process.

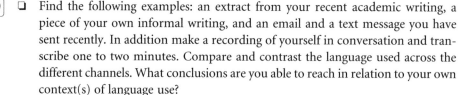

Activity ✪

❏ Find the following examples: an extract from your recent academic writing, a piece of your own informal writing, and an email and a text message you have sent recently. In addition make a recording of yourself in conversation and transcribe one to two minutes. Compare and contrast the language used across the different channels. What conclusions are you able to reach in relation to your own context(s) of language use?

❏ Alternatively, if you are a regular emailer or texter, or have (permitted) access to someone else's emails or text messages, print out or copy down a sample of the emails or text messages received over a period of a week. Analyse them for their language and style. If these are very different (in the case of email) from the messages which were sent to me and are reproduced above, how do you account for the differences? Could they be connected with age, sex, first language, professional status, type of email list subscribed to, or something else?

CORE APPROACHES TO ENGLISH AS AN INTERNATIONAL LANGUAGE (EIL)

According to Anna Szabo, President of the Brazilian English language organisation Braz-TESOL, the debate over whether learners of English should opt for American or British varieties is losing importance. Instead, she thinks, in future 'language learners will look for efficient schools that can teach them clear, understandable and communicative language without demanding either specifically American or British versions' (*EL Gazette* no. 201, October 1996: 8). The problem here, though, is that our knowledge of what constitutes 'clear, understandable and communicative language' for EIL listeners (largely non-native speakers of English from other L1s) is still in its infancy. This unit will explore some perspectives.

A core approach to EIL pronunciation

Core approaches to EIL pronunciation take as their starting point the fact that for various reasons, the world's two prestige accents of English, Received Pronunciation (RP) and General American (GA) no longer provide the best goals for L2 learners. This is particularly true of RP, whose L1 speakers now constitute less than 3 per cent of the British population (Trudgill 2001).

Not only is RP a minority accent, but its origins in the English public school system and a social élite from London and the Home Counties is nowadays felt to be more of an embarrassment than an advantage in many parts of the world including Britain. In some countries (such as Australia) and some contexts (such as youth media) it is even stigmatised. More importantly as far as EIL is concerned, RP is not one of the easiest accents for an L2 learner to acquire either productively, because of its large number of diphthongs, non-rhotic 'r', complex word stress rules, and tenuous relationship with spelling, or receptively because of its extensive use of weak forms. In addition, teachers with regional accents have become less willing to adopt RP or GA (General American) for teaching purposes. Meanwhile, learners are more frequently voicing a desire to preserve something of their L1 accent as a means of expressing their own identity in English rather than identifying with its NSs. The problem until very recently, however, has been the lack of any realistic alternative. But with the advent of the latest core approaches, the situation looks set to change.

Core approaches to EIL pronunciation have taken three main directions:

1   A contrived core: Gimson's rudimentary international pronunciation

The earliest direction taken by core approaches to EIL pronunciation was one of contrivance. Gimson devised an artificial phonological core by simplifying the existing inventory of RP sounds and reducing the number of phonemes from 44 to 29. His 'rudimentary international pronunciation (RIP)' (1978) was designed specifically for the emerging category of EIL speakers of that time: people who needed to be able to speak English as a *lingua franca* in relatively predictable work situations.

2   An empirical core: Jenner's 'International English'

The second approach is to try to identify what all L2 varieties of English *already* have in common and to establish the shared component as an 'International English'. Scholars arguing along these lines, such as Bryan Jenner (1997), believe that there is a single phonological system shared by all speakers of English around the world, regardless of whether their English is a first, second or subsequent language.

Activity

This approach, if ultimately successful, will have the advantage of representing almost all the world's varieties of English without distinguishing their origins. On the other hand, it has a number of disadvantages. Before reading on, note down or discuss any disadvantages you can think of.

Potential disadvantages of an 'International English' (IE) core approach:

1   It will require a very substantial pronunciation corpus to be gathered from all the main varieties of English used internationally around the world. This will take many years and be cumbersome to collect.
2   Assuming that an underlying IE core exists, is the actual process of identifying it going to further the cause of mutual intelligibility? Or would it be fair to argue that the act of collating an IE core will make no difference – because what is *not* shared among varieties of English has more impact on mutual intelligibility than what *is* shared among them? So would it be true to say that an IE core, if it could be collected, may be of great academic interest to phoneticians and phonologists, but will not of itself solve the problem of mutual intelligibility?

3   An empirical and contrived core: Jenkins' 'Lingua Franca Core'

The third main approach is a combination of empirical and artificial approaches. The **Lingua Franca Core** (LFC) is the most fully researched and detailed attempt that has as yet been made to provide EIL speakers with a core intended to guarantee the mutual intelligibility of their accents.

The core features

1   The consonant inventory with the following provisos

❏   some substitutions of /θ/ and /ð/ are acceptable (because they are intelligible in EIL)
❏   rhotic 'r' rather than non-rhotic varieties of 'r';
❏   British English /t/ between vowels in words such as 'latter', 'water' rather than American English flapped [ɾ];
❏   allophonic variation within phonemes permissible as long as the pronunciation does not overlap onto another phoneme, e.g. Spanish pronunciation of /v/ as [β] leads in word-initial positions to its being heard as /b/ (so 'vowels' is heard as 'bowels' etc.).

2   Additional phonetic requirements

❏   aspiration following word-initial voiceless stops /p/ /t/ and /k/, e.g. in [pʰɪn] ('pin') as compared with /spɪn/ ('spin'), otherwise these stops sound like their voiced counterparts /b/ /d/ and /g/;

❏ shortening of vowel sounds before fortis (voiceless) consonants and maintenance of length before lenis (voiced) consonants, e.g. the shorter /æ/ in 'sat' as contrasted with the longer /æ/ in 'sad', or the /i:/ in 'seat' as contrasted with that in 'seed'.

3 Consonant clusters

❏ no omission of sounds in word-initial clusters, e.g. in <u>pr</u>omise, <u>str</u>ing;
❏ omission in middle and final clusters only permissible according to L1 English rules of syllable structure, e.g. fa<u>cts</u>heet' can be pronounced 'facsheet' but not 'fatsheet' or 'facteet';
❏ /nt/ between vowels as in British English 'wi<u>nt</u>er' pronounced /wɪntər/ rather than American English where, by deletion of /t/, it becomes /wɪnər/;
❏ addition is acceptable, e.g. 'product' pronounced [pərɒdʌkʊtɔ] was intelligible to non-native speaker interlocutors, whereas omission was not, e.g. 'product' pronounced /pɒdʌk/.

4 Vowel sounds

❏ maintenance of contrast between long and short vowels e.g. between 'l<u>i</u>ve' and 'l<u>ea</u>ve';
❏ L2 regional qualities acceptable if they are consistent, except substitutions for the sound /ɜ:/ as in 'b<u>ir</u>d', which regularly cause problems.

5 Production and placement of tonic (nuclear) stress

❏ appropriate use of **contrastive stress** to signal meaning. For example, the difference in meaning in the utterances 'I came by TAXi' and 'I CAME by taxi' in which nuclear stress is shown in upper case. The former is a neutral statement of fact, whereas the latter includes an additional meaning such as 'but I'm going home by bus'.

The non-core features:

1 The consonant sounds /θ/, /ð/ and the allophone [ɫ].
2 Vowel quality e.g. the difference between /bʌs/ and /bʊs/ as long as quality is used consistently.
3 Weak forms, i.e. the use of schwa instead of the full vowel sound in words such as 'to', 'fr<u>o</u>m', '<u>of</u>', 'w<u>as</u>', 'd<u>o</u>'; in EIL the full vowel sounds tend to help rather than hinder intelligibility.
4 Other features of connected speech, especially assimilation, e.g. the assimilation of the sound /d/ at the end of one word to the sound at the beginning of the next, so that /red peeɪnt/ 'red paint') becomes /reb peeɪnt/.
5 The direction of pitch movements whether to signal attitude or grammatical meaning.
6 The placement of wordstress which, in any case, varies considerably across different L1 varieties of English, so that there is a need for receptive flexibility.
7 Stress-timed rhythm.

(core and non-core taxonomies taken from Jenkins 2002)

128

 Activity Study the core itself and then the list of features which have been excluded from it, and decide:

1 whether you think the LFC principle is in itself a good one;
2 whether you agree, from your own experience of listening to English, with the fine details;
3 whether you think it is feasible to ask EIL speakers for whom English is either their first or second/subsequent language to learn such a core.

Activity To demonstrate how the LFC works in practice, here is an extract from my data. Each line of alphabetic transcript is followed by a line where any item which was pronounced differently from the way it would be pronounced by a native speaker is written under the corresponding word in phonetic transcript. Study the extract and note which items a teacher would correct and which they would regard as features of the speaker's L2 regional accent according to the LFC.

Korean subject, social interaction task

(T) indicates that the Taiwanese interlocutor spoke briefly at this point.
Yes, the capital of Korea is Seoul and now, right now, I'm living in Seoul. But
                                          ɪzə
actually I was born in the southern part of Korea but, I studied in Seoul and after
æktʊæɾi   pʌt   bɒt   aːptə
finish at the school and finishing my study I got a job at Seoul so-in Seoul, so I now
pɪnɪʃ æ̃tə skʊ   gɒd
live in Seoul (T) Ah my family. Yeah. Actually, right now I'm living with my wife
                                          æktʊæɾi   waɪp
and my son, but . . . the concept of family is very different I think here and in my
                                                                       sɪŋk
country. In my country when I, when we say about family, uh we think that we have
                                                      pæmɪlɪ   sɪŋk
father, I have my father and my mother and my sisters and my brothers, all equally,
paːdə   mɒdə   sɪstəs
and . . . uh I have three sisters and (T)
                    sri

(Jenkins 2000: 65)

A core approach to EIL lexicogrammar

As Gimson's RIP represents an early attempt to produce a core phonology for EIL so, too, there is a precedent for work in lexicogrammar. For example, Quirk's (1982) Nuclear English in many ways parallels Gimson's RIP. Quirk's aims were for his Nuclear English to be:

❏ easier and faster to learn than full English
❏ communicatively adequate
❏ amenable to extension in the course of any further learning

To achieve this, Quirk advocated dispensing with

❑ items which are 'disproportionately burdensome' such as question tags, e.g. 'I'm late, <u>aren't I</u>? 'She used to work here, <u>didn't she</u>'?
❑ items which are 'semantically inexplicit' such as non-defining relative clauses, e.g. 'I chatted with the captain, <u>who</u> was later reprimanded' (= <u>and</u> he was later reprimanded or <u>as a result</u> he was later reprimanded?);
❑ items which are completely ambiguous such as many modal verbs, e.g. 'Able Baker 123 <u>may</u> land at O'Hare in five minutes' (= the flight <u>will possibly</u> land or <u>has permission</u> to land?).

Like Gimson's RIP, Quirk's Nuclear English relies heavily on prescription, makes little allowance for sociolinguistic variation according to the regional backgrounds of its learners, and prioritises the needs of NS listeners rather than being genuinely international. In addition, because they are entirely contrived and intuitive, neither Nuclear English nor the RIP necessarily remove those items that are most problematic for L2 learners.

According to Willis (1999), if we want to ensure the mutual intelligibility of lexicogrammar in EIL, then we have to go for one of six options in teaching the language. Think about the pros and cons of each of these options. How far do you agree with them? Do you think the options are mutually exclusive?

Option 1: Teach standard (British?) English
Option 2: Define a form of 'international English' and teach that
Option 3: Offer a range of Englishes in the classroom
Option 4: Offer successful L2 speakers of English as models
Option 5: Give learners exposure largely to native-speaker English but place a very low premium on conformity
Option 6: Include the study of language and dialects in a language teaching programme

---

The following is a short extract from Seidlhofer's VOICE (Vienna-Oxford International Corpus of English – see Seidlhofer 2001a, 2001b). It is a conversation between R, a German L1 speaker of English and S, a French L1 speaker of English. They are engaged in a collaborative task in which they have to select one of twelve pictures for the front of a calendar to be sold in aid of a third world charity. Read through the dialogue and identify any specifically non-native speaker features of English. Which of these, if any, do you think have the potential to impede successful communication? Of those which do not, which do you think could be features of the **emerging lexicogrammar** of English as a Lingua Franca (ELF), a variety of English developing through interaction among non-native speakers from different first languages?

1	R	I think on the front xx on the front page should be a picture who-which only
2		makes p-people to er spend money, to the charity
3	S	yes
4	R	and I think er yeah maybe
5	S	I think a picture with child
6	R	Yeah, child are always good to
7	S	Yes
8	– R	to trap people spend money
9	S	Yes. I think, erm, let me see, erm . . .
10	R	I don't know . . . but maybe we should er choose a picture who gives the
11		impression that this child needs needs the money or
12	S	So I think, then that's my, this one, no
13	R	Yeah it's quite happy
14	S	Yeah, she's happy er .. Maybe this one
15	R	Yeah.
16	S	He look very sad . . . and he has to carry heavier vase
17	R	Mm, that's right.
18	S	Too heavy for him, or . . .
19	R	Hm hm
20	S	But also this one, even if he's smiling
21	R	Yeah, that's right . . . And maybe this one can show that the that the chari-er
22		charity can really help
23	S	Uh huh
24	R	and that the charity can er make a smile on a on a chil – on on a child's face
25	S	Yes
26	R	Yeah I think this one would be
27	S	A good one
28	R	It would be good
. . .		long pause
–		self-correction
–R		continuation
xx		unintelligible

Activity How would you go about deciding whether certain items used by L2 speakers of English (ELF/EIL) should be classified as simplification errors in need of correction or as pidgin-type simplifications which are evidence of evolving ELF varieties of English?

❏   These are the lexicogrammatical 'sins' which Seidlhofer lists as regularly occur-
ring in her corpus (VOICE) without causing any miscommunication:

❏   using the same verb form for all present tense verbs, as in 'you look very sad'
and 'he look very sad' ('3rd person -s')

❏   not putting a definite or indefinite article in front of nouns, as in 'our countries have signed agreement about this'

❏   treating 'who' and 'which' as interchangeable relative pronouns, as in 'the
picture who' or 'a person which'

❏   using just the verb stem in constructions such as 'I look forward to see you
tomorrow' ('gerund')

❏   using 'isn't it?' as a universal tag question (i.e. instead of, e.g. 'haven't they?'
and 'shouldn't he?') as in 'You're very busy today, isn't it?'

(from Jenkins, Modiano and Seidlhofer 2001: 16)

On the other hand, Seidlhofer identifies as the greatest causes of miscommunication
in EIL both gaps in a speaker's vocabulary, and what she calls 'unilateral idiomaticity',
when one speaker uses utterances that are idiomatic in native-speaker English and therefore difficult for many non-native speakers to understand, e.g. 'Would you like us
to give you a hand?' instead of 'Can we help you?' (Jenkins, Modiano and Seidlhofer
2001: 16).

❏   Willis (1996, 2003) considers that it is more important for EIL speakers to convey
their meaning accurately than to conform accurately to the lexicogrammatical
patterns of native speakers. Do you agree?

❏   Crystal (1995: 299) lists the following invariant question tags used by different
groups of English speakers around the world:

> is it? (Zambia, South Africa, Singapore, Malaysia)
> isn't it? (South Asia, Wales, Papua New Guinea, West Africa)
> not so? (West Africa, South Asia, Papua New Guinea)
> no? (SW USA, Pueblo)

We could add 'innit', used increasingly in informal spoken English by young British
speakers. Many other languages make use of invariant question tags. For example,
French 'n'est-ce pas?' and 'non?', German 'oder?', Spanish '¿no?' Quirk. Willis and
Seidlhofer have all identified English variant question tags as candidates for regularisation in ELF. What do you think is/are the most likely to be used, and why?

❏   Invite responses and a discussion to this quotation:

> There really is no justification for doggedly persisting in referring to an item
> as 'an error' if the vast majority of the world's L2 English speakers produce and
> understand it. Instead, it is for L1 speakers to move their own receptive goal posts
> and adjust their own expectations as far as *international* (but not *intranational*)
> uses of English are concerned.

(Jenkins 2000: 160)

ASIAN ENGLISHES IN THE OUTER CIRCLE

In this unit we explore in greater detail recent developments in English use in two Asian settings, India and Hong Kong. In particular we will consider roles of and attitudes towards the local variety. These two settings have been selected because while they have a certain amount in common, there are important differences both in the ways in which English functions in these multilingual contexts and in the attitudes of its users towards their own English.

Indian English*

India has approximately 37 million proficient speakers of English, the highest number of (non-creole) English speakers in the world after the US and UK and, in addition, there are around a further 200 million Indians with some degree of knowledge of English. The earliest English language policy for India was enshrined in **Macaulay's** famous **Minute** of 1835, passed shortly after he arrived in Calcutta to take his seat on the Supreme Council of India:

> We must at present do our best to form a class who may be interpreters between us and the millions whom we govern; a class of persons, Indian in blood and colour, but English in taste, in opinions, in morals, and in intellect. To that class we may leave it to refine the vernacular dialects of the country, to enrich those dialects with terms of science borrowed from Western nomenclature, and to render them by degrees fit vehicles for conveying knowledge to the great mass of the population.
>
> (quoted in Bailey 1991: 138)

This became the British government's official language policy in India, giving the English language priority in Indian administration, education and society. English-medium universities and schools and an English press were established in India, and contributed to the gradual encroachment of English on Indian languages and a role as the official language and primary *lingua franca* of the country.

In the post-independence era from 1947, in an attempt to acknowledge the strength of nationalist feeling especially in the pro-Hindi camp, the 1950 constitution of India declared Hindi the official national language, but allowed English to continue to be used for official purposes for a further fifteen years, after which it was gradually to be replaced by Hindi. This policy proved unsuccessful, in part because of anti-Hindi feeling in southern India, and in 1967 the Official Languages (Amendment) Act provided that English would be the 'associate' official language and could continue to be used alongside Hindi in all official matters at the national level. In addition, the constitution recognised eighteen regional languages as having the right to function as the official languages of individual states.

In practice, however, there is something of a contradiction between government policy and language use, as English continues to be used as the primary *de facto* official national language and is also the official language of many of the states in the south and north-east. In fact, in the post-independence period there has been a steady growth in the use of English in the country with English nowadays being used primarily for communication among Indians rather than with native speakers of English. This is not primarily on account of anti-Hindi feeling in these parts of the country, although its role as a *neutral* language of wider communication certainly plays a part. More important is its perceived usefulness both within India and internationally; the fact that English has not killed off India's indigenous languages but functions in a complementary relationship with them; and the steady growth of an Indian English identity which finds expression in a linguistic variety with its own grammatical, lexical, phonological and discoursal norms.

In adapting to local cultural norms, Indian English has developed its own varietal characteristics through the interaction of Indian languages and social behaviours with those of English. These characteristics differ in quite major ways from British English and would still be considered 'deviant' by those who take an interlanguage/ fossilisation view of the indigenised varieties of English (see B7). The Indianisation of English essentially involves on the one hand adaptations of existing features of British and on the other, the use of transferred mother-tongue items where British English lacks the scope to express a particular concept – or, to put it another way, where British English is 'deficient'. At the discoursal level, Indian English also makes considerable use of code switching and code mixing.

Here are some examples of Indian English (all taken from Parasher 2001). What are the lexical, grammatical, discoursal and any other features which identify these as specifically Indian English usage?

1 Newspaper advertisement

> Brahmin girl, divorcee kashyapa, 35, B.Com.H, 5'3',
> very fair, respectable family, issueless, Govt. employee
> UDC Hyderbad Rs.5,000/-p.m., required
> well settled broad-minded life partner from same caste.
> Write Box No. –
>
> (*Deccan Chronicle*, 5 October, 1997)

2 Politeness formulae

> a   . . . it will not be out of place to request you to send us the details of
>   chemicals etc . . .
> b   Kindly please advise me.
> c   I invite your kind attention.
> d   I respectfully submit the following few lines for favour of your kind
>   consideration.

3 Honorifics

> Helloji
> Thank youji
> Doctorji
> Doctor Sahib

4 Code switching and code mixing

> A   Good morning.
> B   Good morning
> A   Kya haal hen. (How are you?)
>   Kayi din se aap dikhai nahin diye.
>   (I haven't seen you for a long time.)
> B   Men Dilli gaya hua tha, ek selection committee ki meeting thi.
>   (I was away in Delhi. There was a Selection Committee meeting.)

Finally, growing acceptance of English as an Indian language is not universal and is still the subject of considerable debate. Below is a letter to the editor of the *Maharashtra Herald*, an English daily newspaper published in Pune which responds to an interview published a few days earlier. It is followed by a second letter sent to the editor four days later in reply to the first. Read the two letters and decide first which writer you support and why, and second, how you would have answered the writer of the first letter, bearing in mind what you have read in this unit:

> *Mother tongue supreme*
> This refers to writer Ruchira Mukherjee's assertion that, 'People are beginning to think in English' (MH, October 5).
>
>> Well, the question is: Can an Indian really think in English? As far as thinking is concerned, one can only think in one's mother tongue.
>>   Since English is an alien tongue to every Indian, no Indian can claim to think in English. Because it is linguistically next to impossible to be equally at ease with a target language, which English is, for every Indian.
>>   I've been speaking Persian right from my childhood. In fact Persian was the first language I picked up. My Persian is as good as that of a native speaker of Iran and Central Asia and it's replete with typical native idiosyncracies and idioms of written and colloquial Persian.

Yet Persian is not the language of my consciousness, though I do my written work mostly in this language.

My mother tongue, which is Bengali, always comes to me naturally and it predominates my thinking process. Likewise, however good one may be at English, he can't have that native sensibility.

You can never iron out the ingrained impressions of your respective mother tongue which at times prevail over English or for that matter, any language learnt at a relatively later stage. English will always play second fiddle to an Indian's linguistic mental make up.

(*MH*, 13 October 1998, quoted in D'souza 2001: 148)

What's mother tongue?

Sumit Paul's letter 'Mother Tongue Supreme' of October 13 is not correct. He wonders if an Indian can 'really think in English'.

First of all, I would like to define mother tongue. The mother tongue of an Indian can be French or English or anything. One's mother tongue is that which one learns from infancy. (For example, a language learnt from one's parents.)

Secondly, if one's parents are, let us say, Bengali, but never spoke to the child in Bengali but only in English, then the mother tongue of the child would be English and not Bengali. A language cannot be inherited, it is taught and learnt.

How can Sumit Paul claim that English is 'an alien tongue to every Indian'? Sumit is not a spokesman for Indians. I personally know many Indians whose parents' language is Hindi or Malayalam or so on, but whose own mother tongue is English, or rather family language is English.

They excel in English about above else. Many times, even when neither the mother tongue nor family language is English, the person excels in English above all else. Many service officers' families are good examples.

Paul assumes that every Indian first learns his parents' language and then English. And that an Indian has to be better at the parents' language than English. He further assumed that everybody learns first the language of his parents' race, and that it is the same as the language spoken by the parents, and that it is called the mother tongue!

(*MH*, 17 October 1998, quoted in D'souza 2001: 149)

Activity ✪

❏ In your view, is Indian English a new language? If so, would you describe it as a single language, a mixed or hybrid language, a new variety, or something else?
❏ What are the implications of linguistic varieties such as Indian English for the study of languages in isolation and for the study of bi- and multilingualism? Has the time come when Englishes can be studied primarily as they are used in bilingual and multilingual societies or is it still helpful to study them in monolingual use?

Hong Kong English

Hong Kong has a population of over six million, of which almost two million speak English (Crystal 1997), though this assumes there has been no major change in the figures since Hong Kong ceased to be a British crown colony and became a Special Administrative Region in 1997. It was a British colony from 1842 up until this point, and for the first hundred years of colonial rule, the British and Chinese communities led separate lives as a result of language barriers, racial prejudice and cultural differences. On those occasions when they did make contact, it was mainly for business purposes, and communication was for the most part conducted in pidgin English (Evans 2000: 198).

During the years of British sovereignty up to the First World War, English was largely restricted in Hong Kong to colonial use and, in particular, to the domains of government, the law, the professions and education. Then, during the period between the two world wars, a Western-educated Chinese élite started to become involved in business and the professions, and by the 1960s, English had metamorphosed from a colonial language used only by a small Chinese élite to an important language of wider communication in the region. This was primarily the result of 'the transformation of Hong Kong from a colonial backwater into a leading centre of business and finance' (Evans 2000: 198). And because English had, during the same period, emerged as the international *lingua franca*, a much larger number of ethnic Chinese needed to be proficient in the language.

Despite the growth in English use amongst the Hong Kongese (and we should not forget that it is spoken by almost a third of the population, compared to the 4 per cent of non-native speakers in India who have a proficient knowledge of the English language), it appears that Hong Kong English does not have widespread acceptance as a variety of English. Its existence is acknowledged but it is apparently not the variety to which Hong Kong English speakers aspire. Instead, despite the reservations of linguists, the majority, and particularly English teachers, remain firmly attached to British English norms of correctness.

Nevertheless, as Bolton (2000: 267) asks, is it not the case that 'conditions now exist for a recognition of the autonomy of Hong Kong English, on a par with other Englishes in the Asian region?' He goes on to provide evidence of both a Hong Kong accent (as does Hung 2000) and a Hong Kong English lexis. As regards vocabulary, a number of Hong Kong English items are included in the Macquarie dictionary (see B7 for a description of the dictionary).

Activity ✪

The following are examples of entries cited by Bolton (2000: 280). If you are not familiar with Hong Kong English, can you guess their meanings (the key is at the end of this section)?

 1 ABC
 2 Ah
 3 astronaut
 4 BBC
 5 big brother
 6 black hand
 7 black society
 8 bo lei
 9 Buddha's delight
10 Canto-speak
11 Canto star
12 char siew
13 China doll
14 Chinglish
15 chit

As yet, however, there are few reference works such as dictionaries and pedagogic grammars which acknowledge the existence of a local Hong Kong variety of English. And, as Bolton points out, even in those regions where such reference works already exist, for example Singapore and the Philippines, they have not received a wholly favourable reception. In Hong Kong itself, moreover, the attitudes among teachers of English suggest that it will be some time before the local variety is used as a pedagogic model. In a study into attitudes, Hong Kong teachers were asked where they looked for models of correctness and acceptability (Tsui and Bunton 2000). The vast majority who responded (of which two-thirds were native speakers of English) cited native-speaking countries, particularly Britain, and tended to be cautious or even critical of local Hong Kong sources. The term 'Hong Kong English' did not occur in any of the (1,234) responses, and there were no favourable references to deviations from native-speaker norms. Clearly there is a considerable way to go before Hong Kong English is regarded as a legitimate variety.

Key

 1 an Australian-born Chinese/American-born Chinese
 2 an informal term of address: *Ah Sam/Ah Chan*
 3 a public servant in the most senior career grade in the Hong Kong Civil service
 4 a British-born Chinese
 5 a Chinese kinship term referring to the eldest male sibling in a family, or a recruiter or protector in a Chinese secret society or triad
 6 a behind-the-scenes mastermind who plans political or criminal activities
 7 a Chinese secret society or triad
 8 a variety of strong black tea
 9 a vegetarian dish of bean curd, nuts, tiger lilies and a hair-like seaweed which is particularly popular at Chinese New Year, as the Cantonese name of the seaweed (*fat choi* or 'hair vegetable') sounds very similar to the New Year greeting wishing prosperity

10 the Cantonese language
11 a singer of Cantonese pop songs
12 Chinese-style roast pork
13 a pretty young Chinese woman of submissive demeanour
14 any variety of English strongly influenced by Chinese, or any variety of Chinese featuring a high proportion of English loanwords
15 bill

C8

LANGUAGE KILLER OR LANGUAGE PROMOTER?

In this final unit of Section C, we will consider two very different perspectives on the effects of the global spread of English: first, its potential to cause the deaths of other languages; and second, its role within a framework of bilingualism.

English as a killer language

David Crystal begins his book *Language Death* (2000) by asking some key questions. Try to answer them before looking at Crystal's answers below:

1   How many languages are there in the world today?
2   At what rate are they dying off?
3   How many of the world's languages are spoken by fewer than 1,000 people?
4   How many indigenous languages are there in North America?

Recent estimates of the number of languages in the world vary between 3,000 and 10,000, but by most definitions of a 'language' the figure lies between 6,000 and 7,000.

Over the next century, something like two languages will die each month. A quarter of the world's languages are spoken by fewer than 1,000 people. Though estimates vary, there may still be close to 200 indigenous languages in use in North America.

Trudgill points this out in his review of another book on the subject, Grenoble and Whaley's *Endangered Languages* (1998),

> One of the greatest cultural tragedies ever to befall the human race is taking place before our eyes but no one is paying attention. There are members of the British intelligentsia who profess to be concerned about language and who agonise over utter trivialities such as the failure of the nation to use *hopefully* or to place *only* "correctly". Here is what they should be worrying about: of the world's 6,000 or so languages, as many as 3,000 are in the process of dying out, and another 2,400 are endangered.
>
> (*The Times Higher*, May 8 1998: 26; emphasis in original)

The first stage in the process of reversing **language death** is to identify the cause. Although no one factor is likely to prove singly responsible for the dramatic loss of languages which we are currently witnessing, one cause is frequently named by endangered language experts as bearing the greatest share of responsibility: the English language. The English language, of course, does not exist in a vacuum, but must be considered within the framework of globalisation as a whole. That is, English operates in a global context in which the most politically and economically powerful English speakers – those in the Inner Circle countries – have to now benefited massively and dispropor- tionately from the spread of the language.

❏ To what extent has exploitation by the countries of the 'centre' been responsible for causing speakers of other languages, especially the smaller languages, to replace their mother tongues with English for some or even all important lan- guage functions?

❏ How far has the endemic monolingualism of the Inner Circle countries played a part in the process?

✪ **Activity**

Here are some quotations taken from various writings on endangered languages. Read them and decide – with the help of first-hand knowledge if you speak or are familiar with an endangered language yourself – how far you agree or disagree with them. You might also like to refer back to the discussion of the 'English Only' campaign in the USA in C1.

✪ **Activity**

> Europeans who came from polities with a history of standardizing and promoting just one high-prestige speech form carried their "ideology of contempt" for subordinate languages with them when they conquered far-flung territories, to the serious detri- ment of indigenous languages. And in addition [. . .] Europeans [. . .] seriously con- founded technological and linguistic development [. . .]. Unable to conceive that a people who lacked a rich material culture might possess a highly developed, richly complex language, they wrongly assumed that primitive technological means implied primitive linguistic means [. . .]
>
> Two other European beliefs about language are also likely to have had an un- favorable impact on the survival of indigenous languages in the very considerable portions of the globe where a standardized European language became the language of the dominant social strata [. . .] Particularly widespread and well established is a belief in a linguistic survival of the fittest, a social Darwinism of language. This belief encourages people of European background to assume a correlation between adaptive and expressive capacity in a language and that language's survival and spread. Since their own languages are prominent among those which have both survived and spread, this is of course a self-serving belief.
> [. . .]
> The second of the additional beliefs disadvantageous to indigenous languages in regions dominated by speakers of European languages may actually be more charac- teristic of Anglophones than of speakers of other European languages. Anglophones however are particularly thickly distributed in regions that once had large numbers of indigenous languages, so English single-handedly threatens a disproportionate num- ber of other languages. The belief in question is that bilingualism (and by extension

multilingualism, all the more so) is onerous, even on the individual level. This belief is so widespread, in fact, that it can be detected even among linguists.

(Dorian 1998: 9–11)

Most Western countries participate in murdering the chances that they might have to increase the linguistic diversity in their countries, because they do not give immigrants and refugees much chance of maintaining and developing their languages. Development co-operation also participates, with very few exceptions, in murdering small languages and supporting subtractive spread of the big killer languages, especially English. 'Subtractive spread' means that new languages are not learned in addition to the language(s) people already have, but instead of them, at the cost of the mother tongue(s). The whole homogenisation process that globalisation is made to 'demand' has to be problematised and nuanced before it is too late.

(Skuttnab-Kangas 1999: 6–7)

Those who control particular linguistic resources are in a position of power over others. Linguistic capital, like all other forms of capital, is unequally distributed in society. The higher the profit to be achieved through knowledge of a particular language, the more it will be viewed as worthy of acquisition. The language of the global village (or McWorld, as some have called it) is English: not to use it is to risk ostracization from the benefits of the global economy.

(Nettle and Romaine 2000: 30–1)

Educational policy is another striking example of misguided strategies imported from the West into developing countries. Believing that tribal languages stood in the way of unity and were not suitable as languages of education and technology essential for western-style development, most newly independent countries did not develop their own languages, but continued using the languages of their former colonizers even when most of their citizens did not know them. Western policies and practices have generally reinforced European languages [. . .] Development agents sent into the field rarely bother to learn the local languages, which leads to communication problems. The World Bank and International Monetary Fund seldom make reference to the possible role indigenous languages might play in development. The use of western school curricula in developing countries tends to devalue traditional culture and excludes formal study of traditional knowledge systems. Younger members of the culture are educated to believe that traditional knowledge is not worth learning because it will not lead to a job.

(Nettle and Romaine 2000: 160–4)

'Globalisation is the wave of the future', more than one recent newspaper headline (not to mention the received popular wisdom) has announced, and, to some extent, this is so. But globalisation is both a constructive and a destructive phenomenon, both a unifying and a divisive one, and it is definitely not a culturally neutral or impartial one. In our day and age, it is definitely the globalisation of pan-Western culture (and pop-consumer culture in particular) that is the motor of language shift. And since America-dominated globalisation has become the major economic, technological and cultural thrust of worldwide modernisation and Westernisation, efforts to safeguard threatened languages (and, therefore, inevitably, contextually weaker languages) must oppose the very strongest processes and powers that the world knows today. That, in a word, is exactly why it is so hard to save threatened languages.

(Fishman 2001: 6)

English-knowing bilingualism

Bilingualism and multilingualism, though threatened to some extent by language death, and though regarded as aberrations by English mother-tongue speakers in the UK and US, are the *de facto* norm throughout the rest of the world. Speakers of 'big' languages, particularly English, meanwhile, have long been reluctant to acquire other languages, have expected others to make the effort to learn 'their' language, and have viewed code switching as a sign of linguistic incompetence. However, bilingualism will by definition play a critical role in the prevention of language death so long as efforts are made to persuade learners of English that they should become practitioners of **English-knowing bilingualism** (see Pakir 1991, Kachru 1982/1992): that is, that they are made aware of the value of maintaining within their linguistic repertoires their indigenous language(s) for local identity functions alongside their English.

If English-knowing bilingualism is to become the recognised rather than begrudgingly tolerated world norm, however, it will be crucial for the (largely monolingual) mother-tongue English speech communities to embrace the concept – and not merely as an acceptable practice for non-English mother-tongue 'others', but as one in which they themselves engage. Such an engagement will enable 'citizens of the UK, the USA, Canada, Australia, New Zealand, and other largely English-speaking countries . . . to avoid being the monolingual dinosaurs in a multilingual world' (Brumfit 2002: 11). Moreover, with bilingualism will come flexibility and accommodation skills of the sort these citizens have always expected of English-speaking 'others' whenever English is spoken in cross-cultural contexts.

As was clear in the quotation from Hilary Footitt in A6, people need to speak second languages in order to develop intercultural competence. This is not to say that people need necessarily to *acquire* these cultural practices along with the languages: it will depend on whether they will be speaking a particular language with its native speakers. In the case of learners of English for local (Outer Circle) or international (Expanding Circle) use this is generally not so, and there is rarely an imperative for them to learn British, American or Australian culture along with the English language. Indeed, it would be counterproductive for them to make a one-to-one cultural link between the English language and the cultural practices of any one of its minority groups of mother-tongue speakers, when their goal is to use English in predominantly non-English mother-tongue contexts. But awareness of the existence of difference is another matter and this is an area in which English mother-tongue speakers have much catching up to do.

English monolingualism is not only a problem for cross-cultural communication at the international level, however. Within the Inner Circle countries there are, through immigration, increasingly large numbers of non-L1 English speakers. In Britain, around one person in fourteen is now from an ethnic minority group and this trend is predicted to continue. In the US, the numbers are far greater, as a result of both more extensive immigration and the existence of the indigenous population. But in both communities, the learning of another language – any language – would help to reduce that fear of the 'other' which is bred out of ignorance of difference, and which often leads to racist attitudes and behaviours, and to campaigns such as 'English Only'. Better still would be the learning of one of the community languages of the immigrant population, or one of the heritage languages of the indigenous peoples, a practice which has begun recently in New Zealand, where the Maori language is being taught in some **Pakeha** (New Zealander of European origin) schools. Despite the latter example, though, the expectation is overwhelmingly that immigrant and indigenous minorities (which in some cases are very large minorities) should learn the lingua-cultural practices of the L1 English population.

The monolingual emphasis among English L1 speakers can cause problems in international contexts, when English is used as a medium for communication which does not relate to intranational (either Inner or Outer Circle) functions. The problem is hierarchical. That is, educated (but monolingual!) L1 English speakers, unaware of the superiority of the bilingual's linguistic repertoire and skills, assume the right to the senior position in the English language hierarchy. English for international use thus has at its pinnacle and serving as global models the varieties of English used by a small minority of (L1) English speakers. Yet many of these are among the least linguistically able EIL speakers in the world, the least able to exercise **accommodation** skills (adjusting their language to facilitate communication), and the most biased against other varieties of the English language whether non-standard L1 or standard/non-standard L2.

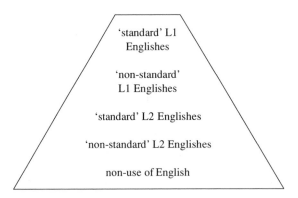

Figure C8.1 Traditional hierarchy of Englishes

On the other hand, if we reconceptualise the hierarchy by taking into account the advantages of English-knowing bilingualism and of what is involved in being an English-using bilingual, we come up with a very different hierarchy. This time, we prioritise the varieties of English spoken by its bilingual speakers, be they L2 or (though less likely) L1 speakers. In addition, we put intranational (local) varieties at the equivalent level in the hierarchy, be they ENL or ESL varieties, rather than adopting the traditional practice of placing Inner Circle standard Englishes above Outer Circle ones.

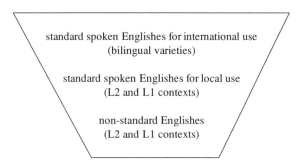

standard spoken Englishes for international use
(bilingual varieties)

standard spoken Englishes for local use
(L2 and L1 contexts)

non-standard Englishes
(L2 and L1 contexts)

Figure C8.2   Reconceptualised hierarchy of Englishes

One final point to make about English-using bilinguals is that the code switching of those who speak international (EIL/ELF) rather than intranational (ESL) varieties of English does not, as is sometimes claimed, serve purely communicative functions. Rather, it is also frequently used as a means of promoting identity and self expression. Matsuda (2000: 52–3), for example, reports the following comments from participants in her study of Japanese-English bilinguals:

❏ I use Japanese when I request something. Japanese is softer . . . don't you think so? And when I apologize . . . well, I might use English if I don't really feel like apologizing. A Japanese apology sounds more sincere (Keiko).
❏ I think my personality differs in English and Japanese. I'm more *wild* when I speak English . . . I mean, more outgoing and not so *conservative*. Yeah, I'm more *conservative* in Japanese. I feel '*this is me*' when I can say something in English (Chikako).
❏ My personality changes from Japanese mode to English mode. I'm more sarcastic and joking all the time and outgoing and, well, that's when I'm speaking English. In Japanese, I'm quieter (Eriko).

Again, it is the monolingual mindset which is unable to grasp the fact that a language does not have to be a mother tongue in order to be capable of expressing aspects of a speaker's social identity. And if English remains the world's primary international language, the expressive function is likely to become increasingly central to its international use.

❏ In the year 2000, a Conservative member of the UK parliament, the shadow **Activity** health secretary Liam Fox, launched a verbal attack on overseas doctors in the UK, arguing that 'Their English language skills are not up to scratch and patients are suffering as a result' (*Guardian* 28 August 2000, p. 2). He announced that a Conservative government, if elected, would introduce 'a tough English language test that might apply to overseas doctors already working in Britain'. The ensuing debate was heated, with some arguing that overseas doctors from outside the EU already had to pass stringent English language tests, and that the charge amounted to racism. On the other hand, others claimed, for example, that overseas doctors 'cannot communicate with patients because they cannot understand the everyday language' (Letter to the editor, *Guardian*, 4 September 2000), or called into question the overseas doctors' English accents. To what extent do you believe that racism was involved? And do you think that if the British nation was not so predominantly monolingual, the same charges would have been made?

❑ Look back to the two hierarchies of English as an International Language. Do you agree with the manner in which the traditional hierarchy has been recast? What advantages and disadvantages do you see in each case, and what implications does the second hierarchy have for the future development of English?

SECTION D

EXTENSION
READINGS IN WORLD ENGLISHES

HOW TO USE THE READINGS

The readings in this final section of the book have been selected in order to provide a range of perspectives on the themes of the individual units. You will not necessarily agree with their conclusions, but the purpose of the readings is to engage you critically and encourage you to read still further, so that you are able to develop your own informed views on the subject in hand. After each reading there are suggestions of issues to consider and prompts for discussion.

The numbering of the readings corresponds to the numbering of the sections in the previous three parts of the book. Thus, the reading which follows this introduction in D1 relates to the material in A1, B1 and C1, the reading in D2 to the material in A2, B2 and C2, and so on.

D1

THE DISCOURSES OF POSTCOLONIALISM

In his earlier book, *The Cultural Politics of English as an International Language* (1994), Alastair Pennycook charted the colonial background underlying the contemporary place of English as the world's primary international language. His 1998 book, *English and the Discourses of Colonialism*, starts with the British departure from Hong Kong in 1997 which, in theory, signalled the ending of mainstream British colonialism. Pennycook demonstrates in this book, however, the extent to which he believes colonialism still permeates both British discourses and those of the postcolonial territories. In the following extract, he looks critically at some of the arguments that are often put forward to justify why the English language 'deserves' its place as the global *lingua franca*.

Our marvellous tongue

Alastair Pennycook (reprinted from *English and the Discourses of Colonialism*, London: Routledge, 1998: 133–44)

The wondrous spread of English
The nineteenth century was a time of immense British confidence in their own greatness, and writing on English abounded with glorifications of English and its global spread. [. . .] Although the fervent triumphalism that appears so evident in [. . .] earlier descriptions of the spread of Empire and English is a less acceptable aspect of more recent discourses on the spread of English, I would like to suggest that the same celebratory tone seems to underlie recent, supposedly neutral descriptions of English. Thus, it is interesting to compare Rolleston's (1911) description of the spread of English with Crystal's (1987) from the *Cambridge Encyclopedia of Language*:

> The British flag waves over more than one-fifth of the habitable globe, one-fourth
> of the human race acknowledges the sway of the British Monarch, more than one
> hundred princes render him allegiance. The English language is spoken by more

people than that of any other race, it bids fair to become at some time the speech of the globe, and about one-half of the world's ocean shipping trade is yet in British hands. (1911, p. 75)

English is used as an official or semi-official language in over 60 countries, and has a prominent place in a further 20. It is either dominant or well established in all six continents. It is the main language of books, newspapers, airports and air-traffic control, international business and academic conferences, science, technology, medicine, diplomacy, sports, international competitions, pop music, and advertising. Over two-thirds of the world's scientists write in English. Of all the information in the world's electronic retrieval systems, 80% is stored in English. English radio programmes are received by over 150 million in 120 countries. (Crystal 1987: 358)

The similarities become more obvious when we turn to other books and articles on English. Bryson's (1990) book *Mother Tongue: The English Language* starts: 'More than 300 million people in the world speak English and the rest, it sometimes seem, try to' (p. 1). [. . .] Claiborne (1983) opens his book *The life and times of the English language: The history of our marvellous tongue* with:

By any standard, English is a remarkable language. It is, to begin with, the native tongue of some 300,000,000 people – the largest speech community in the world except for Mandarin Chinese. Even more remarkable is its geographical spread, in which it is second to none; its speakers range from Point Barrow, Alaska, to the Falkland Islands; from Hong Kong to Tasmania . . . English is also by far the most important 'second language' in the world. It is spoken by tens of millions of educated Europeans and Japanese, is the most widely studied foreign tongue in both the USSR and China, and serves as an 'official' language in more than a dozen other countries whose populations total more than a thousand million . . . English is the lingua franca of scientists, of air pilots and traffic controllers around the world, of students hitchhiking around Europe, and of dropouts meditating in India and Nepal. (Claiborne 1983: 1–2)

and so on and so on.
[. . .]
According to Simon Jenkins (1995), attempts to introduce artificial languages have failed because 'English has triumphed. Those who do not speak it are at a universal disadvantage against those who do. Those who deny this supremacy merely seek to keep the disadvantaged deprived.' As we shall see later, this notion of 'linguistic deprivation' for those who do not speak English and even for those who do not speak it as a native language starts to have very particular significance within this discourse.

At times, too, the descriptions of this global spread start to use terms even more reminiscent of the prose of George (1867) or de Quincey (1862) and their talk of 'destiny' and the inevitable spread of English being like a mighty river flowing towards the sea. An editorial in *The Sunday Times* (UK) (10 July 1994), responding to the attempts in France to limit the use of English in various public domains, thunders against the French for opposing the 'European lingua franca which will inevitably be English'. To oppose English is pointless, the editorial warns, since 'English fulfills its own destiny as Churchill's "ever-conquering language". With every shift in international politics, every turn of the world's economies, every media development and every technological revolution, English marches on'. The editorial then returns to slightly more sober language:

> No other country in Europe works itself into such a frenzy about the way English eases the paths of multi-national discussion and assumes an ever-growing role as the language of power and convenience. The Germans, Spanish and Italians have accepted the inevitable. So, further afield, have the Russians, Chinese and Japanese. If you want to get ahead, you have to speak English. Two billion people around the world are believed to have made it their second language. Add that to 350m native English speakers in the United States, Britain and the Commonwealth, and you have an unstoppable force.

After these remarkable claims for the global spread of English and its inevitable path towards ascendancy, the editorial goes on to reassert that France must acknowledge 'the dominance of Anglo-American English as the universal language in a shrinking world', and that 'no amount of protectionist legislation and subsidies can shut out the free market in the expression of ideas'. 'Britain,' it asserts, 'must press ahead with the propagation of English and the British values which stand behind it' with the British Council ('Once a target for those unable to see no further than the end of their nose, it now runs a successful global network with teaching as its core activity in 108 countries'), the BBC (which 'is told to exploit its reputation and products abroad as never before') helping with 'the onward march of the English language'. As we shall see, this juxtaposition of the spread of English with the protectionism of the *Academie Française* is a frequently repeated trope of these discourses.

An article in *U.S. News & World Report* (18 February 1985) called 'English: Out to conquer the world' starts with the usual cataloguing of the spread of English:

> When an Argentine pilot lands his airliner in Turkey, he and the ground controller talk in English. When German physicists want to alert the international scientific community to a new discovery, they publish their findings in English-language journals. When Japanese executives cut deals with Scandinavian entrepreneurs in Bangkok, they communicate in English. (p. 49)

and so on and so on. The article also derides those who would oppose the 'inevitable' spread of English, for 'English marches on. "If you need it, you learn it", says one expert'. Despite various attempts to counter the spread of English, 'the world's latest lingua franca will keep spreading. "It's like the primordial ooze," contends James Alatis, . . . "its growth is ineluctable, inexorable and inevitable"' (p. 522). [. . .]

Clearly, there is quite a remarkable continuity in the writing on the global spread of English. Bailey (1991: 121) comments that 'the linguistic ideas that evolved at the acme of empires led by Britain and the United States have not changed as

economic colonialism has replaced the direct, political management of third-world nations. English is still believed to be the inevitable world language'.
[. . .]

In praise of English

If there are many similarities in the ways the spread of English has been both exhorted and applauded over the last hundred years, there are also interesting similarities in the way the language itself has been praised as a great language. Nineteenth-century writing on English abounded with glorifications of the language, suggesting that on the one hand the undeniable excellence of British institutions, ideas and culture must be reflected in the language and, on the other, that the undeniable superior qualities of English must reflect a people and a culture of superior quality. Thus, the Reverend James George, for example, arguing that Britain had been 'commissioned to teach a noble language embodying the richest scientific and literary treasures,' asserted that 'As the mind grows, language grows, and adapts itself to the thinking of the people. Hence, a highly civilized race, will ever have, a highly accomplished language. The English tongue, is in all senses a very noble one. I apply the term noble with a rigorous exactness'. (George 1867: 4)
[. . .]

A key argument in the demonstration of the superior qualities of English was in the breadth of its vocabulary, an argument which, as we shall see, is still used widely today.

The article 'English out to conquer the world' asks how English differs from other languages: 'First, it is bigger. Its vocabulary numbers at least 750,000 words. Second-ranked French is only two thirds that size . . . . English has been growing fast for 1,000 years, promiscuously borrowing words from other lands' (1985, p. 53). According to Bryson (1990), the numbers of words listed in *Webster's Third New International Dictionary* (450,000) and the *Oxford English Dictionary* (615,000) are only part of the total number of English words since 'technical and scientific terms would add millions more'. Looking at which terms are actually commonly made use of, Bryson suggests that about '200,000 English words are in common use, more than in German (184,000) and far more than in French (a mere 100,000)' (p. 3). Claiborne (1983) asserts that 'for centuries, the English-speaking peoples have plundered the world for words, even as their military and industrial empire builders have plundered it for more tangible goods'. This plundering has given English

> the largest, most variegated and most expressive vocabulary in the world. The total number of English words lies somewhere between 400,000 – the number of current entries in the largest English dictionaries – and 600,000 – the largest figure that any expert is willing to be quoted on. By comparison, the biggest French dictionaries have only about 150,000 entries, the biggest Russian ones a mere 130,000. (Claiborne 1983: 3)

Simon Jenkins (1995) explains that:

> English has not won the battle to be the world's language through a trial of imperial strength. As the American linguist Braj Kachru points out, English has achieved

its hegemony through its inherent qualities, by 'its propensity for acquiring new identities . . . its range of varieties and above all its suitability as a flexible medium for literary and other types of creativity'.

The subtitle to Jenkins' article ('The triumph of English') is 'Our infinitely adaptable mother tongue is now the world's lingua franca – and not before time.'

Apart from clearly supporting a simple argument about the superiority of English, this view of the richness of English puts into play several other images of English that are extremely important: the notion of English as some pure Anglo-Saxon language, the idea that English and English speakers have always been open, flexible and integrationist, and the belief that because of their vast vocabulary, speakers of English are the ablest thinkers. The first of these emerges in 'English out to conquer the world' when the article suggests that 'All-told, 80 per cent of the world stock is foreign-born (p. 53). The implications of this statement seem to be that 'English' refers to a language of Anglo-Saxon purity, a language that despite all its borrowings and enrichments is, at heart, an Anglo-Saxon affair. This effort to construct some clear Anglo-Saxon lineage for English has a long history. [. . .] Writing in 1901, Earle argued that:

> We do not want to discard the rich furniture of words which we have inherited from our French and classic eras; but we wish to wear them as trophies, as the historic blazon of a great career, for the demarcation and amplification of an imperial language whose thews and sinews and vital energies are essentially English. (cited in Crowley 1989: 74)

According to Burnett (1962: 75), 'the long process of creating the historic seedbed of the English language actually began with the arrival of the first Indo-European elements from the continent'. Claiborne (1983: 5) goes further and claims that 'the story of the life and times of English' can be traced from 'eight thousand years ago to the present'. Although both these claims – that 80 per cent of English could be foreign and that the language can be traced back over 8,000 years – seem perhaps most remarkable for the bizarreness of their views, they also need to be taken very seriously in terms of the cultural constructions they produce, namely a view of English as some ethnically pure Anglo-Saxon or Aryan language. Bailey (1991: 270) comments that '"Restoring" a racially pure language to suit a racially "primitive" nation is an idea that reached its most extreme and dreadful consequence in Hitler's Reich, and its appearance in images of English has not been sufficiently acknowledged'.

The second image that emerges here is that to this core of Anglo-Saxon has been added – like tributaries to the great river of English, as many writers like to describe this – words from languages around the world, suggesting that English and British people have always been flexible and keen to borrow from elsewhere to enrich the language. This image of English is then used to deride other languages for their lack of breadth and, especially when people have sought to safeguard languages from the incursions of English, to claim that English is democratic while other languages are not. Most commonly this argument is used against the French for their attempts to legislate against the use of English words.

[. . .]

Thus, the image of English as a great borrowing language is used against any attempts to oppose the spread of English, the argument being that the diverse vocabulary of English is a reflection of the democratic and open nature of the British people, and that reactions against English are nothing but evidence that other people are less open and democratic. 'English need not be protected by French Academies, Canadian constitutions or Flemish language rioters,' Simon Jenkins (1995) tells us. 'The world must just take a deep breath and admit that it has a universal language at last.' But Jenkins is of course merely repeating an old image of English, one that the linguist Jespersen was quite happy with: 'The English language would not have been what it is if the English had not been for centuries great respecters of the liberties of each individual and if everybody had not been free to strike out new paths for himself.' (Jespersen 1938/1982: 14). And this linguistic democracy is, as ever, far superior to the narrow-minded protectionism of the French:

> the English have never suffered an Academy to be instituted among them like the French or Italian Academies . . . In England every writer is, and has always been, free to take his words where he chooses, whether from the ordinary stock of everyday words, from native dialects, from old authors, or from other languages, dead or living. (Jesperson 1938/1982: 15)

The notion of English as a great borrowing language also seems to suggest a view of colonial relations in which the British intermingled with colonized people, enriching English as they communed with the locals. Such a view, however, is hardly supported by colonial history. Kiernan (1969: 148) mentions Macartney's observation of the British 'besetting sin of contempt for the rest of mankind' and that 'while other foreigners at Canton mingled socially with the Chinese, the British kept aloof'. Kiernan goes on to suggest that 'the *apartheid* firmly established in India was transferred in a great measure to China. Everyone has heard of the "Dogs and Chinese not admitted" notice in the park' (Kiernan 1969: 156). In Hong Kong, he points out, 'the position of the Chinese as subjects under British rule increased British haughtiness'. He quotes from Bowring in 1858 as observing that 'the separation of the native population from the European is nearly absolute: social intercourse between the races wholly unknown' (Kiernan 1969: 156). As Metcalf (1995) shows with respect to India, this apartheid policy extended to the division of cities, with railway lines often built to separate the 'native areas' from the white preserves, and houses built with extensive verandahs, gardens and gateways in order to keep the colonized at bay. These observations are backed up by Wesley-Smith's (1994) analysis of 'anti-Chinese legislation' in Hong Kong. Looking at the 'considerable body of race-based discriminatory legislation' in Hong Kong, Wesley-Smith points to one of the central aims of much of this legislation: the separation of Chinese and Europeans. In 1917, Governor May [. . .] wrote to the secretary of state about the importance of maintaining the Peak area as an all-European reserve: 'It would be little short of a calamity if an alien and, by European standards, semi-civilized race were allowed to drive the white man from the one area in Hong Kong, in which he can live with his wife and children in a white man's healthy surroundings' (cited in Wesley-Smith 1994: 100).

Alastair
Pennycook

If, then, the British tended to mingle with colonized or other people far less than did other Europeans, it is unlikely that the English language was in fact such an open, borrowing language as is claimed. Indeed, Bailey (1991: 61) argues that the British 'sense of racial superiority made English voyagers less receptive to borrowings that had not already been, in part, authenticated by other European travelers'. Thus, he goes on:

> Far from its conventional image as a language congenial to borrowing from remote languages, English displays a tendency to accept exotic loanwords mainly when they have first been adopted by other European languages or when presented with marginal social practices or trivial objects. Anglophones who have ventured abroad have done so confident of the superiority of their culture and persuaded of their capacity for adaptation, usually without accepting the obligations of adapting. Extensive linguistic borrowing and language mixing arise only when there is some degree of equality between or among languages (and their speakers) in a multilingual setting. For the English abroad, this sense of equality was rare. (Bailey 1991: 91)

There are, therefore, serious questions to be asked about the image of democratic English put into play by the construction of English as a borrowing language. Indeed, the constant replaying of this image of English as an open and borrowing language, reflecting an open and borrowing people, is a cultural construct of colonialism that is in direct conflict with the colonial evidence.

The third, and probably most insidious, view produced by the insistence on English having a far larger vocabulary than other languages relates to thought. Having stated that English has far more words than German or French, Bryson (1990) goes on to argue that:

> The richness of the English vocabulary, and the wealth of available synonyms, means that English speakers can often draw shades of distinction unavailable to non-English speakers. The French, for example, cannot distinguish between house and home, between mind and brain, between man and gentleman, between 'I wrote' and 'I have written'. The Spanish cannot differentiate a chairman from a president, and the Italians have no equivalent of wishful thinking. In Russia there are no native words for efficiency, challenge, engagement ring, have fun, or take care. (Bryson 1990: 3–5)

Now it is important to note here that this is not merely an argument that different languages cut the world up differently but rather that English, with its larger vocabulary, cuts the world up better. Claiborne (1983: 4), having also claimed a larger vocabulary for English than for other languages, goes on to suggest that 'Like the wandering minstrel in *The Mikado*, with songs for any and every occasion, English has the right word for it – whatever "it" may be'. Thus:

> It is the enormous and variegated lexicon of English, far more than the mere numbers and geographical spread of its speakers, that truly makes our native tongue marvellous – makes it, in fact, a medium for the precise, vivid and subtle expression of thought and emotion that has no equal, past or present. (Claiborne 1983: 4)

**Alastair
Pennycook**

In case the implications of this are not clear, Claiborne goes on to claim that English is indeed 'not merely a great language but the greatest' (p. 4) and that 'Nearly all of us do our thinking in words, which symbolize objects and events (real or imagined) . . .' (p. 6). Clearly, then, in this view, if you are a speaker of English, you are better equipped than speakers of other languages to think about the world. In this view, English is a window on the world. According to Burnett (1962: 20–1), 'not only in Asia and Africa, but in Europe, crisscrossed by linguistic frontiers and dissected by deep-rooted cultural loyalties, people of all classes now look to English as a window, a magic casement opening on every horizon of loquacious men'.

[. . .]

ISSUES TO CONSIDER

❏ The journalist Simon Jenkins quotes Kachru in the extract above. Given that Kachru is, himself, far from being a glorifier of British colonialism but is, rather, a pioneer of language rights for the descendants of those whom the British colonised, how do you interpret his words? And do you agree with him? If you want to follow up Kachru's views on this subject, see the 'Further reading' section on p. 208 and especially his article 'The paradigms of marginality' (1996). Bamgboṣe (1998) also deals with this theme.

❏ An article in the *Observer* (28 November 1999) listed ten items relating to global inequality. Among these are the following:

> ❏ The 48 least developed countries accounting for just 0.4 per cent of world trade
> ❏ Nearly 75 per cent of the world's telephone lines being in the West though it has only 17 per cent of the global population
> ❏ On the Internet, 80 per cent of websites being written in English, understood at best by just 10 per cent of the global population
> ❏ The cost of a computer in the US being an average one month's salary pay. In Bangladesh it is the equivalent of eight years' salary.

How far (if at all) do you think the spread of English in colonial and postcolonial times has contributed to this situation?

❏ Pennycook is highly critical of the view that English dissects the world differently (and, for some writers, better) than do other languages, and that when people speak English as an L2 they, too, dissect the world through the filter of the English language. What evidence is there to support or contradict this view? In your opinion, does it depend, at least to some extent, on whether or not English is spoken within the L2 speaker's own country? If you speak English as an L2 yourself, compare your use of the mother tongue with your use of English. Areas typically discussed in this regard include kinship and colour terminology and the use of taboo and euphemistic language.

❑   In the extract, Pennycook is damning of the view that the English language and its L1 speakers are flexible and adaptable. What is your view on this subject? Do you have any evidence of this flexibility/adaptability or the lack of it?

<hr/>

D2

THE STATUS OF PIDGINS AND CREOLES

D1 presented Pennycook's views on the way postcolonial discourses continue to reproduce colonial perspectives on the way English is (or should be) used around the world. In the next reading, we see how this perspective is not by any means restricted to the dominant (L1) English-speaking countries, but has been adopted by the countries once colonised by them. In other words, these ex-colonies are in a sense colluding in the degrading and marginalisation of their own varieties of English. Whether this is the result of 'linguistic insecurity' (a term coined many years ago by the socio-linguist William Labov to describe how people feel about their language variety when it is constantly denigrated), or whether it is simply a case of pragmatism, to the extent that speakers of Standard English reap better financial rewards, is not at all clear. As you read the article by Charles Alobwede d'Epie, bear this issue in mind.

Banning Pidgin English in Cameroon?

Charles Alobwede d'Epie (reprinted from *English Today* Vol.14 No.1, 1998: 54–60)

At least one household, gathering, or educational institution is banning Pidgin English (PE) in Cameroon every passing minute. This banning ranges from the mild hush-ing down of PE users, through stern verbal orders, to written 'decrees'. This may explain why there is a rapidly growing number of children whose first language (what would have been known as mother tongue) is English.

Mbassi Manga's 1973 survey of language acquisition among anglophone chil-dren revealed two macro-patterns – the rural and the urban. The rural pattern was characterized by what he called Home Language dominance. In other words, in rural areas, children acquired the Home Language (HL) first, then PE and finally educated English (EdE), thus giving the pattern HL → PE → EdE. The urban areas on their part had a pattern marked by PE dominance, giving the formula PE → HL → EdE or PE → EdE → HL. The micro-pattern involved a reversal of the basic order of the macro-patterns or/and a revelation of distinctive linguistic features in pockets of given urban centres like Bamenda up-station, Buea G.R.A., and Limbe Bota.

The Koenig, Chia and Povey socio-linguistic survey of the major urban centres of Cameroon (1977–78) led to the discovery of the following percentages of children who acquired English and PE as their first languages respectively:

Charles
Alobwede
d'Epie

Table [D2.1]   Percentages of children who acquire English/Pidgin English as L1

	English	Pidgin English
Bamenda	1%	22%
Mamfe	0%	25%
Kumba	1%	19%
Buea	7%	26%
Limbe	4%	31%

Source: Koenig, Chia and Povey 1983

In this current survey, I have used the principles used in the 1977–78 survey and have come out with these figures:

Table [D2.2]   Percentages of children who acquire English/Pidgin English as L1

	English	Pidgin English
Bamenda	3.5%	24%
Mamfe	1%	25%
Kumba	3%	22%
Buea	13%	28%
Limbe	9%	30%
Douala	6%	10%
Yaounde	8%	15%

Source: d'Epie 1998

These figures contrast the geometrical progression of the acquisition of EdE as a first language, with the arithmetical progression of the acquisition of PE as a first language. The dynamics of EdE therefore show that the unofficial banning of PE is steadily gaining ground.

Who bans Pidgin English?

The Cameroon government does not encourage the use of PE in schools. Yet, there is no official text banning it anywhere. The Koenig *et al.* survey revealed that where children acquired EdE as their first language, the pattern of language acquisition was EdE→(PE)+(HL). In other words, PE and HL were optional. In such cases, some children ended up being monolingual in English especially if they were whizzed off to Britain before making contact with other children in post-primary school institutions.

Most of the children in the survey were the children of ministers and high civil servants married to educated wives. The educated wife is of paramount significance

**Charles
Alobwede
d'Epie**

in the acquisition of EdE as a first language. I have not used the label *mother tongue* because EdE as a child's first language may not fit the description of mother tongue. I shall rather use the term *Status Mother Tongue (SMT)* to describe a situation in which a well-educated top brass family with a sound HL and PE background shuns both languages in preference to English. This imposes English on the child even though neither of his parents call it his/her mother tongue.

SMT is no longer the monopoly of the top brass of society. The growing number of single-mother graduates (and their likes) is a major force in SMT acquisition. This explains why SMT percentages are high in Buea, Limbe, Douala and Yaounde – cities with a high concentration of single-mother graduates who are either employed or are engaged in petty business. They rent enclosed studios or houses, have SMT-speaking babysitters and because of the economic crisis, live secluded lives – conditions suitable for imposing an SMT on children. Single-mother graduates are a very conscious group. Those doing petty business see it as a temporary measure for survival and hope for a better tomorrow. They reinforce their SMT by sending their children to expensive private schools where PE and HL are banned.

Another group that bans PE is that of the *New Found Status* – uneducated men married to uneducated wives – people who because of their noble birth, wealth or position at work commune with the top brass of society. This is the most dogmatic group in the banning process. Although they try to counterpoise their handicap by banning PE and HL in their homes, their children are usually bilingual in either PE and EdE or HL and EdE, since they themselves are incapable of SMT. This group spends heavily on their children's education in expensive private schools, sometimes schools meant for the children of ministers and diplomats.

Bonny Kfua of Bamenda issues the following decree in 'Time is up for Pidgin English':

> Anyone reading through an essay or letter written by a class seven pupil will admit that the cry of fallen standards in our schools is a reality. Whatever might have pushed the British and Catholic Church to use pidgin as a vehicle of communication, it is high time someone courageously put an end to the widespread use of Pidgin English in Cameroon

[. . .]

The relationship between PE and EdE

[. . .]

Mbassi-Manga traces the history of PE right back to 1400 when the Portuguese traders, employing the services of English servants, traded with the coastal regions of Cameroon. The English servants spoke or introduced a workaday language that was later known as PE, because of the origins of its speakers and the heavy presence of English words in the language.

Baptist missionaries came to Cameroon in 1841 and opened the first English school in 1844. Thus, from 1400 to 1844 Cameroon coastal regions were under

Charles
Alobwede
d'Epie

the sway of PE. Within this time, the language was establishing its grammar, structure and lexis, and developing its synchronic and diachronic varieties as any other
native language (since the traders were not settlers who could have influenced its
evolution otherwise). Any language that has survived the turbulence of linguistic
evolution and has co-existed with another for 444 years cannot be considered an
appendix of the newcomer. This paper therefore considers PE in the light of Ngome's
views. PE is not a type of English as American or Australian Englishes are types
of English, nor does it have a diglossia relationship with English as High and Low
Arabic have to Arabic. It is simply a hybrid African language – a language which
English speaking missionaries had to learn, as they learnt Douala, Ewondo, and
other HLs in Cameroon for evangelical purposes.

PE enjoyed unchallenged leverage during the Portuguese trade (1400–1600)
and the slave trade (1600–1800). The abolition of these trades triggered the
opening up of free trade. This coincided with the opening up of plantations and
the subsequent annexation of Cameroon by Germany (1884) and thus the colonial
epoch. The Germans found both PE and English well in place but since PE was the
workaday language (the language of the labourers) and their immediate concern was
labour, they used it. Upon their defeat in the Second World War and the institution of British administration, the English language came in again in full force.

The co-existence of PE and EdE at these epochs had great sociolinguistic consequences. From 1400 to 1800, PE operated in an unmarked society, but, with
the introduction of EdE, the society became stratified, and that engendered the
phenomenon of 'who spoke what language to whom?' in multilingual situations.
This dichotomy became more marked in the plantations where the few whites and
blacks who spoke and wrote English used it as an order-giving language and the
masses who spoke PE used it as an order-obeying language. Furthermore, planta-
tion society was stratified into white overlords and black underdogs. The blacks
were further classified (according to their English language competence) into Senior
Service, Intermediate Service, and General Labour. Each group had salary scales,
and was assigned living quarters with facilities commensurate to it.
[. . .]

These attributes stigmatized the PE speaker as he found himself quarantined
not only because he spoke PE but also because it exposed him to a lifestyle and
morals associated with slovenliness, vulgarity and debasement. He found himself
split between maintaining his language (PE) loyalty, and aspiring to belong to the
EdE group. He unconsciously transferred the latter to his progeny and as such,
openly or privately, individually or collectively banned PE.

Is PE the cause of fallen standards?

Talk of fallen standards presupposes that there were once high standards.
Respondents cite the performance of educational institutions between 1945 and
1960 and those between 1960 and 1996. These two periods, they say, indicate
colonial stability and educational growth after the war, as well as the relative calm
and educational expansion after independence. According to the respondents, the
Standard Six pupils (end of primary school) of 1945–1960 spoke and wrote better

**Charles
Alobwede
d'Epie**

English than their 1960–1996 counterparts (and even secondary school students). One thing no respondent has stated categorically is whether PE was spoken less at that time (1945–1960) than today.

There is, however, a consensus that the 1945–1960 period was characterized by a British-styled, better planned and administered educational policy, better text-books, limited enrolment, advanced school age and duty-conscious teaching staff. The 1960–1996 period was characterized by an educational policy restrained by political constraints. This, coupled with unrestricted enrolment, tender school age and general laxity in administration, produced adverse results.

[. . .]

Substandard English in Cameroon has had different names – Broken English, Poor English, Bush English, Joinjoin English, Bad English. Each reflects the fluid-ity of the borderline between levels of competence. [. . .]

Bad English has nothing to do with native/non-native, educated/non-educated and monolingual/multilingual dichotomies. It is simply a reality with the English language.

The English language reality

Norman Fairclough [1989] claims that what is today known as Standard English developed from the East Midland dialect associated with the merchant class in London at the end of the medieval epoch. According to him, its beginnings were modest – it was used in very few places for very few purposes by very few people. This humble beginning gave it its cult characteristic – the language of the few for the few by the few. Associated with commerce, and therefore power, it gradually "took over" major social institutions, pushing out Latin and French, vastly extending the purposes it was used for and its formal resources as a result, and coming to be accepted (if not always widely used) by more and more people.

A language that was capable of sacking Latin and French at the time was a no-nonsense language. It was this language that the British used in conquering the world and establishing the greatest empire man has ever known. As it spread, it subjugated native languages and took over their major social, judiciary, adminis-trative and economic institutions. It spread vertically rather than horizontally – thus remaining the language of the few by the few for the few, and in spite of British colonial policy of indirect rule, its intrinsic power acculturated its non-native speakers, depersonalized them and made them think and reason like Englishmen. Fishman echoes this by quoting Sekou Touré thus:

> The education that was given to us was designed to assimilate us, to deperson-alize us, to Westernize us – to present our civilization, our culture, our own sociological and philosophical concepts, even our humanism as the appreciation of a savage and almost conscious primitivism – in order to create a number of complexes in us which would drive us to become more (English) French than the (English) French themselves.

And even after independence, most of those who possessed the language to an agreeable degree could not afford to lose it because they saw in it an enviable

**Charles
Alobwede
d'Epie**

asset – good jobs, positions of political and economic power and above all, the core remnant of colonialism. Whitely beautifully states:

> There are leaders and democrats who still look upon the English way of life as a superior culture, and therefore English as the language of 'culture'. They seize every opportunity to speak English and flaunt their knowledge of English before peasants and workers in the fields and offices. Some of them will even proudly assert that they can only think in English . . . They do so because they subconsciously wish they were Englishmen.

The English language is a colonial heritage, and the leaders are the epitomes of the heritage. Colonialism was characterized by white supremacy (segregation), exploitation, oppression and vindictiveness. Although the leaders fought against these ills in their struggle for independence, they themselves had unconsciously incorporated them in their lifestyles and thus inherited a superiority complex which they could not mortgage. They could not as such liberalize the English language. They had to maintain it as a cult language, a capitalist language, a language of power by the few for the subjugation of the majority. This explains why PE, which is a non-ethnic language and which is acquired freely by the majority, could not be adopted as the language of governance after independence. The English language is a protected language, a language of the status quo. Its value depends on its being closed, and this depends on its being expensive, difficult and time-consuming to learn.

Can PE survive?
The hostility against PE and the growing number of SMT children tend to suggest that with time, PE would decline. However, Lesley Milroy believes that:

> Many bidialectal and bilingual communities maintain, in a parallel way, low status dialects or languages in their repertoires which have the capacity to persist, often over centuries, in the teeth of powerful pressures from a legitimized norm. Social psychologists have concluded that it is the capacity of these low status varieties to symbolize solidarity and group identity, values important to their users, which account for their persistence.

PE has been a low status language under German, French and British administrations, and under each, in spite of the odds, it has shown the capacity to survive. Its survival rests on solid grounds. For one thing, it is the only language in Cameroon which expresses Cameroonian reality without provoking vertical or horizontal hostilities. Secondly, it is conveniently flexible and as such can be acquired at no cost. Finally, because of its horizontal spread, it is the language of consensus.

The controversy as to whether PE should be encouraged or discouraged rests on the language policy of the country. Cameroon has adopted English as her second official language. Some respondents think that, because PE vies for position and threatens the effective use of English, it (PE) should be discouraged. But is that discouragement ideal for the country? It is estimated that more than 70% of our population speaks PE. To discourage PE is to alienate 70% of the population from the basic collective identity.

Charles
Alobwede
d'Epie

This is where Cameroon language policy seems to have failed. The choice of French and English as official languages has relegated the HLs and PE to the background of international communication and divided the country into two linguistic loyalties. In choosing French and English, our leaders thought of avoiding the ethnic conflict which might result if they chose one HL in preference to another. They also thought that the two languages, as languages of worldwide communication, would be instrumental in the economic, political and administrative growth of the country. But is this true today, more than 30 years after independence and the use of French and English as official languages?

Cameroon's underdevelopment could be blamed on factors other than linguistics. But I stress the linguistic factor in agreeing with Fishman that:

> A common indigenous language in the modern nation state is a powerful factor for unity. Cutting across tribal and ethnic lines, it promotes a feeling of single community. Additionally it makes possible the expression and development of social ideas, economic targets and cultural identity easily perceived by citizens. It is, in a word, a powerful factor for mobilization of people and resources for nationhood.

Cameroon elites and masses function at opposing realms of thought because they use codes of opposing status. This retardatory factor would have been eliminated if, upon independence, Cameroon had realized the divisive nature of English and had adopted and developed a neutral indigenous language (PE) to function alongside EdE. This would have reduced the present stigma on PE and would have made it a participatory language for development. In East Africa, Tanzania is developing Swahili for such purposes. In the Philippines, Pilipino is functioning side by side with English. In Paraguay, a local language Guarani is being developed with the aim of using it to increase national awareness.

The division of a nation into high status language elites and low status language masses destroys national unity and cohesion; it leads to segregated quarters, schools, and so on. It enhances the exploitation of the masses by the minority and leads to the masses resisting policies formulated in the high status language. The masses identify the high status language and its objectives as belonging to exploiters, segregationists and oppressors. A language situation that recreates a colonial stereotype is what Orwell would call a decadent civilization – a civilization that leads to politico-economic and linguistic collapse.

ISSUES TO CONSIDER

❑   In his controversial book *Language is Power*, John Honey (1997) argues that 'apparently egalitarian notions of Black English and other dialects can limit access to standard English – and hence power – for minority groups' (back cover). In your view, is this a valid argument for banning Pidgin English in Cameroon? You might like to look back to the arguments and counter-arguments of Bisong and Phillipson regarding English in Africa, in C1.

❑ D'Epie, while supporting the maintenance of Pidgin English in the Cameroon education system, reveals certain prejudices in the way he conceptualises 'correct' English and 'bad' English. How 'standard' do you find the author's own use of English (e.g. his punctuation, and his mixing of formal and colloquial styles)?

❑ Is there to some extent a parallel between the situation in Cameroon and that in the UK? Are both guilty of 'golden age syndrome' and unable to cope with natural language change? Or are language standards genuinely in decline? If so, to what do you attribute the cause?

❑ The following is an extract from the autobiographical *School Days* by Patrick Chamoiseau, in which he describes his school experiences in Martinique. Although the unfamiliar standard language he was forced to use at school in place of his native creole was French, the feelings he describes so graphically must have been very similar to those of children compelled to use Standard English. How strong a 'case' does Chamoiseau make here for the use of creole in education?

But everything went well: no one had to speak, to write, to explain this-or-that. It was the Teacher who talked. And now the little boy realized something obvious: *the Teacher spoke French.* Mam Ninotte used snippets of French on occasion (a half-word here, a quarter-word there), bits of French that were automatic and unchanging. And the Papa, when he made a rum punch, ceremoniously unfurled a French that was less a language than an esoteric tool used for effect. As for the Big Kids, their natural mode of expression was Creole, except with Mam Ninotte, other grownups, and most particularly the Papa. A certain respectful distance was maintained through the rituals of formality when speaking to them. And everything else for everyone else (pleasures, shouts, dreams, hatreds, the life in life ...) was Creole. This division of speech had never struck the little boy before. French (to which he didn't even attach a name) was some object fetched when needed from a kind of shelf, outside oneself, but which sounded natural in the mouth, close to Creole. Close through articulation. The words, the sentence structure. But now, with the Teacher, speaking traveled far and wide along a single road. And this French road became strangely foreign. The articulation changed. The rhythm changed. The intonation changed. Words that were more or less familiar began to sound different. They seemed to come from a distant horizon and no longer had any affinity with Creole. The Teacher's images, examples, references did not spring from their native country anymore. The Teacher spoke French like the people on the radio or the sailors of the French line. And he deliberately spoke nothing else. French seemed to be the very element of his knowledge. He savored this smooth syrup he secreted so ostentatiously. And his language did not reach out to the children, the way Mam Salinière's had, to envelop, caress, and persuade them. His words floated above them with the magnificence of a ruby-throated hummingbird hovering in the breeze. *Oh, the Teacher was French!*

D3 WHO OWNS ENGLISH TODAY?

Henry Widdowson

The ownership debate

In C3, you read the views of scholars such as Kachru, who argue that we need a paradigm shift in the teaching and testing of English, to reflect the fact that the majority of people who learn and use English today are not native speakers and do not even use it to communicate with them. In the paper that follows, Henry Widdowson argues in the strongest terms that native speakers of English no longer 'own' English or have the right to determine how it is, or should be, spoken around the world.

The ownership of English

Henry Widdowson (The Peter Strevens Memorial Lecture delivered at the 1993 IATEFL International Conference, Swansea and reprinted from the *Annual Conference Report* 1993: 5–8)

[. . .] I want to talk about how the English we teach is to be defined and how this is related to its position as an international language.

To start with, who determines the demarcation of the subject itself? We are teaching English and the general assumption is that our purpose is to develop in students a proficiency which approximates as closely as possible to that of native speakers. But who are these native speakers?

The English perhaps. And why not? A modest proposal. England is where the language originated and this is where the English live. The language and the people are bound together by both morphology and history. So they can legitimately lay claim to this linguistic territory. It belongs to them. And they are the custodians. If you want real or proper English, this is where it is to be found, preserved and listed like a property of the National Trust.

Of course, English of a kind is found elsewhere as well, still spreading, a luxuriant growth from imperial seed. Seeded among other people but not ceded to them. At least not completely. For the English still cling tenaciously to their property and try to protect it from abuse. Let us acknowledge (let us concede) that there are other kinds of English, offshoots and outgrowths, but they are not real or proper English, not the genuine article.

As an analogy, consider the French. They have, until just recently, successfully denied others the right to use the appellation 'Champagne' for any wine that does not come from the region of that name, where Dom Perignon first invented it. There may be all kinds of derivative versions elsewhere, excellent no doubt in their way, but they are not real or proper Champagne, even though loose talk may refer to them as such. Similarly, there is real English, *Anglais réal*, Royal English, Queen's English, or (for those unsympathetic to the monarchy) Oxford English. The vintage language.

I do not imagine that such a view would gain much support in present company. The response is more likely to be outrage. You cannot be serious. Well, not entirely, it is true. As I have expressed it, in somewhat extravagant terms, this position is one which very few people would associate themselves with. It is

Henry
Widdowson

reactionary, arrogant, totally unacceptable. And the argument is patently absurd. Perhaps as I have expressed it. But then why is it absurd? The particular associations of England, Queen and country and Colonel Blimp which I invoked to demonstrate the argument also in some respects disguise it. If we now remove the position from these associations and strip the argument down to its essential tenets, is it so readily dismissed? Is it indeed so uncommon after all? I want to suggest that the ideas and attitudes which I have presented in burlesque are still very much with us in a different and less obvious guise.

To return briefly to Champagne. One argument frequently advanced for being protective of its good name has to do with quality assurance. The label is a guarantee of quality. If any Tom, Dick or Harry producing fizzy wine is free to use it, there can be no quality control. Recently an English firm won a court case enabling it to put Champagne on its bottles containing a non-alcoholic beverage made from elderflowers. The Champagne lobby was outraged. Here, they said, was the thin end of the wedge. Before long, the label would be appearing on bottles all over the place containing concoctions of all kinds calling themselves Champagne, and so laying claim to its quality. The *appellation* would not be *controlée*. Standards were at stake.

They have a point. And the same point is frequently made about English. In this case, you cannot, of course, preserve exclusive use of the name and, indeed, it would work against your interests to do so (of which more later), but you can seek to preserve standards by implying that there is an exclusive quality in your own brand of English, aptly called 'standard English'. What is this quality, then? What are these standards?

The usual answer is quality of clear communication and standards of intelligibility. With standard English, it is argued, these are assured. If the language disperses into different forms, a myriad of Englishes, then it ceases to serve as a means of international communication; in which case the point of learning it largely disappears. As the language spreads, there are bound to be changes out on the periphery; so much can be conceded. But these changes must be seen not only as peripheral but as radial also, and traceable back to the stable centre of the standard. If this centre does not hold, things fall apart, mere anarchy is loosed upon the world. Back to Babel.

In itself, this argument sounds plausible; and it is difficult to refute. But for all that, there is something about it which is suspect. Let us replay it again. Standard English promotes the cause of international communication so we must maintain the central stability of the standard as the common linguistic frame of reference.

To begin with, who are 'we'? Obviously the promoters of standard English must themselves have standard English at their disposal. But to maintain it is another matter. This presupposes authority. And this authority is claimed by those who possess the language by primogeniture and due of birth, as Shakespeare puts it. In other words, the native speakers. They do not have to be English, of course. That would be too restrictive a condition, and one it would be tactless to propose, but they have to be to the language born. Not all native speakers, you understand. In fact, come to think of it, not most native speakers, for the majority

Henry
Widdowson

of those who are to the language born speak non-standard English, and have them-selves to be instructed in the standard at school. We cannot have any Tom, Dick or Harry claiming authority, for Tom, Dick and Harry are likely to be speakers of some dialect or other. So the authority to maintain the standard language is not consequent on a natural native speaker endowment. It is claimed by a minor-ity of people who have the power to impose it. The custodians of standard English are self-elected members of a rather exclusive club. Now it is important to be clear that in saying this, I am not arguing against standard English. You can accept the argument for language maintenance, as indeed I do, without accepting the authority that claims the right to maintain it. It is, I think, very generally assumed that a particular subset of educated native speakers have the natural entitlement to custody of the language. That the preservation of its integrity is in their hands: their right and their responsibility. It is this which I wish to question. Not in any spirit of radical rebellion against authority as such, but because I think such ques-tioning raises a number of crucial issues about the learning and teaching of the language.

Consideration of who the custodians are leads logically on to a consideration of what it is exactly that is in their custody. What is standard English? The usual way of defining it is in reference to its grammar and lexis: it is a variety, a kind of superposed dialect which is socially sanctioned for institutional use, and there-fore particularly well suited to written communication. In its spoken form it can be manifested by any accent. So it is generally conceded that standard English has no distinctive phonology. The same concession is not, however, extended to its graphology. On the contrary, it is deviant spelling which, in Britain at least, is most frequently singled out for condemnation. There is something of a contradic-tion here. If standard English is defined as a distinctive grammatical and lexical system which can be substantially realized in different ways, then what does spelling have to do with it? It is true that some spelling has a grammatical function (like apostrophe s which distinguishes the possessive form from the plural) but most of it does not. If you are going to ignore phonological variation, then, to be con-sistent, you should surely ignore graphological variation as well, and overlook it as a kind of written accent.

The reason it is not overlooked, I think, is that standard English, unlike other dialects, is essentially a written variety mainly designed for institutional purposes (education, administration, business and so on). Its spoken version is secondary, and typically used by those who control these institutions. This means that although it may not matter how it is spoken, it emphatically does matter how it is written. Furthermore, since writing, as a more durable medium, is used to express and establish institutional values, deviations from orthographic conventions undermine in some degree the institutions which they serve. They can be seen as evidence of social instability: a sign of things beginning to fall apart. So it is not surpris-ing that those who have a vested interest in maintaining these institutions should be so vexed by bad spelling. It is not difficult to identify words through their unorthodox appearance. What seems to be more crucial is that good spelling rep-resents conformity to convention and so serves to maintain institutional stability.

Henry Widdowson

Similar points can be made about grammatical features. Since language has built-in redundancy, grammatical conformity is actually not particularly crucial for many kinds of communicative transaction. What we generally do in the inter-pretative process is actually to edit grammar out of the text, referring lexis directly to context, using lexical items as indexical clues to meaning. We edit grammar back in when we need it for fine tuning. If the reason for insisting on standard English is because it guarantees effective communication, then the emphasis should therefore logically be on lexis rather than grammar. But the champions of stand-ard English do not see it in this way: on the contrary, they focus attention on grammatical abuse. Why should this be so? There are, I think, two reasons. Firstly, it is precisely because grammar is so often redundant in communicative trans-actions that it takes on another significance, namely that of expressing social identity. The mastery of a particular grammatical system, especially, perhaps, those features which are redundant, marks you as a member of the community which has developed that system for its own social purposes. Conversely, of course, those who are unable to master the system are excluded from the community. They do not belong. In short, grammar is shibboleth.

So when the custodians of standard English complain about the ungrammatical language of the populace, they are in effect indicating that the perpetrators are outsiders, non-members of the community. The only way they can become members, and so benefit from the privileges of membership, is to learn standard English, and those privileges include, of course, access to the institutions which the community controls. Standard English is an entry condition and the custodi-ans of it the gatekeepers. You can, of course, persist in your non-standard ways if you choose, but then do not be surprised to find yourself marginalized, per-petually kept out on the periphery. What you say will be less readily attended to, assigned less importance, if it is not expressed in the grammatically approved manner. And if you express yourself in writing which is both ungrammatical and badly spelled, you are not likely to be taken seriously. You are beyond the pale. Standard English, then, is not simply a means of communication but the symbolic possession of a particular community, expressive of its identity, its conventions and values. As such it needs to be carefully preserved, for to undermine standard English is to undermine what it stands for: the security of this community and its institutions. Thus it tends to be the communal rather than the communicative fea-tures of standard English that are most jealously protected: its grammar and spelling.

I do not wish to imply this communal function is to be deplored. Languages of every variety have this dual character: they provide the means for com-munication and at the same time express the sense of community, represent the stability of its conventions and values, in short, its culture. All communities possess and protect their languages. The question is, which community and which culture have a rightful claim to ownership of standard English? For standard English is no longer the preserve of a group of people living in an off-shore European island, even if some of them still seem to think that it is. It is an international language. As such, it serves a whole range of different communities and their institutional purposes, and these transcend traditional communal and cultural boundaries. I am

Henry
Widdowson

referring to the business community, for example, and the community of researchers and scholars in science and technology and other disciplines. Standard English, especially in its written form, is their language. It provides for effective communication, but at the same time, it establishes the status and stability of the institutional conventions which define these international activities. These activities develop their own conventions of thought and procedure, customs and codes of practice; in short, they in effect create their own cultures, their own standards. And obviously for the maintenance of standards it is helpful, to say the least, to have a standard language at your disposal. But you do not need native speakers to tell you what it is.

[. . .]

As I indicated earlier, the custodians of standard English express the fear that if there is diversity, things will fall apart and the language will divide up into mutually unintelligible varieties. But things in a sense have already fallen apart. The varieties of English used for international communication in science, finance, commerce and so on are mutually unintelligible. As far as lexis is concerned, their communicative viability depends on the development of separate standards, and this means that their communication is largely closed off from the world outside.

The point, then, is that if English is to retain its vitality and its capability for continual adjustment, it cannot be confined within a standard lexis. And this seems to be implicitly accepted as far as particular domains of use are concerned. Nobody, I think, says that the abstruse terms used by physicists or stock-brokers are non-standard English. It is generally accepted that communities or secondary cultures which are defined by shared professional concerns should be granted rights of ownership and allowed to fashion the language to their needs.

The same tolerance is not extended so readily to primary cultures and communities, where the language is used in the conduct of everyday social life. Lexical innovation here, equally motivated by communal requirement, is generally dismissed as dialect. Take, for example, the two words *depone* and *prepone*. The first is a technical legal term and therefore highly respectable. The second, *prepone*, is not. It is an Indian English word of very general currency, coined to contrast with 'to postpone'. To postpone an event means to put it back, to prepone an event is to bring it forward. The coinage exploits the morphology of English in an entirely regular way. It is apt. But it is also quaint. An odd Indian excrescence: obviously non-standard. And yet there is clearly nothing deviant in the derivational process itself and, indeed, we can see it at work in the formation of the related words *predate* and *postdate*. But these are sanctioned as entirely ordinary, proper, standard English words. What, then, is the difference? The difference lies in the origin of the word. Prepone is coined by a non-native speaking community, so it is not really a proper English word. It is not pukka. And of course the word *pukka* is itself only pukka because the British adopted it.

Where are we then? When we consider the question of standard English what we find, in effect, is double standards. The very idea of a standard implies stability and this can only be fixed in reference to the past. But language is of its nature unstable. It is essentially protean in nature, adapting its shape to suit

changing circumstances. It would otherwise lose its vitality and its communicative
and communal value. This is generally acknowledged in the case of specialist domains
of use, but is not acknowledged in the case of everyday social uses of the language. So it is that a word like *depone* is approved and a word like *prepone* is not.
But the basic principle of dynamic adaption is the same in both cases. And in both
cases, the users of the language exploit its protean potential and fashion it to their
needs, thereby demonstrating a high degree of linguistic capability. In both cases
the innovation indicates that the language has been learned, not just as a set of
fixed conventions to conform to, but as a resource for making meaning; and making meaning which you can call your own. This, surely, is a crucial condition. You
are proficient in a language to the extent that you make it your possession, bend
it to your will, assert yourself through it rather than simply submit to dictates of
its form. It is a familiar experience to find oneself saying things in a foreign language because you can say them rather than because they express what you want
to say. You feel you are going through the motions, and somebody else's motions
at that. You are speaking the language but not speaking your mind. Real proficiency is when you are able to take possession of the language and turn it to
your advantage. This is what mastery means. So in a way, proficiency only comes
with non-conformity, when you can take the initiative and strike out on your own.
Consider these remarks of the Nigerian writer, Chinua Achebe:

> I feel that the English language will be able to carry the weight of my African
> experience . . . But it will have to be a new English, still in Communion with
> its ancestral home but altered to suit its new African surroundings.

Achebe is a novelist and he is talking here about creative writing. But the point
I have been making is that all uses of language are creative in the sense that they
draw on linguistic resources to express different perceptions of reality. English is
called upon to carry the weight of all kinds of experience, much of it very remote
indeed from its ancestral home.

The new English that Achebe refers to is locally generated, and although it
must necessarily be related to, and so in communion with, its ancestral origins in
the past, it owes no allegiance to any descendants of this ancestry in the present.
And this point applies to all other new Englishes which have been created to
carry the weight of different experience in different surrounding, whether they are
related to specialist domains of use or to the contexts of everyday life. They are
all examples of the entirely normal and necessary process of adaption, a process
which obviously depends on non-conformity to existing conventions or standards.
For these have been established elsewhere by other people as appropriate to quite
different circumstances. The fact that these people can claim direct descent from
the founding fathers has nothing to do with it. How English develops in the world
is no business whatever of native speakers in England or anywhere else. They have
no say in the matter, no right to intervene or pass judgement. They are irrelevant. The very fact that English is an international language means that no nation
can have custody over it. To grant such custody of the language, particularly, one
might add, to a nation disposed to dwell on the past, is necessarily to arrest its

development and so undermine its international status. It is a matter of considerable pride and satisfaction for native speakers of English that their language is an international means of communication. But the point is that it is only international to the extent that it is not their language. It is not a possession which they lease out to others, while still retaining the freehold. Other people actually own it.

[. . .]

[A]s soon as you accept that English serves the communicative and communal needs of different communities, it follows logically that it must be diverse. An international language has to be an independent language. It does not follow logically, however, that the language will disperse into mutually unintelligible varieties. For it will naturally stabilise into a standard form to the extent required to meet the needs of the communities concerned. Thus it is clearly vital to the interests of the international community of, for example, scientists or business people, whatever their primary language, that they should preserve a common standard of English in order to keep up standards of communicative effectiveness. English could not otherwise serve their purpose. It needs no native speaker to tell them that. Furthermore, this natural tendency towards standardization will be reinforced by the extending of networks of interaction through developments in telecommunications and information technology. For there is little point in opening up such amazing new transmission systems if what you transmit makes no sense at the other end. The availability of these new channels calls for the maintenance of a common code. And these are therefore likely to have greater influence on stabilizing the language than the pronouncements of native speakers.

The essential point is that a standard English, like other varieties of language, develops endo-normatively, by a continuing process of self-regulation, as appropriate to different conditions of use. It is not fixed, therefore, by native speakers. They have no special say in the matter, in spite of their claims to ownership of real English as associated with their own particular cultural contexts of use.

[. . .]

ISSUES TO CONSIDER

❑ Widdowson's paper argues uncompromisingly for precisely the kind of paradigm shift that Kachru calls for. Do you agree with his view that the standard English argument is suspect?

❑ Do you think Widdowson is right in predicting that if English is allowed to develop independently into a number of different standards around the world, 'it will not disperse into mutually unintelligible varieties'? Is this a likely outcome for both spoken and written English?

❑ If you disagree with Widdowson's prediction, what are your reasons?

❑ If you agree, are there any measures that could or should be put in place to improve the degree of success – and if so, who should be responsible for taking such action?

FROM LANGUAGE TO LITERATURE

D4

Chinua Achebe

Although this section focuses on literature rather than language, many of the issues are the same. Underlying the extracts from Achebe and Ngũgĩ is the fundamental and unresolved question of whether the English language is able to (re)present the experience of speakers from other backgrounds, as well as the extent to which the language can or should be modified in the process. As you read through the two extracts, note the main points of disagreement between Achebe and Ngũgĩ on these issues.

The African writer and the English language

Chinua Achebe (reprinted from *Morning Yet On Creation Day*, New York: Anchor, 1975)

I have indicated somewhat off-handedly that the national literature of Nigeria and of many other countries of Africa is, or will be, written in English. This may sound like a controversial statement, but it isn't. All I have done has been to look at the reality of present-day Africa. This "reality" may change as a result of deliberate, e.g. political, action. If it does an entirely new situation will arise, and there will be plenty of time to examine it. At present it may be more profitable to look at the scene as it is.

What are the factors which have conspired to place English in the position of national language in many parts of Africa? Quite simply the reason is that these nations were created in the first place by the intervention of the British which, I hasten to add, is not saying that the peoples comprising these nations were invented by the British.

[. . .]

Of course there are areas of Africa where colonialism divided up a single ethnic group among two or even three powers. But on the whole it did bring together many peoples that had hitherto gone their several ways. And it gave them a language with which to talk to one another. If it failed to give them a song, it at least gave them a tongue, for sighing. There are not many countries in Africa today where you could abolish the language of the erstwhile colonial powers and still retain the facility for mutual communication. Therefore those African writers who have chosen to write in English or French are not unpatriotic smart alecs with an eye on the main chance – outside their own countries. They are by-products of the same process that made the new nation states of Africa.

You can take this argument a stage further to include other countries of Africa. The only reason why we can even talk about African unity is that when we get together we can have a manageable number of languages to talk in – English, French, Arabic.

The other day I had a visit from Joseph Kariuki of Kenya. Although I had read some of his poems and he had read my novels we had not met before. But it didn't seem to matter. In fact I had met him through his poems, especially through his love poem, "Come Away My Love" in which he captures in so few words the trial and tensions of an African in love with a white girl in Britain.

> Come away my love, from streets
> Where unkind eyes divide
> And shop windows reflect our difference.

By contrast, when in 1960 I was travelling in East Africa and went to the home of the late Shabaan Robert, the Swahili poet of Tanganyika, things had been different. We spent some time talking about writing, but there was no real contact. I knew from all accounts that I was talking to an important writer, but of the nature of his work I had no idea. He gave me two books of his poems which I treasure but cannot read – until I have learnt Swahili.

And there are scores of languages I would want to learn if it were possible. Where am I to find the time to learn the half-a-dozen or so Nigerian languages each of which can sustain a literature? I am afraid it cannot be done. These languages will just have to develop as tributaries to feed the one central language enjoying nation-wide currency. Today, for good or ill, that language is English. Tomorrow it may be something else, although I very much doubt it.

Those of use who have inherited the English language may not be in a position to appreciate the value of the inheritance. Or we may go on resenting it because it came as part of a package deal which included many other items of doubtful value and the positive atrocity of racial arrogance and prejudice which may yet set the world on fire. But let us not in rejecting the evil throw out the good with it.

[. . .]

I think I have said enough to give an indication of my thinking on the importance of the world language which history has forced down our throat. Now let us look at some of the most serious handicaps. And let me say straight away that one of the most serious handicaps is *not* the one people talk about most often, namely, that it is impossible for anyone ever to use a second language as effectively as his first. This assertion is compounded of half-truth and half bogus mystique. Of course, it is true that the vast majority of people are happier with their first language than with any other. But then the majority of people are not writers. We do have enough examples of writers who have performed the feat of writing effectively in a second language. And I am not thinking of the obvious names like Conrad. It would be more germane to our subject to choose African examples.

The first name that comes to my mind is Olaudah Equiano, better known as Gustavus Vassa, the African. Equiano was an Ibo, I believe from the village of Iseke in the Orlu division of Eastern Nigeria. He was sold as a slave at a very early age and transported to America. Later he bought his freedom and lived in Engand. In 1789 he published his life story, a beautifully written document which, among other things, set down for the Europe of his time something of the life and habit of his people in Africa in an attempt to counteract the lies and slander invented by some Europeans to justify the slave trade.

D

Chinua Achebe

[. . .]

It is when we come to what is commonly called creative literature that most doubt seems to arise. Obi Wali [. . .] has this to say:

> . . . Until these writers and their Western midwives accept the fact that any true African literature must be written in African languages, they would be merely pursuing a dead end, which can only lead to sterility, uncreativity and frustration.

But far from leading to sterility the work of many new African writers is full of the most exciting possibilities.
[. . .]

[T]ake the poem "Night Rain" in which J.P. Clark captures so well the fear and wonder felt by a child as rain clamours on the thatch-roof at night and his mother walking about in the dark, moves her simple belongings

> Out of the run of water
> That like ants filing out of the wood
> Will scatter and gain possession
> Of the floor . . .

I think that the picture of water spreading on the floor "like ants filing out of the wood" is beautiful. Of course if you have never made fire with faggots you may miss it. But Clark's inspiration derives from the same source which gave birth to the saying that a man who brings home antridden faggots must be ready for the visit of lizards.

I do not see any signs of sterility anywhere here. What I do see is a new voice coming out of Africa, speaking of African experience in a world-wide language. So my answer to the question: *Can an African ever learn English well enough to be able to use it effectively in creative writing?* is certainly yes. If on the other hand you ask: *Can he ever learn to use it like a native speaker?* I should say, I hope not. It is neither necessary nor desirable for him to be able to do so. The price a world language must be prepared to pay is submission to many different kinds of use. The African writer should aim to use English in a way that brings out his message best without altering the language to the extent that its value as a medium of international exchange will be lost. He should aim at fashioning out an English which is at once universal and able to carry his peculiar experience. [. . .]

Allow me to quote a small example from *Arrow of God* which may give some idea of how I approach the use of English. The Chief Priest in the story is telling one of his sons why it is necessary to send him to church:

> I want one of my sons to join these people and be my eyes there. If there is nothing in it you will come back. But if there is something there you will bring home my share. The world is like a Mask, dancing. If you want to see it well you do not stand in one place. My spirit tells me that those who do not befriend the white man today will be saying *had we known* tomorrow.

Now supposing I had put it another way, Like this for instance:

I am sending you as my representative among these people – just to be on the safe side in case the new religion develops. One has to move with the times or else one is left behind. I have a hunch that those who fail to come to terms with the white man may well regret their lack of foresight.

The material is the same. But the form of the one is *in character* and the other is not. It is largely a matter of instinct, but judgment comes into it too.

[. . .]

One final point remains for me to make. The real question is not whether Africans could write in English but whether they *ought to*. Is it right that a man should abandon his mother-tongue for someone else's? It looks like a dreadful betrayal and produces a guilty feeling.

But for me there is no other choice. I have been given this language and I intend to use it. I hope, though, that there will always be men, like the late Chief Fagunwa, who will choose to write in their native tongue and ensure that our ethnic literature will flourish side-by-side with the national ones. For those of us who opt for English there is much work ahead and much excitement.

Writing in the *London Observer* recently, James Baldwin said:

> My quarrel with English language has been that the language reflected none of my experience. But now I began to see the matter another way . . . Perhaps the language was not my own because I had never attempted to use it, had only learned to imitate it. If this were so, then it might be made to bear the burden of my experience if I could find the stamina to challenge it, and me, to such a test.

I recognise, of course, that Baldwin's problem is not exactly mine, but I feel that the English language will be able to carry the weight of my African experience. But it will have to be a new English, still in full communion with its ancestral home but altered to suit its new African surroundings.

The language of African literature

Ngũgĩ wa Thiong'o (reprinted from *Decolonising the Mind: The Politics of Language in African Literature*, London: James Currey, 1986)

It was after the declaration of a state of emergency over Kenya in 1952 that all the schools run by patriotic nationalists were taken over by the colonial regime and were placed under District Education Boards chaired by Englishmen. English then became the language of my formal education. In Kenya, English became more than a language: it was *the* language, and all the others had to bow before it in deference.

Thus one of the most humiliating experiences was to be caught speaking Gĩkũyũ in the vicinity of the school. The culprit was given corporal punishment – three to five stokes of the cane on bare buttocks – or was made to carry a metal plate around the neck with inscriptions such as I AM STUPID or I AM A DONKEY. Sometimes the culprits were fined money they could hardly afford. And how did the teachers catch the culprits? A button was initially given to one pupil who was supposed to hand it over to whoever was caught speaking his mother tongue. Whoever had the button at the end of the day would sing who had given it to him and the ensuing process would bring out all the culprits of the day. Thus children were turned into witch-hunters and in the process were being taught the lucrative value of being traitor to one's immediate community.

The attitude to English was the exact opposite: any achievement in spoken or written English was highly rewarded; prizes, prestige, applause; the ticket to higher realms. English became the measure of intelligence and ability in the arts, the sciences, and all the other branches of learning. English became the main determinant of a child's progress up the ladder of formal education.

As you may know, the colonial system of education in addition to its apartheid racial demarcation had the structure of a pyramid: a broad primary base, a narrowing secondary middle, and an even narrower university apex. Selections from primary into secondary were through an examination, in my time called Kenya African Preliminary Examination, in which one had to pass six subjects ranging from Maths to Nature Study and Kiswahili. All the papers were written in English. Nobody could pass the exam who failed the English language paper no matter how brilliantly he had done in the other subjects. I remember one boy in my class of 1954 who had distinctions in all subjects except English, which he had failed. He was made to fail the entire exam. He went on to become a turn boy in a bus company. I who had only passes but a credit in English got a place at the Alliance High School, one of the most elitist institutions for Africans in colonial Kenya. The requirements for a place at the University, Makerere University College, were broadly the same: nobody could go on to wear the undergraduate red gown, no matter how brilliantly they had performed in all the other subjects unless they had a credit – not even a simple pass! – in English. Thus the most coveted place in the pyramid and in the system was only available to the holder of an English language credit card. English was the official vehicle and the magic formula to colonial elitedom.

Literary education was now determined by the dominant language while also reinforcing that dominance. Orature (oral literature) in Kenyan languages stopped. In primary school I now read simplified Dickens and Stevenson alongside Rider Haggard. Jim Hawkins, Oliver Twist, Tom Brown – not Hare, Leopard and Lion – were now my daily companions in the world of imagination. In secondary school, Scott and G.B. Shaw vied with more Rider Haggard, John Buchan, Alan Paton, Captain W.E. Johns. At Makerere I read English: from Chaucer to T.S. Eliot with a touch of Graham Greene.

Thus language and literature were taking us further and further from ourselves to other selves, from our world to other worlds.

What was the colonial system doing to us Kenyan children? What were the consequences of, on the one hand, this systematic suppression of our languages and the literature they carried, and on the other the elevation of English and the literature it carried? To answer those questions, let me first examine the relationship of language to human experience, human culture and the human perception of reality.

Ngũgĩ wa Thiong'o

Language, any language, has a dual character: it is both a means of communication and a carrier of culture. Take English. It is spoken in Britain and in Sweden and Denmark. But for Swedish and Danish people English is only a means of communication with non-Scandinavians. It is not a carrier of their culture. For the British, and particularly the English, it is additionally, and inseparably from its use as a tool of communication, a carrier of their culture and history. Or take Swahili in East and Central Africa. It is widely used as a means of communication across many nationalities. But it is not the carrier of a culture and history of many of these nationalities. However in parts of Kenya and Tanzania, and particularly in Zanzibar, Swahili is inseparably both a means of communication and a carrier of the culture of those people to whom it is a mother-tongue.

[. . .]

But there is more to it: communication between human beings is also the basis and process of evolving culture. In doing similar kinds of things and actions over and over again under similar circumstances, similar even in their mutability, certain patterns, moves, rhythms, habits, attitudes, experiences and knowledge emerge. Those experiences are handed over to the next generation and become the inherited basis for their further actions on nature and on themselves. There is a gradual accumulation of values which in time become almost self-evident truths governing their conception of what is right and wrong, good and bad, beautiful and ugly, courageous and cowardly, generous and mean in their internal and external relations. Over a time this becomes a way of life distinguishable from other ways of life. They develop a distinctive culture and history. Culture embodies those moral, ethical and aesthetic values, the set of spiritual eyeglasses, through which they come to view themselves and their place in the universe. Values are the basis of a people's identity, their sense of particularity as members of the human race. All this is carried by language. Language as culture is the collective memory bank of a people's experience in history. Culture is almost indistinguishable from the language that makes possible its genesis, growth, banking, articulation and indeed its transmission from one generation to the next.

Language as culture [. . .] has three important aspects. Culture is a product of the history which it in turn reflects. Culture in other words is a product and a reflection of human beings communicating with one another in the very struggle to create wealth and to control it. But culture does not merely reflect that history, or rather it does so by actually forming images or pictures of the world of nature and nurture. Thus the second aspect of language as culture is as an image-forming agent in the mind of the child. Our whole conception of ourselves as a people, individually and collectively, is based on those pictures and images which may or may not correctly correspond to the actual reality of the struggles with nature and nurture which produced them in the first place. But our capacity to confront the world creatively is dependent on how those images correspond or not to that reality, how they distort or clarify the reality of our struggles. Language as culture is thus mediating between me and my own self; between my own self and other selves; between me and nature. Language is mediating in my very being. And this brings us to the third aspect of language as culture. Culture transmits or imparts those images of the world and reality through the spoken and written language, that is through a specific language. [. . .] Written literature and orature are the main means by which a particular language transmits the images of the world contained in the culture it carries.

Language as communication and as culture are then products of each other. Communication creates culture: culture is a means of communication. Language carries culture, and culture carries, particularly through orature and literature, the entire body of values by which we come to perceive ourselves and our place in the world. How people perceive themselves affects how they look at their culture, at their politics and at the social production of wealth, at their entire relationship to nature and to other beings. Language is thus inseparable from ourselves as a community of human beings with a specific form and character, a specific history, a specific relationship to the world.

So what was the colonialist imposition of a foreign language doing to us children?

The real aim of colonialism was to control the people's wealth [. . .]. But its most important area of domination was the mental universe of the colonised: the control, through culture, of how people perceived themselves and their relationship to the world. Economic and political control can never be complete or effective without mental control. To control a people's culture is to control their tools of self-definition in relations to others.

For colonialism this involved two aspects of the same process: the destruction or the deliberate undervaluing of a people's culture, their art, dances, religions, history, geography, education, orature and literature, and the conscious elevation of the language of the coloniser. The domination of a people's language by the languages of the colonising nations was crucial to the domination of the mental universe of the colonised.

Take language as communication. [. . .] Since the new language as a means of communication was a product of and was reflecting the 'real language of life' elsewhere, it could never as spoken or written properly reflect or imitate the real life of that community. This may in part explain why technology always appears to us as slightly external, *their* product and not *ours*. The word 'missile' used to hold an alien far-away sound until I recently learnt its equivalent in Gĩkũyũ, *ngurukuhi*, and it made me apprehend it differently. Learning, for a colonial child, became a cerebral activity and not an emotionally felt experience.

But since the new, imposed languages could never completely break the native languages as spoken, their most effective area of domination was [. . .] the written. The language of an African child's formal education was foreign. The language of the books he read was foreign. Thought, in him, took the visible form of a foreign language. So the written language of a child's upbringing in the school (even his spoken language within the school compound) became divorced from his spoken language at home. There was often not the slightest relationship between the child's written world, which was also the language of his schooling, and the world of his immediate environment in the family and the community. [. . .] This resulted in the disassociation of the sensibility of that child from his

Ngũgĩ wa Thiong'o

natural and social environment, what we might call colonial alienation. The alienation became reinforced in the teaching of history, geography, music, where bourgeois Europe was always the centre of the universe.

This disassociation, divorce, or alienation from the immediate environment becomes clearer when you look at colonial language as a carrier of culture.

[. . .]

Since culture does not just reflect the world in images but actually, through those very images, conditions a child to see that world in a certain way, the colonial child was made to see the world and where he stands in it as seen and defined by or reflected in the culture of the language of imposition.

And since those images are mostly passed on through orature and literature it meant the child would now only see the world as seen in the literature of his language of adoption. From the point of view of alienation, that is of seeing one-self from outside oneself as if one was another self, it does not matter that the imported literature carried the great humanist tradition of the best in Shakespeare, Balzac, Tolstoy, Gorky, Brecht, Sholokhov, Dickens. The location of this great mirror of imagination was necessarily Europe and its history and culture and the rest of the universe was seen from that centre.

But obviously it was worse when the colonial child was exposed to images of his world as mirrored in the written languages of his coloniser. Where his own native languages were associated in his impressionable mind with low status, humiliation, corporal punishment, slow-footed intelligence and ability or down-right stupidity, non-intelligibility and barbarism, this was reinforced by the world he met in the works of such geniuses of racism as a Rider Haggard or a Nicholas Monsarrat; not to mention the pronouncement of some of the giants of western intellectual and political establishment, such as Hume ('. . . the negro is naturally inferior to the whites . . .'), Thomas Jefferson ('. . . the blacks . . . are inferior to the whites on the endowments of both body and mind . . .'), for Hegel with his Africa comparable to a land of childhood still enveloped in the dark mantle of the night as far as the development of self-conscious history was concerned. Hegel's statement that there was nothing harmonious with humanity to be found in the African character is representative of the racist images of Africans and Africa such a colonial child was bound to encounter in the literature of the colonial languages. The results could be disastrous.

[. . .]

In history books and popular commentaries on Africa, too much has been made of the supposed differences in the policies of the various colonial powers, the British indirect rule (or the pragmatism of the British in their lack of a cultural programme!) and the French and Portuguese conscious programme of cultural assimilation. These are a matter of detail and emphasis. The final effect was the same: [. . .] Chinua Achebe's gratitude in 1964 to English – 'those of us who have inherited the English language may not be in a position to appreciate the value of the inheritance'. The assumptions behind the practice of those of us who have abandoned our mother-tongues are not different either. [. . .] It is the final triumph of a system of domination when the dominated start singing its virtues.

ISSUES TO CONSIDER

❏ In his book *Decolonising the Mind* Ngũgĩ (1986: xiv) declares: 'This book, *Decolonising the Mind*, is my farewell to English as a vehicle for any of my writings. From now on it is Gĩkũyũ and Kiswahili all the way. However, I hope that through the age-old medium of translation I shall be able to continue dialogue with all.' Achebe, on the other hand, argues eloquently in favour of writing in English, but in one adapted to its 'New English' users. With which of these two perspectives do you find yourself in greater sympathy?

❏ Achebe argues above that 'the price a world language must be prepared to pay is submission to many different kinds of use'. How far do you agree in terms of both literary and non-literary use? It might help you, as regards non-literary use, to refer back to the earlier sections of strand 4, especially B4.

❏ How similar do you find Ngũgĩ's views on the link between language and culture to those of Pennycook (see D1)? On the other hand, in what respects do Achebe's views seem to you to be closer to those of Bisong (see C1)?

IS LANGUAGE STILL POWER?

The book *Language is Power* (Honey 1997) promotes the author's belief that 'schoolchildren should be given maximum access to standard English' (p. 5), and attacks what he sees as the obstacle to such access: 'the consensus that has existed among linguists . . . for at least three decades now, around the hypothesis that I will call "linguistic equality", the notion that all languages, and all dialects of any language, are equally good'. This 'liberal orthodoxy', Honey believes, far from protecting underprivileged children, has 'inflicted lasting educational damage' on them (back cover) and is in need of remediation in both Britain and the US.

In 1998 a book taking a rather different view was published: *Language Myths* edited by the linguist Laurie Bauer and the sociolinguist Peter Trudgill. This book sets out to do precisely the opposite of Honey's. That is, its twenty-one articles each take a particular belief about 'correct' English, and demonstrate its mythical nature. The article reproduced below focuses on English grammar, discussing it in precisely the 'liberal' manner so despised by Honey. It is followed by two articles which appeared in May 2001 in the Singaporean newspaper, *The Straits Times*, one by the prescriptivist Alfred Lee lamenting the deterioration in the use of English by its native speakers in Britain, the other a response two days later from the non-prescriptivist Dennis Bloodworth.

Bad grammar is slovenly

Lesley Milroy (reprinted from Laurie Bauer and Peter Trudgill (eds) *Language Myths*, London: Penguin, 1998: 94–101)

**Lesley
Milroy**

Like most language myths this one begs a number of questions, such as the following:

What is meant by 'bad grammar'?

What is meant by 'grammar'?

Can particular sentences of the English language reasonably be described as 'slovenly' – or 'lacking in care and precision', according to one dictionary definition? The quest for answers exposes the myth to critical scrutiny.

Newspaper features, letter columns and the mailboxes of the BBC are good places to find complaints about bad grammar. A rich harvest may be gathered if language use becomes the subject of public debate or if current educational policies are focusing on English teaching and testing. In Britain recently many judgemental remarks have been aired about 'Estuary English', the name given to a variety of the language which is spreading both socially and geographically.

Examples of specific constructions often described as bad grammar can be placed in at least three categories. The first, exemplified in sentences (1)–(3) along with the (presumed) correct form in italics, regularly occur in the speech and writing of educated people.

(1) Who am I speaking to? / *To whom am I speaking?*

(2) Martha's two children are completely different to each other /
    Martha's two children are completely different from each other.

(3) I want to quickly visit the library / *I want to visit the library quickly.*

Two well-known 'errors' appear in (1), namely the preposition in the sentence final position and the nominative form of the relative pronoun 'who' rather than the oblique form 'whom' which is prescribed after a preposition. In (2) the expression 'different to' is used rather than the prescribed 'different from'; and in (3) there is a 'split infinitive'. In fact, the 'correct' versions were prescribed as such relatively recently in the history of the language, as part of the flurry of scholarly activity associated with the codification of the English language in the eighteenth century. Since the goal of codification is to define a particular form as standard, this process entailed intolerance of the range of choices which speakers and writers had hitherto taken for granted. In earlier centuries all these 'errors' appeared in highly sophisticated writing; in 1603, for example, Thomas Decker wrote 'How much different art thou to this cursed spirit here?'

Different rationalizations were introduced to support these new prescriptions. The model of Latin was invoked to argue that a preposition should not end a sentence, that the inflected form of *who* should not appear anywhere other than in the subject of the sentence, and that an infinitive should not be split. The reason advanced by one writer of a popular manual of correctness for preferring 'different from' is that 'different to' is illogical, since no one would say 'similar from'. But it is not difficult to construct an equally logical argument in support of 'different to', since it falls into a set of words with comparative meanings such as *similar, equal, superior*, which require *to*. Not only are prescriptive arguments difficult to sustain, but if taken seriously they are likely to create problems. For example, 'Who am I speaking to?' is normal in most contexts, while 'To whom am I speaking?' will generally be interpreted as marking social distance. Thus the real difference between these forms is stylistic; both are good English sentences in appropriate contexts. Sometimes an attempt to follow the prescribed rules produces odd results.

(4) A good author needs to develop a clear sense of who she is writing for.
(5) A good author needs to develop a clear sense of for whom she is writing.

The prescription which outlaws (4) and yields (5), does not work because it is not based on a principled analysis of the structure of English but is a response to cultural and political pressures. By the eighteenth century Britain needed a standardized language to meet the needs of geographically scattered colonial government servants and to facilitate mass education. It did not too much matter which of a set of variants emerged as standard, as long as only one was specified as such. The prescribed standard was codified in grammars (such as Robert Lowth's) and dictionaries (the most famous being Dr Johnson's). No systematic grammar of English existed at that time, but Latin had a particular prestige as the lingua franca of scholars throughout Europe; hence the appeal not only to logic but to the model of Latin to justify particular prescriptions. But as we shall see shortly, English rules are very different from Latin rules, though equally complex; like all Germanic languages, English quite naturally places prepositions in sentence final position.

By 'bad grammar' then is sometimes meant expressions which are not in line with even unrealistic prescriptions. But what is grammar? Our myth refers to a *prescriptive* grammar, which is not a systematic description of a language, but a sort of linguistic etiquette, essentially an arbitrary set of *dos* and *don'ts*. [. . .]

Prescriptive rules are never as complex as properly formulated descriptive rules, and are easily dealt with by descriptive grammars. For example, *different from/to* would simply be specified as options; the split infinitive would not be an issue since the infinitive form of the verb is *visit*, not *to visit*; 'Who am I speaking to?' would be viewed as a normal sentence following the rules of English.

Sentences like (11) and (12) are also subject to popular criticism:

(11) So I said to our Trish and our Sandra, 'Yous wash the dishes.'
(12) Was you watching the game when the rain started?

Unlike (1)–(6), which are regularly used by educated speakers and writers, both of these are characteristic of low-status speakers. They were recorded respectively in Belfast and London, although the grammatical patterns which they illustrate are found elsewhere. It is the low social status of these speakers, indexed by details of their language use, which seems in this case to form the basis of negative evaluation. In such a way is social class prejudice disguised as neutral intellectual commentary, and for this reason one linguist has described linguistic prescriptivism as the last open door to discrimination. But note that (11) makes a systematic distinction between 'you' (singular) and 'yous' (plural) similar to many languages of the world but lacking in Standard English. Thus (11) cannot be argued to be in any sense linguistically impoverished (another common rationalization in defence of prescribed variants). Languages and dialects simply vary in the meaning distinctions they encode, regardless of their social status.

Note that (12) is a perfectly formulated question. Earlier in the history of English *was* and *were* in such sentences were acceptable alternatives (recall that the process of standardization has narrowed the range of socially and stylistically acceptable linguistic choices). But if we ask whether such sentences are 'slovenly' ('lacking in care and precision') we must surely concede that the care and precision needed to implement the question-formation rule is considerable, placing in perspective the triviality of requiring *were* with a plural subject.

Let us look finally at two sentences which seem to be subject to criticism for yet a different reason:

(13) Me and Andy went out to the park.
(14) it's very awkward/it's difficult mind you/with a class of thirty odd/occasionally with the second form/you'll get you know/well we'll we'll have erm a debate/

Neither (13) nor (14) are clearly marked as belonging to a particular region, but between them they display a number of characteristics of informal spoken English. Uttered by an adolescent boy, (13) is criticized on the grounds that the wrong pronoun case (*me* instead of *I*) is used inside a conjoined phrase. Speakers are so conscious of this Latin-based prescription that even linguistically self-conscious and quite prescriptively minded individuals sometimes hypercorrect and use *I* where *me* is prescribed (a particularly large number of complaints about these patterns of pronoun use are received by the BBC). Thus Margaret Thatcher once announced, 'It is not for you and I to condemn the Malawi economy,' and Bill Clinton pleaded, 'Give Al Gore and I a chance.' But a systematic analysis of English grammar reveals underlying rules which permit variation between *me* and *I* only within conjoined phrases. Thus, adolescent boys do not habitually say 'Me went out to the park,' Clinton would not plead 'Give I a chance,' and not even Margaret Thatcher would have said 'It is not for I to condemn the Malawi economy.' With respect to *prescriptive* rules, there is often such a disparity between what speakers believe is correct and what they actually do; but *descriptive* rules are neither subject to violation nor are they part of our conscious knowledge of language.

Although conversation is often thought to be unstructured, ungrammatical and slovenly (presumably when judged against the norms of writing or formal speech), its complex organizational principles are quite different from those of planned spoken or written discourse; it is not simply spoken prose. Transcribed from a coffee-break conversation between two teachers, (14) is typical of informal conversation in its chunks (marked by slashes), which do not correspond to sentences of written English. Also in evidence are fillers such as *erm*, hesitations (marked by full stops), repairs, repetitions, and discourse tokens such as *you know, mind you*. Most of these features are attributable to conversation's interactive, online mode of production, and the two discourse tokens function as 'participation markers', signalling to the interlocutor that interactional involvement or response is expected. Thus, it hardly seems appropriate to describe even the apparently unstructured utterance (14) as 'slovenly'.

So what are we to say in conclusion about our current 'myth'? 'Bad grammar' is a cover term to describe a number of different kinds of English expressions. Some are widely used by educated speakers and writers but are outlawed by traditional prescriptions which are difficult to sustain; some appear to attract covert social prejudice by virtue of their association with low-status groups; and some follow the very characteristic but still rule-governed patterns of informal speech. All are perfectly grammatical, providing evidence of a complex body of rules which constitute mental grammars, the unconscious knowledge which speakers have of their own language. In comparison, the prescriptions which are recommended as 'good grammar' are revealed as at best marginal and frequently as unrealistic and trivial.

English to get English lessons

Alfred Lee (reprinted from the *Straits Times*, Tuesday 15 May 2001)

A society has been set up to teach the English language to adults in England.

Retired newspaper sub-editor John Richards was so appalled at public misuse of apostrophes that he formed the Apostrophe Protection Society.

After news of his society was revealed, hundreds of people, including teachers, writers, academics and others rushed to support his campaign and to join his society.

They have now decided to expand the aims of the organisation – and to highlight common errors in English made by English people.

"English people are supposed to write excellent English – but many can't," said Mr Richards, 75.

"My local fruiterer writes on posters that he sells bunch's of banana's. The public library has a sign saying that it has CD's. The largest supermarket in town promises 1000's of products at reduced prices."

"I was so irritated by the mistakes in the use of apostrophes that I had to do something."

Headmaster Anthony Macrory said the group had "a tremendous fight on our hands, with the Internet and e-mails responsible for 'weblish' and mobile phone text messages undoing all that is taught in English classes".

In "weblish", e-mails are often sent in lower case or all in capital letters, because Internet users are too lazy to use the capital letter key.

Punctuation is often left out. It is as though apostrophes, full stops and initial capital letters for proper nouns never existed, he said, adding that in the world of text messages, abbreviations and acronyms fly through cyberspace.

"Good English has nothing to do with messages that read RUF2T – Are you free to talk?; CUL8R – See you later; IJC2SaILuvU – I just called to say I love you," he said.

A recent survey placed the literacy of adults in England among the lowest of any developed country.

When Britain's education authority tried to fill some administrative posts, only six of 33 candidates with A-level qualifications passed a test in literacy.

One 19-year-old applicant, asked to write a short essay on how he would organise a campaign against the use of narcotics, started by saying: "I wud reed all the leaflets and complied a questionair concerning how the bodies system was effected by drugs."

As Mr Tony Maher of the Plain English Campaign put it: "Sadly, there is a huge army of grown-up English people who are illiterate."

"They cannot spell properly and their grammar and punctuation are atrocious."

Professor Roger Holliday, an English expert, said he believed that things have been going downhill in Britain ever since the Rolling Stones sang, "I Can't Get No Satisfaction".

CHECKLIST: Common mistakes

- ❏ **Split infinitives:** Its five-year mission is *to boldly go* where no man has has gone before. Should be: To go boldly.
- ❏ **You, I and me:** *Between you and I,* Nicole Kidman and Tom Cruise were always going to separate. Should be: between you and me.
- ❏ **To lay and lie:** I *always lay* down to sleep after a big meal. Should be: Always lie.
- ❏ **Who or whom:** *Who do you think* you are kidding, Mr Hitler? Should be: Whom do you think.
- ❏ **Herewith:** Enclosed *herewith with* this letter, please find another one. Should be: Delete the with.
- ❏ **Prepositions:** That was the Prime Minister I gave my vote *to*. The sentence should not end with a preposition.

Go on, dare to boldly split the infinitive

Dennis Bloodworth (reprinted from the *Straits Times*, Thursday 17 May, 2001)

I was fascinated by the box ("Checklist: Common mistakes") which accompanied the report, "English to get English lessons" (ST, May 15).

The Straits Times listed splitting infinitives as one common mistake that people make. But what do the pundits say about this?

In his Penguin Dictionary Of Troublesome Words, Bill Bryson writes that "one (misconception) is the belief that the split infinitive is a grammatical error. It is not. Another is that the split infinitive is widely condemned. That too is untrue".

He cites, as an example of the folly of religiously avoiding a split infinitive, this sentence from The Times (of London): "The education system had failed adequately to meet the needs of industry and commerce". Failed adequately? Well, thank goodness for that – or, no, wait a minute . . .

Sir Ernest Gowers writes about the split infinitive: "Broadminded grammarians have described it as . . . a bad rule, and many people (including so good a writer as Bernard Shaw) have regarded it as a mere fetish".

Eric Partridge quotes H.W. Fowler, who said that, though not desirable in itself, the split infinitive was preferable to ambiguity and "patent artificiality", citing as an example, "in not combining to forbid flatly hostilities". Forbid flatly hostilities? What on earth does it mean?

Fowler himself points out that to avoid that patent artificiality, Byron wrote "to slowly trace the forest's shady scene" and Thomas Hardy, "she wants to honestly and legally marry that man".

He quotes sentences from Bernard Levin, Anita Brookner, John Updike, Julian Barnes, Iris Murdoch and others to show that when literary sense and rhythm and grace, clarity and style demanded it, they were ready to split with the best, and to hell with academic nitpickers.

The Times commented in fun in 1992: "The most diligent search can find no modern grammarian to pedantically, to dogmatically, to invariably condemn a split infinitive".

The ST box correctly attacks "Between you and I". But then it denounces "I always lay down to sleep after a big meal". It should be "always lie", you say. But you are not "always" right. If you are talking about the past, it is "lay" that is correct.

Next comes "who or whom". Your checklist quotes "Who do you think you are kidding, Mr Hitler?", saying it should be "whom do you think . . ." Spot on.

Except that (if I remember rightly) this was the first line of a music-hall ditty sung during World War II in Cockney, and might well have begun (phonetically) not with "who" or "whom" at all, but "'Oo do you fink . . . , Mr' itler?" And anyway that was about 60 years ago.

Do you really consider it a valid example of bad English today that you should pass on to Singaporeans in your newspaper? Are you suggesting that instead of "Who do you think you're talking to?", they should learn to say "To whom do you think you are talking?"

And what about these examples from Fowler that flout the rigid rules you echo: "Who wouldst thou strike?" (The Bible) and "To who, my Lord?" (Shakespeare).

Gowers quotes Addison ("Who would I see there?") and Winston Churchill ("Moves made to displace their leader by someone whom they imagined would be a more vigorous President"). Partridge simply wants to abandon "whom" altogether.

Finally, we come to prepositions: A sentence should not end with a preposition, says your box.

Really? Bryson writes: "Anyone who believes that it is wrong to end a sentence with a preposition . . . is about a century out of date . . . Today, happily, it is universally condemned as a ridiculous affectation".

Gowers: "Do not hesitate to end a sentence with a preposition if your ear tells you it is where the preposition goes best . . . no good writer ever heeded the rule, except Dryden".

Fowler: "One of the most persistent myths about prepositions is that they . . . should not be placed at the end of a clause or sentence". Shakespeare obviously would have agreed with him; take "Who servest though (sic) under?" Or "Who do you speak to?"

Dennis Bloodworth

Pundits have asked how else would you write "This bed hasn't been slept in" or "What is the world coming to?". Winston Churchill reputedly gave his opinion on the matter by saying "This is the sort of English up with which I will not put".

So what have you scored? According to my calculations, two out of six – all right, two and a half. I certainly wouldn't advise you to take the hot seat in Who Wants To Be A Millionaire?

But, more seriously, your London correspondent Alfred Lee has excelled by finding yet another story that puts the British in a bad light, this one about their ignorance of their own language. The ignorance is real enough, unhappily.

But, surely, that is all the more reason for not misleading poor Singaporeans with bogus dogma when they are already struggling with the wiles of English, the writing of which is an art, not a geometrical theorem in a secondary-school exam.

I feel that Mr Lee should at least make sure that his sources know what they are talking about. Or do you really believe that sentence ought to read "know about what they are talking"? Bunkum!

ISSUES TO CONSIDER

❑ How far do you agree with Milroy and Bloodworth, and how far do you think that Honey's and Lee's positions (which are shared by many members of the British general public and right-wing press) are valid? In particular, do you believe that standard language use still provides people with power, and vice versa, or do you think that things are changing, e.g. among younger users of English?

❑ In Mugglestone's view (1995: 49), 'Prescriptive ideology . . . in spite of its professed egalitarianism, instead merely reinforces notions of the cultural hegemony of one social group above others.' She describes as '"fictions of empowerment"' the attempts of eighteenth-century elocutionists such as Thomas Sheridan and John Walker to encourage the disadvantaged to 'emulate their "betters"' on the grounds that use of the standard would be a social leveller. Do you agree with Mugglestone (and therefore disagree with Honey) that the 'language is power' argument actually works against rather than for the disadvantaged in society?

❑ What about the way Milroy herself writes? To what extent does she practise or not practise what she preaches? Identify instances of 'grammatical' and ungrammatical' use according to prescriptive rules.

❑ Milroy mentions speech/writing differences. In your view, do her arguments hold good for both, or are they more appropriate to one or other channel? (You might like to refer back to the section on speech and writing in C5.)

❑ Milroy talks about native-speaker intuitions. Consider this in the light of what has been said earlier in this strand about the New Englishes. Do you find it surprising that a sociolinguist should argue that native speakers of English have intuitions about the grammar of the language and not consider the possibility that speakers of New Englishes may have intuitions about their own varieties of English?

❑ Prepare a questionnaire that will enable you to compare the attitudes of older and younger groups in your own country towards specific so-called 'incorrect' usages (using either your own examples or those provided above by Milroy, Bloodworth and Lee), and to the present-day grammatical competence in general of native speakers of English. After you have administered your questionnaire to a sufficient number of respondents (I suggest a minimum of six for each of the two groups), look for patterns relating to the age of the respondents. Do you think you would obtain different responses if you asked these questions in a native speaker English-speaking country if yours is a non-native English-speaking one, or vice versa? Why might this be?

WHAT DOES IT MEAN TO SPEAK AN INTERNATIONAL VARIETY OF ENGLISH?

This unit contains four extracts. The first is from an article by Marko Modiano, 'International English in the global village' published in *English Today*. It was followed in the journal by six solicited comments, two of which are included here. Finally, Modiano's reply to his critics is reproduced.

International English in the global village

Marko Modiano (reprinted from *English Today* Vol.15 No.2, 1999: 23–5)

[. . .]
As English takes on the responsibilities of a *lingua franca*, non-native speakers are taking a more active role in the development of the language, not only in respect to the manner in which they develop educational models for the teaching of local varieties, but also in their understanding of how the language is used in cross-cultural communication. Understandably, when observing the language as it is used internationally, they experience a great deal of multiplicity, not only in pronunciation and vocabulary, but also in other respects. This indicates, as I see it, that in the teaching of EIL [English as an International Language], emphasis should be placed on a descriptive as opposed to a prescriptive model. Such positioning is in direct contrast to the near-native proficiency BrE [British English] educational standard which has been successfully promoted and practiced in many parts of the world.
[. . .]
    From an EIL perspective, Kachru's conceptualization of "inner circle varieties" is problematical. Kachru's model, for example, is interpreted in different ways, depending on the manner in which the observer views the language. The centralized

Marko Modiano

position of the major varieties might be taken as a given by some observers of the English language, while it may be considered inaccurate among proficient speakers of the language living and working outside of this privileged circle. Moreover, in allowing the "major varieties" a symbolic central positioning, it is easy to assume that all of the speakers of these varieties are proficient in the language in a more global sense. This is not the case. A large number of L1 speakers living in regions where the major varieties are rooted do not speak varieties which are easily comprehensible internationally (assuming that they are incapable of code-switching). These speakers are not as worthy of a central position when compared to other speakers of the language, whether they be L1 speakers of standardized varieties or second/foreign language speakers who are excellent communicators in an international context. For these reasons I find Kachru's model less useful when viewing the development of EIL.

Granted, the paradigm of inner, outer and expanding circle is an excellent point of departure for determining the development of the language in various parts of the world. Indeed, the legitimization and codification process starts with the *recognition* and *communicative value* of local varieties. Moreover, a break with near-native proficiency models in language education is in fact a logical step (Kachru 1982). We must ease off outmoded beliefs in the superiority of BrE, and indeed even AmE, and instead embrace a more modern understanding of the language. In view of the excellent work carried out in this field, my aim is not to devalue the Kachru model. Nevertheless, Kachru's definition of the inner circle re-establishes the notion that the language is the property of specific groups, and that correct usage is determined by experts who speak a prestige variety. This inner-circle position indicates that English is a language which comes from a geographical location, the spread being the result of the historic exploits of specific peoples. Moreover, Kachru's paradigm supports a belief that the language is associated with distinctive frames (in this case, with the Anglo-American and Christian sphere of influence). These assumptions are, in my opinion, indicative of an antiquated view of the English language.

It is clear, in historical terms, that English is an Indo-European language. As a Germanic language it is based in the tongues once spoken by the northern Germanic tribes who brought their language and culture to the island of Britain after the withdrawal of the Roman legions. England then served as home for these Germanic nomads who migrated across the channel. From there, many of these people continued, not only to unsettled areas, but also to populated regions where the language continued to evolve. In the post-colonial era, increasing numbers of people are adopting the language, not only to communicate with native speakers, but also for communication within their own communities. These new speech communities have developed cultural activities such as literature and film in English. They often conduct government and law proceedings in English. Scientific research, as well, is published in English. Moreover, there are quite often domestic news services and television and radio programming in English [. . .]

As a result, English now has relevance to vast numbers of people living outside the confines of the "English speaking world" (defined, as it is by some, as the regions where the major varieties are dominant). Thus, the spread of English has not been restricted in any geographical sense, and in time the language has come to influence life in many parts of the world. Michael Toolan, discussing "New English" as the "English used in mainstream public discourse in countries where English is a major native language" and "Global" as "public international English", notes that "these two standard Englishes are increasingly treated not as Anglo-Saxon and metropolitan properties, found by or shared with others, but as resources owned by larger constituencies of users . . . In the case of Global, its non-English majority of users are increasingly claiming ownership of it" (1997: 3). This indicates, clearly, that there is a growing awareness of the role which non-native speakers play in the development of EIL.

[Modiano goes on to describe his 'Centripetal circles of international English' which places those who are 'proficient in international English' whether native speaker or non-native speaker at the centre, surrounded by those who have 'native and foreign language proficiency', with his third circle being occupied by learners of English and his outermost circle by 'people who do not know English'. See A3 for further details and diagram.]

Replies to Modiano

Loreto Todd (reprinted from *English Today* Vol.15 No.2, 1999: 30–1)

It has become a truism of contemporary descriptions of English that it is the most widely used language the world has ever known. Because of its extensive use, scholars have, inevitably perhaps, tried to pigeonhole it. Traditional descriptions offered a binary division: as mother tongue and other tongue, with 'other tongue' being segmented further into such categories as 'second language', 'third language', 'foreign language', 'link language', 'working language'.

While linguists have endeavoured to provide increasingly subtle classifications, based on circles (concentric, spoked or parabolic), speakers and writers have been largely indifferent to whether they were in some privileged inner circle of standard speakers or some expanding outer circle of not-quite-standard users. They have, it would appear, been content to use the language – and to mould it – to suit their individual needs. As early as the 1940s, Raja Rao in his foreword to *Kanthapura* realised that his medium, Indian English, could not and *should* not be identical with that of mother tongue speakers, and Chinua Achebe expressed the views not only of Nigerians when he insisted:

> So my answer to the question '*Can an African ever learn English well enough to be able to use it effectively in creative writing?*' is certainly yes. If on the other hand you ask '*Can he ever learn to use it as a native speaker?*', I should say, I hope not. It is neither necessary nor desirable for him to be able to do so. The price a world language must be prepared to pay is submission to many different kinds of use (*Transition*, 1965: 29–30).

Loreto Todd

Modiano's paper is, I am sure, a well-intentioned attempt to impose a degree of order on the apparently chaotic systems subsumed by the label 'English'. However, he should be aware of certain facts:

❏ Local varieties are not and have not been regarded as 'sub-standard' for at least a generation.
❏ Most users of the language are aware of the difference between their spoken 'language of slippered ease' and the register required for formal occasions.
❏ Phrases like 'inner circle' and comments like 'These speakers are not worthy' are judgmental and largely unhelpful. Are dialect speakers to be expelled to a 'place of darkness, where there shall be weeping and gnashing of teeth'?
❏ Writers and speakers know, and have known for a long time, that the English language belongs to no one country or group or race or class. They are also aware that certain 'rules' must be followed if full international communication is to continue.

The English language, in its many forms, is today a medium for speakers in every continent. It is used by people who are multilingual and by those who have lost their ancestral mother tongue. For many, it is selected almost unthinkingly as the natural medium, but others echo the viewpoint of James Joyce's Stephen Daedalus in *Portrait of the Artist as a Young Man*:

> [This] language, so familiar and so foreign, will always be for me an acquired speech. I have not made or accepted its words. My voice holds them at bay. My soul frets in the shadow of his language. (Joyce 1969: 189)

In modifying English, they have found it possible to keep alive a world view that might otherwise have disappeared, for there is some truth in the claim that the Irish playwright Brian Friel makes through the character Hugh Mór:

> [It] can happen that a civilisation can be imprisoned in a linguistic contour that no longer matches the landscape of . . . fact. (*Translations*, p. 43)

But I shall also highlight the sadness and pain of all people who have lost or are losing their mother tongues. They carry an extraordinary emotional burden: namely that we can lose an entire civilisation when we lose a language. As George Steiner points out: "Each [dying language] takes with it a storehouse of consciousness" (1975: 54).

Every one of us probably feels a sentimental attachment to the notion that a multilingual country is rich in linguistic resources and that we should be wary about following any plan that might limit or destroy such resources for ever. More and more of us, however, are choosing to write in English and, wittingly or unwittingly, we are diminishing the linguistic richness of the planet. It is certainly true that the Irish, the Africans, the Asians, the Amerindians and the people from the Caribbean have not been content to take and use a ready-made English. Rather, many of them have transmuted English into a hybrid tongue, a half-way house between their indigenous mother tongues and this infinitely useful lingua franca. My concern is that successive generations will move closer and closer to

International English, helping people to understand each other better but, in the process, causing the slow death, not only of their languages, but of their cultures.

Alan S. Kaye

Alan S. Kaye (reprinted from *English Today* Vol.15 No.2, 1999: 31–3)

What exactly is meant by the term 'International English' (IE), or, as it is referred to in this essay, 'English as an International Language' (EIL), assuming that there is, in fact, such an English variety which exists on a par with British, American, Canadian, New Zealand, Australian, South African, etc., counterparts? How does one say for example 'What's your name?', 'I love you', or 'Pass me the salt, please!', in each of the aforementioned? We can point to the phonetic differences among these different dialects, and we can even compare their narrow phonetic transcriptions, including intonational structure; however, the words in each of the illustrative sentences remain the same in each variety mentioned.

Trying to elucidate the exact nature of what the designation IE must involve, we can complicate the picture slightly by focusing on other kinds of English, such as Indian, Pakistani, Sri Lankan, Kenyan, and Nigerian English, etc., and we can make matters even more involved by mentioning the various English pidgins and creoles from around the world. Each of the aforementioned varieties of English can, I think, be precisely defined, giving illustrative examples for each. Of course, there are many subdialects, including sociolects for each of these, depending on the age, educational level, sex, profession and, most importantly, level of proficiency of the speaker, among other factors which need not concern us here.

What then does the term IE actually entail? It is much easier, I think, to say what IE *is not* than what it is. It may not be spoken, presumably, with an 'Indian' (i.e. retroflex), East/West/South African, Middle Eastern (Arabic, Iranian, Kurdish) accent, etc. IE is supposed to be accentless – or is it? From the phonetic point of view, as is well known, there are numerous possibilities for pronouncing English, depending on the country or region in which it is being used. It is unrealistic to expect IE to be otherwise. It, too, has a wide range of different acceptable pronunciations. The grammatical systems of IE are also similarly linked to the various national, regional, and local dialects. In other words, if we may legitimately make reference to IE at all in any meaningful taxonomic way, it must be viewed as being directly tied to the way in which English is used in a particular area. The IE of someone from India is surely recognizably different from the IE spoken by an Australian or a Briton. In fact, the IE of a Briton can be generally trichotomized into a Scots, Welsh and English variety.

Let us now specifically address the author's contentions. According to Modiano, IE is spoken by native as well as non-native speakers. In this regard, it is similar to all other varieties of English. Natives code-switch from their native dialect, while non-natives speak it in accordance with their levels of proficiency representative of distinct interlanguages. With reference to this latter point, the author maintains: 'Understandably, when observing the language as it is used internationally, [non-natives] experience a great deal of multiplicity, not only in pronunciation and vocabulary, but also in other respects'. Further, an implicit value judgement is proffered by Modiano on IE as he defines it to be 'a general term which includes all of the varieties which function well in cross-cultural communication', and 'this speaker of EIL need not necessarily be an L1 speaker'.

But what is meant by 'function well'? I do not agree with the author's pronouncement that 'good [IE] communicators are easily recognizable, and that the same can be said of their opposite'. The word 'good' reflects a prescriptive indoctrination, and I fully support the author's enlightened perspective that 'in the teaching of EIL, emphasis should be placed on a descriptive as opposed to a prescriptive model'. Thus, I have difficulty comprehending how a proficient non-native IE speaker can be better equipped to 'define and develop English as a tool in cross-cultural communication'. Is not the very concept of a non-native IE fuzzy and ill-defined? Is it not axiomatic in modern linguistics that native speakers play the sole role in defining a language and its dialects, at least insofar as grammatical utterances and correct pronunciation are concerned? While I certainly agree that English has many non-native speakers with various levels of proficiency and competence, it remains unclear how their ill-defined data can be used along with native-speaker input of all varieties of the language to produce an accurate description of IE.

To sum up, there are many insurmountable problems with Modiano's designation IE. To better understand how we might deal with this subject in the future, let me offer the example of Modern Standard Arabic (MSA), an artificial, superposed variety of this Middle Eastern language in use in the Arab world today in formal contexts. It is important, first of all, to realize that MSA has no native speakers. Thus its phonology, for example, is interrelated with that of the speaker's well-defined spoken vernacular. An Arab's intuition of MSA is, therefore, directly dependent on his/her colloquial dialect. However, a non-native speaker has little or no influence, in my opinion, on the contemporary structure of the language: that is, on MSA's current development. If the term IE is to have any legitimacy among linguists, then it should perhaps designate an artificial, superposed variety of the language. What would be very interesting to study about this particular sense of IE is the influence of the non-native speaker on the structure and vocabulary of the language.

Rethinking ELT

Marko Modiano (reprinted from *English Today* Vol.16 No.2, 2000: 30–4)

Loreto Todd contends that "speakers and writers have been largely indifferent to whether they were in some privileged inner circle of standard speakers or some expanding circle of not-quite-standard users". In fact, how one "positions" speakers and writers of English in such paradigms profoundly affects their lives because such theorizing has considerable impact on the development and implementation of the educational norms. For language planners, there is an awareness that the use of specific educational standards (which have previously been established through the power-politics of the "privileged inner circle"), indeed, profoundly affect the cultural contexts which accompany the learning of a foreign tongue, and thus the language behavior of learners.

D

Marko
Modiano

Moreover, in claiming that "local varieties are not and have not been regarded as 'sub-standard' for at least a generation", Todd, I am afraid, is being far too generous in her appraisal of the players in our profession. It is true, at least in the literature, that there is an understanding that all forms of English are equally valid mediums of communication. The notion that all languages and varieties are capable of being the vehicle of advanced thought, high technology, and literature is currently being promoted. In practice, however, it is evident that there are those who insist on BrE with RP because they are convinced that it best equips the student with the skills required to get on in the world. John Honey, in his *Standard English and its Enemies* (1997), presents such an argument. We know that there is an aversion on the part of some native speakers to accents both native-tongue and non-native speaker-based. Such prejudice is found among English language practitioners working in Europe who in upholding traditional practices effectively promote the notion that other forms of the tongue are less prestigious in comparison to "proper" English. This attitude, which creates systems of exclusion as opposed to inclusion, is still with us.

[. . . T]here is a movement in the UK toward greater acceptance of accents. [. . .] But despite the liberalization policies of the BBC and of the British educational establishment to promote greater acceptance of the many accents flourishing in the UK, it is nevertheless the case that some accents are not very useful for cross-cultural purposes (as is the case with regional dialects). When I state that the native speaker who is not able to effectively communicate cross-culturally lacks the skills required of those who occupy a central position in my paradigm, it is not my intention that such individuals, as Todd claims, should "be expelled to a place of darkness, where there shall be weeping and gnashing of teeth". The point which begs to be made here is that there is no difference between native and non-native speakers in this respect. That is to say, if it is the case that speakers of English who are not capable of communicating cross-culturally must learn a form of EIL if they want to access the global village, this is equally valid for all speakers of the language. Many non-native speakers have experienced feelings of inadequacy and frustration because they feel marginalized by those who possess more "prestigious" forms of English, and this is something which has been exploited in traditional educational settings to coerce students into embracing Eurocentric notions of "high status" accents and language usage. Moreover, there has been little effort to elevate the standing of non-native accents beyond the role of the comprehension exercise.

It appears to be the case that Todd wants native speakers who are not able to speak a form of EIL to be treated differently from non-native speakers in the same situation. Addressing the lack of logic in this standpoint is one of the central tenets of my paradigm. It is of paramount importance, when constructing parameters for a lingua franca, that all of the speakers of the language are on equal footing. Thus, it is equally regrettable, both for the native as well as the non-native speaker, when systems of marginalization are operative. I certainly applaud all of the efforts being made in the UK to bring speakers of regional accent into the fold of educational and public life. Such liberalization processes, which are certainly valid for domestic purposes, are equally valid processes of democratization for a lingua franca.

Marko
Modiano

There is another point that Todd makes which I am convinced needs to be challenged, and that is her claim that "writers and speakers know, and have known for a long time, that the English language belongs to no one country or group or race or class". If Todd is referring to "writers and speakers" active in contemporary sociolinguistic studies, her observation is, for the most part, true. But there are still rather large groups, lay-people as well as academics and other professionals, who feel that English is something which is possessed by the British or the native speaker of the so-called major varieties (AmE, BrE, NZE, AusE, SAfE, CanE). Others, they argue, speak something less "acceptable". This becomes a problem when such notions are adopted by non-native and native speaking language instructors who use this view to enforce traditional practices in their ELT activities.

Alan S. Kaye questions whether EIL is a variety in the sense that AmE or BrE are varieties. As stated above, it is apparent that EIL is not at this point in time a variety. Instead, it is a conceptualization of a lingua franca, and promotes educational practices supportive of cross-cultural communication. To answer a simple question with a simple answer, "what's your name?" in EIL is "what's your name?". The same is true of "I love you", and "pass me the salt, please". This is because these phrases are part of what is referred to as "core English", which in my view are those features of the language often used and commonly understood by the majority of native and competent non-native speakers.

In delineating what is *not* EIL, Kaye presumes that it may not be spoken with a number of accents. This is, naturally, not the case. There are a good many speakers of English who have an "Indian" or "Middle Eastern" accent who are perfectly capable of communicating in an international context. As is the case with *all* accents in my paradigm, and this holds true for both native as well as non-native speakers, those who are capable of making themselves understood internationally without too much effort on the part of the interlocutor can be defined as speakers of a form of EIL. The understanding is that there are no systems of exclusion beyond the realm of understandability. A taxonomy for pronunciation (and lexical usage) must then, by necessity, be first of all descriptive, and secondly, designed to accommodate a tolerable number of alternatives. This is already the case in the standard college dictionaries, where alternative pronunciations and listings of synonyms are the rule rather than the exception. EIL, by necessity, will also include alternatives, the criterion being that the forms are comprehensible to the majority of native and non-native speakers of the language.

One problem, moreover, is that Kaye, like many of his colleagues, is not willing to accept a claim that such a selection of features can, nevertheless, be the foundation of an educational model. Here, we need to allow the practical and functional sensibility which all of us possess to take the upper hand. We know instinctively when a feature of language is useful in communication. We have a great deal of experience. This is true of both native and non-native speakers. As to how this leads to defining the language as a lingua franca, it is apparent, and certainly true for the EU, that while most native speakers primarily use the language to communicate with other native speakers, the non-native speakers have

D

Marko
Modiano

the language as a tool for cross-cultural communication. Thus, as a rule, it is the *non-native speaker* who has the most experience in the use of the lingua franca as a medium of cross-cultural communication. The competent non-native speaker must, for such reasons, be actively involved in the development of EIL educational strategies.

It is not axiomatic, as Kaye claims, "that native speakers play the sole role in defining a language and its dialects, at least insofar as grammatical utterances and correct pronunciation are concerned". Such a view, while prevalent in traditionalist thinking, stems from the time when language was underpinned by ideologies intimately tied to the nation-state and the use of language as a marker of cultural and national identity. Perceiving language as something which has a geographical seat, which is culture-specific, and which is "possessed", is the mind-set of the traditionalist constituency. For the lingua franca, where there are now large groups of non-native speakers who use the language for intra-national purposes and where there are large numbers of non-native speakers (speaking English as a foreign language) who have achieved high levels of proficiency, it is apparent that the linguistic behavior of the competent non-native speaker can be seen to be highly relevant to the formation of educational standards.

Furthermore, the usage of the competent non-native speaker, when based on EIL educational practices, because it is potentially *composite* in nature, and not necessarily culture specific (that is to say, not perceived as a "copy" of a native-tongue variety), is in turn more neutral and hopefully less likely to dilute cultural diversity and plurality in regions where endangered languages are struggling for survival. Promoting EIL practices while at the same time supporting the cultivation of indigenous languages is in fact one of the few ways a lingua franca, at least theoretically, can coexist with the local language(s). With traditional educational practices and the integration motivation which it promotes (something theoretically more engaging when compared with learning the language for "instrumental" purposes), I fear that the lingua franca in this form more effectively channels the student's focus away from the indigenous tongue and more toward the acquired language. The ontological dimension, the "colonization of the mind" which takes place, is more extensive, in my opinion, in comparison to the intrusion experienced when acquiring English with utilitarian motivation.

ISSUES TO CONSIDER

❑   Read the extract from Modiano's first article and note down any points which interest you and which you strongly agree/disagree with. Do you find it surprising that the author was born and brought up in America or do you detect a pro-American bias in his writing?

❑   Then go on and read the solicited responses to Modiano's first article. Where do your own sympathies lie? Note down the main reasons why you support Modiano or his commentator in each case.

❏ Think about *your own* variety of English. Which features of pronunciation and/or vocabulary and/or grammar and syntax would be intelligible internationally? How do you know? If you are not sure, how could you find out?

❏ Read Modiano's responses ('Rethinking ELT') to Todd and Kaye and reconsider your answers so far. Have you been influenced into changing your mind? If so, why? If you originally disagreed with these commentators, is there any overlap between Modiano's counter-arguments and yours?

❏ Finally, in the light of all that you have read and thought about in this unit, to what extent would your responses to the three 'objectors' differ from Modiano's?

D7   **ATTITUDES TO LOCAL NORMS**

David Li **Two views of local norms of English**
The first extract in this unit is by a scholar in the Outer Circle (Hong Kong) who focuses on spoken language and cultural/pragmatic aspects of English use. The second extract is by a scholar in the Expanding Circle (Germany) who focuses on written language and grammar. Despite their different linguistic backgrounds and foci, they share a number of concerns and views.

Incorporating L1 pragmatic norms and cultural values in L2: developing English language curriculum for EIL in the Asia-Pacific region

David Li (reprinted from *Asian Englishes* Vol.1 No.1, 1998: 39–46)

[. . .]
The key question is: how should deviations from Anglo-American norms [in ESL] be regarded? There are broadly speaking two types of errors in the language acquisition process. The first type concerns the lexis and grammar of L2, typically at the sentence level. The two approaches to rectifying and explaining errors in early SLA studies – Contrastive Analysis and Error Analysis – have shown that learner errors are most likely to be attributable to some combination of both L1- and L2-related factors (Ellis 1994).

More controversial is the second type, which is related to the pragmalinguistic and sociopragmatic competence of the adult EFL/ESL learner. Apparent deviations in this area include the appropriacy of terms of address and various communicative actions (or speech acts) such as making requests and complaints, and offering apologies (Trosberg 1995).

Consider the use of terms of address among Hong Kong Chinese . . . many bilingual Hong Kong Chinese are known by a Western-style English name (e.g.

Alan, Anson, Jane, Kit, Maysum, Wing, etc.) largely because of their preference for the more egalitarian-sounding subsystem of Western terms of address as a kind of lubricant to help speed up the process of getting acquainted, both in inter- and intra- ethnic encounters. Notwithstanding this general trend, when it comes to selecting an appropriate term of address for one's teachers, many Hong Kong Chinese students feel uncomfortable initiating first-name adddress, even upon their teachers' invitations such as "Please feel free to call me David" (in English or in code-alternated Cantonese, Li 1996).While to my knowledge the extent to which such inhibitions are shared among Hong Kong students has not yet been subjected to systematic inquiry, there is some indication that such inhibitions are real (though unlikely to be universal among Hong Kong youngsters nowadays) for those students who were inculcated such Confucian values as respecting one's teachers and elders' values which continue to be found in Hong Kong primary and sec-ondary school textbooks. This is clearly borne out by the findings of a recent mini questionnaire survey administered to 32 first–year students working toward Bachelor of Arts in Language Information Science at City University of Hong Kong as a prelude to discussing the significance and impact of contextual and pragmatic factors on actual language use. One of the questions concerns the appropriate choice of terms of address as follows:

> As you know, it is very common indeed for Chinese Hongkongers – including teachers – to adopt an English name. Again, how would you address your Chinese teachers in general?
> (a) by their title plus last name (e.g. Ms. Wong);
> (b) by their English names (e.g. Mary);
> (c) avoid calling them directly by their names
> (d) other
> Briefly explain your general preference below.

With the exception of one student who did not respond to this question, 30 of the 31 responses (or 96.7%) indicated clearly that their preferred option was (a), that is, title plus last name. Two reasons cited most often in the students' com-ments have to do with respect and/or politeness in accordance with norms as pre-scribed in Chinese culture – this in spite of their Chinese teachers' invitation to address them by their English first names. The following comments are represent-ative of the students' explanation behind their preference:

> "We should respect our teachers. It seems to me that address my teachers by only their English names is a kind of impolite".
> "Because in traditional Chinese culture, calling one's name directly (especially for the elderly) is very impolite . . ."
> "It is rude to calling teachers by their first name in Chinese culture".
> "Because they are my teachers, so that I cannot call their English names, this shows the different status between us".
> "To show respect to them. If I just call their English names, it seems too informal".
> "I will call them by their title plus last name because sounds more politely and respectfully in Chinese".

David Li

To some extent, very similar preferences of terms of address occur to me in my interactions with colleagues and students. Hence some of my former students who are graduate teachers themselves now continue to address me by title plus last name (i.e., Dr. Li), despite my invitation to shift to reciprocal first-name address (i.e., David). At the same time, I myself often feel hesitant addressing new senior colleagues in the workplace by their first names, notwithstanding their hints, mentioned typically in passing, to use less formal terms of address.

The psychological strain in question may be explained by the clash between two sets of norms: one governing (or favoring) a more hierarchical interpersonal relationship, while the other downplaying it overtly, resulting in a perceptibly more symmetrical relationship. To the balanced bilingual who has been exposed to conflicting sets of pragmatic norms and cultural values, that kind of psychological strain is probably everyday reality, especially in the intercultural workplace. The crux of the problem is that there is no neutral choice, and so the safest, non-committal behavior may well be a kind of pragmatic avoidance, in that the bilingual consciously avoids committing to either set of norms by not using any terms of address at all. This is a fascinating area which remains largely unexplored, and so more empirical research is needed.

To less informed teachers of English who themselves are native speakers of English, it seems most natural to gauge their Asian students' language behaviors against the standard of Anglo-American norms. Consequently, they may be under the impulse to analyze apparent deviations such as non-reciprocation of first-name address as pragmatic failure to master L2 norms (Thomas 1983, Lii-Shih 1994). This view, however, has been called into doubt by scholars in Interlanguage Pragmatics, for it is increasingly being recognized that divergence from L2 norms may well be the learner's conscious choice in an attempt to preserve their socio-cultural identity (Kasper and Schmidt 1996, Siegal 1996, Takahashi 1996) – a practice which in all likelihood is collectively observed by most members in the local community.

This is also the position of many scholars who consider the use of English as an indigenized variety used especially for intraethnic communication (e.g. India), or when communicating with people from other EFL countries (e.g. between Japanese and Koreans). The functions and needs assigned to English in EFL communities are naturally different from those in places where English is used as a native language (Honna 1995, 1997). More specifically, as pointed out by Scollon (1997), "it should be clear that English is less likely to be a major cognitive, social, or cultural influence in the life of a person who has learned it as an adult than in the life of a person who has spoken the language since infancy" (p. 6). Scollon further observes that "English is certainly going to be a different sort of influence in the life of a monolingual speaker than in the life of a bilingual or multilingual speaker of the language" (p. 6). This point has been amply demonstrated in specialized reports and scholarly works within the paradigm of New Varieties of English (see, e.g., Kachru 1989a [= Kachru (ed.) 1992]).

Relevant examples of this kind can be found occasionally in Hong Kong public discourse. This may be illustrated by two announcements of obituary which appeared on the same day in the most popular English newspaper in Hong Kong, the *South China Morning Post*, in late August 1996. The first one occupies more space and includes a picture of the deceased, whose name and face are suggestive of someone from the Indian subcontinent. It can be seen that many of the expressions in this first announcement are characteristic of what may be called Buddhist discourse (e.g., "the Other Shore", "the land of light", "the Lotus feet of the Lord", etc.), which is untypical of English in the *West* [*South China Morning Post* 96.08.30.06; names abbreviated]:

IN MEMORIAM
[Picture of the deceased]
M.H.

In ever-lasting memory of M.H. who passed away on 30th August 1994. Known for his simplicity, his charity, and his humility, he was loved by all who came in contact with him. He has but passed on to the Other Shore, leaving behind the fragrance of his beautiful life and he dwells now in the land of light. Sadly missed and dearly remembered by his children, grand-children, he lives forever in our hearts. May his soul abide at the lotus feet of the Lord!

L.H. and family

The second one is much smaller and is clearly concerned with a person of Anglo-Saxon origin. Here the deceased is attributed the valor of having fought a brave long battle before being overcome by death:

OBITUARY

LOGAN – T.A. died on 28 August 1996 in Scotland. A long battle bravely fought. RIP. Don.

Our contrast bears not so much on the number of words nor the size of the announcement as the types of messages included. Here the first announcement contains expressions that may be obscure to readers who are unfamiliar with Buddhism. Beyond this slight unfamiliar feeling, there are no language (i.e. grammatical) problems in the text. On the other hand, when an elementary EFL learner attempts to express similar ideas, the text would no doubt be marred by grammatical and/or lexical errors, in which case it would take an informed language teacher to tell the boundary between strictly proficiency problems on the one hand and the expression of L1 content in L2 on the other.
[. . .]
   A brief review of current literature in two research paradigms, Contrastive Rhetoric [the subject of the first part of the article, which is omitted here] and New Varieties of English, shows that EFL learners may not converge to pragmatic norms and cultural values in English. This point finds additional support in recent empirical studies in Interlanguage Pragmatics, where L1 pragmatic norms of EFL learners are transferred to L2. Motivated by similar observations, some scholars, including ESOL professionals, have suggested that linguistic innovations and communicative styles in EFL settings should be incorporated into the local English curriculum. Clyne (1981), for example, suggests that "If culture-specific discourse structures really play an important role, they should occupy a prominent place

in teaching programs for second and foreign languages, including languages for special purposes" (p. 65). More than a decade later, Berns (1995) urges changes in the curriculum of English taught in continental Europe in order to develop and better reflect the typical communication styles of "Euro-English" . . . Johnson (1990) advocates a culturally neutral variety of English called "International English" (IE), whereby the curriculum – specified at the levels of phonology, lexis and grammar, as well as elements of communicative competence – aims at training learners to develop language functions needed for both inter- and intra-group communication, especially across national boundaries. Wolfson (1989) argues for sociolinguistic relativity on the grounds that knowledge of the sociolinguistic rules of native speakers is not of major consideration to all learners of English everywhere in the world. Before designing a curriculum for a particular population of language learners, it is important to be quite clear about the purpose to which the language will be put in order to avoid attempting to teach irrelevant information. Above all, we must remember that among the 600 million or so speakers of English in the world today, there is enormous cultural diversity and that different sociolinguistic rules will be relevant for different groups (Wolfson 1989: 30).

Likewise, after detailing mainland Chinese adult learners' resistance to adopting western rhetorical features and organization, Matalene (1985) pleads for accepting "the relativity of our own [American] rhetoric" (p. 806) and, above all, in view of marked differences, she sounds a clear note of warning to those who plan to follow her footsteps in China to beware of inadvertent ethnocentrism:

> The Western writing teacher, coming upon the set phrases again and again, is programmed to respond with her own ready-made remarks: 'Be original', 'Use new language', 'Avoid clichés'. And she is thus counselling her students to write like uneducated barbarians. But Chinese students are too puzzled and too polite to point this out – and they are certainly not in the habit of questioning teachers. (Matalene 1985: 792)

Given the needs and the domains in which English is used in the Asia-Pacific region, it would be unrealistic to expect Asians to develop native-like communicative competence in English. A correlate of this view is that it is simply futile to measure their EFL pragmatic behaviors and discourse competence against the yardstick of native fluency in British, American, or Australian English. Instead, the curriculum should incorporate elements of pragmatic norms and cultural values of the learners' L1.

Towards more fairness in International English: linguistic rights of non-native speakers?

Ulrich Ammon (reprinted from Robert Phillipson (ed.) *Rights to Language. Equity, Power, and Education*, Mahwah, NJ: Lawrence Erlbaum, 2000: 112–16)

[. . .]

In spite of the majority of non-native speakers of the non-inner-circle countries, many of whom use the language actively and regularly in institutional frameworks,

Ulrich
Ammon

the native speakers of the inner-circle countries retain the hold to the yardstick of linguistic correctness. The inner-circle countries' population is usually equalized, at least roughly, with the native speakers of the language. That their command of the language be superior to any others' is by and large taken for granted. Even researchers who are aware of the numerical proportions of speaker groups or who deal with globalization of the language finally stick to this assumption. Crystal (1997: 130–139) or Graddol (1997: 10–11), for instance, go a long way in presenting and justifying the 'New Englishes' of the outer or even the expanding-circle countries and underlining their values, but Graddol is probably right in pointing out that they, in spite of forming 'distinct varieties', often follow an 'underlying model of correctness' of either Britain or the USA (p. 11). Graddol also, like Crystal, finally retains traditional correctness judgments – contrary to what he seems to profess in some sections of his book. This is at least how I read some of his remarks. I see nothing wrong with his ranking *fluency* in spoken English from 'native-like' to 'extremely poor' (p. 11). But he also states, when reporting on the production of a book written in English, that '[t]he development and writing of the book require advanced "native-speaker" skills' (p. 42). Advanced non-native speaker skills wouldn't do, one must conclude. Native-speaker norms remain the final basis of correctness judgments.

Correctness judgment along these lines seems to be particularly rigorous with respect to written scientific or scholarly texts. British or US English language standards relate to different aspects of texts: orthography, vocabulary, grammar, pragmatic and discourse features as well as text structure in the narrower sense. Clyne (1987) has shown that English and German academic texts are structured differently in various respects (linearity/digression (Exkurs), symmetry, advance organizers, and hedging) and that English texts written by Germans tend to retain typical Germain structures which, as a rule, are evaluated negatively by English readers or reviewers (cf. also the literature on comparisons of English and other languages with respect to text structure in Clyne, 1987). The British reviewer of a handbook of German editors found 'some of the English written by non-native speakers so bad (. . .) as to be almost incomprehensible' (cf. Ammon 1989: 267). Similarly, a US reviewer of another book of a German editor, in fact myself, complained about 'near unintelligibility', because 'the grammatical mistakes are so severe.' He also did not appreciate that a 'decidedly German substratum peeks through in many of the papers written in English' (Di Pietro 1990: 301. Cf. for other examples Coulmas 1987: 106ff.).

In contrast to such criticism of British or US reviewers, I am doubtful whether the texts under scrutiny were really unintelligible, or even especially hard to understand. Generally, I dare to assume that unintelligibility is not the main reason why texts in non-native English are often rejected or judged negatively by native speakers. One indication is that the native speakers who 'corrected' or 'polished' my own English language texts have never had serious difficulty understanding them correctly except in a few instances. Similar experiences were confirmed by about a dozen German colleagues whom I queried. One should also be aware of the fact that texts produced by native speakers can contain unclarities too, especially ambiguities, and as a consequence be unintelligible at some points.

**Ulrich
Ammon**

The question of intelligibility of non-native-speaker texts can of course not be answered without comprehensive empirical research. There is evidence with respect to spoken language – and similar results would probably be found with respect to written language – that non-native English is indeed harder to understand for native speakers than is native English (Nelson 1982). It has, however, also been confirmed that 'speakers with shared cultural and linguistic norms obtain higher degrees of intelligibility in their language interactions' (Nelson 1982: 60). Non-native speakers of English understand non-native speakers of the same linguistic background better than non-native speakers of another linguistic background. In addition, non-native speakers of English or any linguistic background probably understand native speakers of British or American Standard English better than they do non-native speakers of another linguistic background other than their own. Nevertheless, there are reasons to assume that native speakers' negative evaluations of non-native-speaker texts are not only, or often not primarily, based on problems with intelligibility. Do they arise from what has been called 'linguicism'? Are they a special type of linguistic prejudice?

Linguicism?

Linguicism has been characterized as using the languages of different groups as defining criteria and as the basis for hierarchization (Skutnabb-Kangas & Phillipson 1994: 104; 1996a). There are various aspects of such hierarchization, and the delimitation of linguicism is not always easy. A clear case of linguicism, which seems widespread in the scientific community, are quality judgments of texts according to the language in which they are written. Vandenbroucke (1989: 1461) assumes with respect to medical dissertations in the Netherlands: 'By the language a thesis is written in you immediately judge its quality,' meaning that a thesis in English is valued more highly – as to its content! – than a thesis in Dutch. Matched-guise technique with written texts in Scandinavia confirmed the possibility of such judgment. Two different texts, each in two language versions: the national Scandinavian language and English, were presented to referees: 'the majority of different aspects of scientific content was assessed to be better in English than in the national language version for both manuscripts' (Nylenna, Riis & Karlsson 1994: 151).

It could also be argued that it is linguicism if native speakers of a prestige language are ranked higher socially (in some way) than non-native speakers. Is it, however, still linguicism if texts in line with native-speaker standards are valued more highly than those with 'deviations' from these standards? Calling this linguicism seems to be justified if the native-speaker standards do not guarantee more communicative efficiency. They in fact may not, at least in the future, with the growing number of non-native speakers. Reasonably safe judgment would of course require comprehensive empirical research. Yet even dealing theoretically with this question in a convincing manner is, to my view, beyond the scope of this short paper, which will therefore be limited to some general suggestions.

Any alternative to native-speaker standards would have to specify in which way they should be extended or changed. Doing away with standards altogether would certainly be no viable option, since it would endanger successful communication.

Ulrich
Ammon

Would it be possible to encorporate special features of non-native English – of Indian, Chinese, Japanese, French, Spanish, German or other Englishes – as elements of International English (or World English)? Which elements could that be? Would these elements have to be explicitly defined in some manual (codex) of International English, so that they could be studied by anyone interested? Or would it suffice to appeal to all the participants in international communication to be as tolerant as possible with respect to any linguistic peculiarity, as long as the text remains intelligible? This appeal would of course also imply very serious attempts at comprehension. Perhaps, new international standards, different from native-speaker standards, would gradually develop on the basis of such a new culture of communication and could finally be codified. There is a bulk of publications dealing with related questions which should be scrutinized for ideas and evidence, like for instance the literature on modified (mostly simplified) English for international communication or on EFL teaching objectives (closeness to native-speaker competence). Harmut Heberland proposed some of these ideas in a much earlier article, in which he suggested to develop a 'new, independent norm of academic English . . . which would be different from US or British English to the degree that speakers of those dialects would have to learn it, if they want to write or speak it properly . . .' and which 'would serve the purposes of its community of speakers better than any existing standard of English would, since it would be far less culture-bound and ethnocentric than all the other Englishes we can choose between today' (Haberland 1989: 936–7).

Language rights?

Those difficult questions will finally have to be answered if any postulate of 'the non-native speakers' right to linguistic peculiarities' (Ammon 1998: 278–282) is to be taken seriously, i.e. put into practice. Obviously, not all linguistic peculiarities are acceptable if communication is to function. It might be for these difficulties, why Skutnabb-Kangas and Phillipson (1994: 102) mention no such 'linguistic human right.' It even seems hard to place any non-native speakers' right to linguistic peculiarities into their system. Rather, any such a right straddles across their 'necessary' and their 'enrichment-oriented rights', depending on the function of English as a non-native language, but doesn't really fit into either. The deeper reason might be that their system of linguistic rights is itself based on the ideal of native-speaker standards or norms.

It seems to me, however, that systematic provision for such a right should seriously be considered in face of the disadvantages of the non-native speakers of English and actually non-native speakers of any prestige language with rigorous standards. Murray and Dingwall (1997: 56) concede that the dominance of English as a language of science 'may give native speakers of English an unfair advantage in the competition to publish results.' When they point out, however, that native speakers of English too need extensive training before they are capable of writing scientific articles, they seem to forget that the Swiss scientists, whose fate they examine, get the equivalent training. It is even a central objective of university courses in Switzerland, particularly seminars. Swiss scientists are therefore,

Ulrich Ammon

as a rule, very well capable of writing scientific texts – but according to their own and not anglosaxon norms. Disadvantaging such users of English could be called 'discrimination' with respect to the non-native speakers' right to linguistic peculiarities, if we had it, and be criticized accordingly. It would of course be necesssary to show functioning alternatives to the present situation.

There have been demands of learners' rights which seem to be related to our suggestions. Thus, Gomes de Matos (1998: 15) postulated for EFL learners '[t]he right (as non-native speakers) to deviate [from native-speaker standards! U.A.] in noncrucial areas that do not affect intelligibility or communication (. . .)' His ideals remain, however, the native-speaker competence or the standards of the inner-circle countries. In contrast, I would like to challenge the inner-circle countries' exclusive control of the standards of International English. It seems to me that there is no real justification for this kind of control in a world with a growing majority of speakers of the language outside the inner-circle countries. In the case of a planned standard, or set of standards, one could think of a transnational institution, perhaps similar to that for Esperanto, to be put in charge. However, an unplanned, spontaneous development of standards through interaction might be more practical. Changes along the suggested lines probably presuppose long-lasting persistence and growing self-confidence on the side of the non-native speakers with respect to their own use of English.

The non-native speakers' right to linguistic peculiarities remains at the moment a rather helpless postulate. It needs more elaboration as well as integration into an extended system of linguistic human rights. It also needs support through political action. It should become part of the agenda of linguistic and other scholarly or scientific associations, or their conferences, and be presented to political parties or institutions, for instance of the European Union. – For a start, the non-native speakers of English could as a minimum try to raise awareness of their problems (cf. Ammon 1990) and demand more linguistic tolerance from the language's native speakers. They should use their growing number as their argument, among others. In fact of these numbers, rigorous enforcement of native-speaker standards amounts to the suppression of a disadvantaged majority by a privileged minority.

ISSUES TO CONSIDER

❏ These two authors share some similar views. How do you explain these similarities? On the other hand, do you find any major differences in their perspectives? And how far do you agree with their conclusions?

❏ In a paper presented at the ICAME (International Computer Archive of Modern and Medieval English) Conference in Louvain, Belgium in May 2001, Christopher Tribble, an Inner Circle scholar, criticises Ammon's claim of 'the non-native speakers' right to linguistic peculiarities' on the grounds that these would place an unnecessary interpretive burden on the reader, and that it is, anyway, also 'unfair' on other writers if Ammon is allowed to invoke his ELF [English as a Lingua Franca] status to get away with what would be considered to be a mistake by any competent copy editor in the case of other writers. The fact of the matter is that writing is difficult for everyone. Is it not a nonsense for an individual writer to assume a special privilege to be peculiar (or, dare I say it, wrong?) on the accidents of L1 status alone?

Do you agree with Tribble's response? Would you want to make any comment about his use of the idiomatic expression 'to get away with' which may not be widely understood by (proficient) non-native-speakers? (Look back to C6 to see what Seidlhofer says about this kind of unilateral idiomaticity.) Is this a minor slip, or does it suggest to you that when Tribble refers to 'the reader' and 'other writers' he still conceives of these as being only native-speakers and native-speaker clones?

❑ In the light of Ammon's request for tolerance and to be allowed 'linguistic peculiarities', how different from standard British English or American English do you find his writing? Is there anything that you find unintelligible? Although Li makes no such request for his own English, his writing contains certain features which are not characteristic of standard British or American English. Again, is there anything you find unintelligible? Make a note of some of the features in both extracts which you think or know are examples of Chinese-English and German-English (i.e. items which are influenced by the writer's L1 whether or not they are currently recognised as being 'legitimate' features of a local English norm).

❑ Do you agree with Ammon's claim that non-native-speakers find the English of those who share the same L1 the most intelligible, followed by the English of native-speakers? Does it make a difference depending on whether it is written or spoken?

❑ If you are bilingual, do you identify with Li's point that 'psychological strain . . . may be explained by the clash between two sets of norms'? Do you find that a lack of 'neutral choice' (e.g. in the use of address terms) leads you to select as 'the safest, non-committal behavior . . . a kind of pragmatic avoidance' in which you consciously avoid 'committing to either set of norms'?

LOOKING AHEAD

D8

Graddol's book, *The Future of English?* is, to my knowledge, the most fully developed and carefully considered examination of the future of English that has been published hitherto. In the following extract from his final chapter, he considers what sort of English is likely to be spoken in the future, which languages may come to rival English at the global level, and the influences that may affect the roles and types of English spoken in years to come.

English in the future

David Graddol (reprinted from *The Future of English?* London: British Council, 1997: 56–9 and 62–3)

Will a single world standard for English develop?

One question which arises in any discussion of global English is whether a single world standard English will develop, forming a supranational variety which must be learned by global citizens of the 21st century. Like most questions raised in this book, this demands a more complicated answer than those who ask probably desire.

There are, for example, at least two dimensions to the question: the first is whether English will fragment into many mutually unintelligible local forms; the second is whether the current 'national' standards of English (particularly US and British) will continue to compete as models of correctness for world usage, or whether some new world standard will arise which supersedes national models for the purposes of international communication and teaching.

The widespread use of English as a language of wider communication will continue to exert pressure towards global uniformity as well as give rise to anxieties about 'declining' standards, language change and the loss of geolinguistic diversity. But as English shifts from foreign-language to second-language status for an increasing number of people, we can also expect to see English develop a larger number of local varieties.

These contradictory tensions arise because English has two main functions in the world: it provides a vehicular language for international communication and it forms the basis for constructing cultural identities. The former function requires mutual intelligibility and common standards. The latter encourages the development of local forms and hybrid varieties. As English plays an ever more important role in the first of these functions, it simultaneously finds itself acting as a language of identity for larger numbers of people around the world. There is no need to fear, however, that trends towards fragmentation will necessarily threaten the role of English as a lingua franca. There have, since the first records of the language, been major differences between varieties of English.

The mechanisms which have helped maintain standard usage in the past may not, however, continue to serve this function in the future. Two major technologies have helped develop national, standard-language forms. The first was printing, the invention of which provided a 'fixity' in communication by means of printed books. According to scholars such as Anderson (1983), such fixity was a necessary requirement for the 'imagined communities' of modern nation states. But with increasing use of electronic communication much of the social and cultural effect of the

David Graddol

stability of print has already been lost, along with central 'gatekeeping' agents such as editors and publishers who maintain consistent, standardised forms of language.

The second technology has been provided by broadcasting, which in many ways became more important than print in the socially mobile communities of the 20th century. But trends in global media suggest that broadcasting will not necessarily play an important role in establishing and maintaining a global standard. Indeed, the patterns of fragmentation and localisation, which are significant trends in satellite broadcasting, mean that television is no longer able to serve such a function. How can there be such a thing as 'network English' in a world in which centralised networks have all but disappeared?

Meanwhile, new forms of computer-mediated communication are closing the gap between spoken and written English which has been constructed laboriously over centuries. And cultural trends encourage the use of informal and more conversational language, a greater tolerance of diversity and individual style, and a lessening deference to authority. These trends, taken together, suggest that a weakening of the institutions and practices which maintained national standard languages is taking place: that the native-speaking countries are experiencing a 'destandardisation' of English.

The ELT industry, however, may play an important role in maintaining an international standard, as Strevens (1992) suggested.

[. . .]

Since the ELT publishers from native-speaking countries are likely to follow markets – most of the large publishers already provide materials in several standards – it will be non-native speakers who decide whether a US model, a British one, or one based on a second-language variety will be taught, learned and used. At the very least, English textbooks in countries where English is spoken as a second language are likely to pay much more attention to local varieties of English and to localise their product by incorporating materials in local varieties of English.

The most likely scenario thus seems to be a continued 'polycentrism' for English – that is, a number of standards which compete. It will be worth monitoring the global ELT market for signs of shifting popularity between textbooks published in different standards.

[. . .]

Will the British 'brand' of English play an important role in the world in the 21st century?

The conventional wisdom is that US English is the most influential variety worldwide. Recent American studies of the cultural consequences of globalisation suggest:

> The global culture speaks English – or, better, American. In McWorld's terms, the queen's English is little more today than a high-falutin' dialect used by advertisers who want to reach affected upscale American consumers. American English has become the world's primary transnational language in culture and the arts as well as science, technology, commerce, transportation, and banking. . . . The war against the hard hegemony of American colonialism, political sovereignty, and

David
Graddol

economic empire is fought in a way which advances the soft hegemony of American pop culture and the English language. (Barber 1996: 84)

By 2000, English was the unchallenged world lingua franca. . . . This language monopoly bestowed upon the United States an incalculable but subtle power: the power to transform ideas, and therefore lives, and therefore societies, and therefore the world. (Celente 1997: 298)

It will be clear from the discussion elsewhere in this book that these commentaries already have a slightly old-fashioned feel to them. The hegemony of English may not be so entrenched as writers such as Barber and Celente fear. But Barber may also be dismissing the position of British English too readily. Much of the negative reaction to English in the world is directed towards the US; most territories in which English is spoken as a second language still have an (ambiguous) orientation to British English . . . British publishers have a major share of the global ELT market and there are signs that even US companies are using the British variety to gain greater acceptance in some world markets. Microsoft, for example, produces two English versions of intellectual property on CD-ROM, such as the *Encarta Encyclopedia*: a domestic (US English) edition and a 'World English edition' based on British English.

The future of British English in the world will depend in part on continued, careful management of its 'brand image'. Some useful groundwork has already been undertaken. The support of 'British Studies' courses in overseas universities, for example, has helped shift the focus from cultural heritage to a more balanced understanding of Britain's place in the modern world. There is also a growing appreciation of the importance of British audio-visual products in projecting an image of Britain as a leader of style and popular culture.

Which languages may rival English as a world lingua franca in the 21st century?

There is no reason to believe that any other language will appear within the next 50 years to replace English as the global lingua franca. The position of English has arisen from a particular history which no other language can, in the changed world of the 21st century, repeat.

We have argued, however, that no single language will occupy the monopolistic position in the 21st century which English has – almost – achieved by the end of the 20th century. It is more likely that a small number of world languages will form an 'oligopoly', each with particular spheres of influence and regional bases.

As trade, people movement and communication between neighbouring countries in Asia and South America become more important than flows between such regions and Europe and North America, so we can expect languages which serve regional communication to rise in popularity. But it is actually very difficult to foresee more precisely what will occur.

For example, we have noted that economic activity, telecommunications traffic and air travel between Asian countries will greatly increase. But there are at least three possible linguistic scenarios which may develop from this. One is that English

**David
Graddol**

will remain the preferred language of international communication within Asia, since the investment in English may be regarded as too great to throw away, or the social elites who have benefited from English in the past may be reluctant to let their privileged position become threatened. Or it may simply be the most common shared language. A second scenario is that Mandarin becomes regionally more important, beginning as a lingua franca within Greater China (for communication between the regions of Hong Kong, Beijing, Shanghai and Taiwan) and building on increased business communication between the overseas Chinese in South-east Asia.

The third scenario is that no single language will emerge as a dominant lingua franca in Asia and a greater number of regional languages will be learned as foreign languages. If intraregional trade is greatest between adjacent countries, then there is likely to be an increased demand for neighbouring languages. In this case, the pattern of demand for foreign languages will look different in each country.

The position of Russian in Central and North Asia is subject to similar problems of prediction. But it does seem clear that the global fortunes of Spanish are rising quite rapidly. Indeed, the trading areas of the south (Mercosur, Safta) are expected to merge with Nafta in the first decade of the new millennium. This, taken together with the expected increase in the Hispanic population in the US, may ensure that the Americas emerge as a bilingual English-Spanish zone.

Which languages will benefit from language shift? Which languages will lose speakers?

This book has identified language shift – where individuals and whole families change their linguistic allegiances – as a significant factor in determining the relative positions of world languages in the 21st century. Although such shifts are relatively slow – often taking several generations to fully materialise – they are surprisingly difficult to predict. Most research in this area has focused on migrant and minority communities who gradually lose their ethnic language and adopt that of the majority community. Little research has been conducted on linguistic migration between 'big' languages such as from Hindi or Mandarin to English. But in the next 50 years or so we can expect substantial language shift to occur as the effects of economic development and globalisation are felt in more countries. This takes us into new territory: there has been no comparable period which can provide an indication of what is to come.

First, the loss of at least 50% and perhaps as much as 90% of the world's languages means that the remaining languages will acquire native speakers at a faster rate than population increase in their communities. English is not the direct cause of such language loss, nor is it the direct benefactor. As regional language hierarchies become more established, there will be a shift towards languages higher in the hierarchy. One of the concomitant trends will be increased diversity in the beneficiary languages: regional languages will become more diverse and 'richer' as they acquire more diverse speakers and extend the range of their functions.

Second, processes of internal migration and urbanisation may restructure residential and employment patterns in multilingual communities on lines of social class rather than ethnolinguistic community. Parasher (1980) showed, for example how the rehousing of ethnic groups brought about by redevelopment created neighbourhoods in which English became the language of inter-ethnic friendship and communication.

Third, economic development is greatly enlarging the numbers of middle class, professional families in the world – those who are most likely to acquire and use English in both work and social forums.

Fourth, the growth of English-medium tertiary education worldwide has created a significant transition point in late adolescence for many second-language speakers at which English may take over from their first language as a primary means of social communication. The nature of English bilingualism in many L2 countries thus suggests that for some speakers English may become a first language during the course of their lives, which would upset the assumption that such language shift can only occur between generations. Migration towards L1 use of English by middle-class professionals may thus take place more rapidly than has hitherto been thought possible. India and Nigeria may experience substantial increase in numbers of first language speakers of English in this way and it is worth remembering that even a small percentage change in these countries would greatly increase the global number of native speakers.

The languages which might benefit most, in terms of larger numbers of native speakers, are Hausa and Swahili in Africa, Malay, regional languages in India and Tok Pisin. Russian, Mandarin and Arabic may also profit. English, at the apex of the hierarchy, is certainly implicated in this 'upgrading' process and will probably continue to act as a global engine of change, encouraging users to shift upwards from small community languages to languages of wider communication.

What gives a language global influence and makes it a 'world language'?

No one has satisfactorily answered the question of what makes a language a 'world' language. It is clear from earlier discussion in this book that sheer numbers of native speakers do not in themselves explain the privileged position of some language.

David Crystal suggests that 'a language becomes an international language for one chief reason: the political power of its people – especially their military power' (Crystal 1997, p. 7). Historically that may have been true: in the future, it will be less clearly military power which provides the international backing for languages, because of changes in the nature of national power, in the way that cultural values are projected and in the way markets are opened for the circulation of goods and services.

What we need is some sense of what makes a language attractive to learners, so that we can identify languages which newly meet such criteria in the future. This would also allow us to chart and ideally anticipate, the decline of erstwhile popular languages.

In this book we have focused on economic and demographic factors. Some combination of these might usefully form a starting point for an understanding of what makes a language acquire importance. The engco model provides an illustration

David
Graddol

of the kind of approach that can be taken. The model calculates an index of 'global influence' taking into account various economic factors which have been discussed earlier, including Gross Language Product and openness to world trade (Traded Gross Language Product). The model also includes demographic factors, such as the numbers of young speakers and rates of urbanisation. Finally, it takes into account the human development index (HDI) for different countries. This is a composite figure produced by the UN, which combines measures of quality of life with those for literacy and educational provision. In this way, HDI provides an indicator of the proportion of native speakers who are literate and capable of generating intellectual resources in the language.

The engco model of global influence thus generates a new kind of league table among languages, which weights languages not only by the number and wealth of their speakers, but also by the likelihood that these speakers will enter social networks which extend beyond their locality: they are the people with the wherewithal and ambition to 'go about' in the world, influence it and to have others work to influence them. The calculations for the mid 1990s for the 'basket' of languages we have surveyed in this book are as shown in Table [D8.1].

Table [D8.1]   Engco model of the global influence of English

1	English	100
2	German	42
3	French	33
4	Japanese	32
5	Spanish	31
6	Chinese	22
7	Arabic	8
8	Portuguese	5
9	Malay	4
10	Russian	3
11	Hindi/Urdu	0.4
12	Bengali	0.09

Note: An index score of 100 represents the position of English in 1995

No strong claims are made for the validity of this index, but it does seem to capture something of the relative relations between world languages which other indices, based crudely on economic factors or numbers of native speakers, do not convey. It shows that English is, on some criteria at least, a long way ahead of all other languages including Chinese.

The advantage of the engco index is the way it can be used to generate projections. As the model is refined and the full demographic and economic projections for the countries concerned are taken into account, league tables will be published for the decades up to 2050. Preliminary results indicate that on this

David Graddol

basis Spanish is one of the languages which will rise most quickly. The nearest rivals to English – German, French and Japanese, will grow much more slowly. The relative positions of the 'top six' are likely to change during the coming decades, but it is unlikely that any other language will overtake English.

The changing status of language will create a new language hierarchy for the world. Figure [D1.1] shows how this might look in the middle of the 21st century, taking into account economic and demographic developments as well as potential language shift. In comparison with the present-day hierarchy there are more languages in the top layer. Chinese, Hindi/Urdu, Spanish and Arabic may join English. French and other OECD languages (German, Japanese) are likely to decline in status. But the biggest difference between the present-day language hierarchies and those of the future will result from the loss of several thousand of the world's languages. Hence there may be a group of languages at the apex, but there will be less linguistic variety at the base. The shift from linguistic monopoly to oligopoly brings pluralism in one sense, but huge loss of diversity in another. This will be offset only in part by an increasing number of new hybrid language varieties, many arising from contact with English.

Figure [D1.1] The world language hierarchy 2050?

Can anything be done to influence the future of English?

Can anything be done by institutions and decision-makers to influence the future of English?

This is a difficult question to answer. There is an argument that global processes are too complex, too overwhelming in their momentum and too obscure in their outcomes to permit the activities of a few people and institutions, even with coherent policies, to make any difference. David Crystal suggests that the English language may have passed beyond the scope of any form of social control:

> It may well be the case . . . that the English language has already grown to be independent of any form of social control. There may be a critical number or

critical distribution of speakers (analogous to the notion of critical mass in nuclear physics) beyond which it proves impossible for any single group or alliance to stop its growth, or even influence its future. If there were to be a major social change in Britain which affected the use of English there, would this have any real effect on the world trend? It is unlikely. (Crystal, 1997, p. 139)

Even if the English language cannot, in any comprehensive sense, be managed, there is an argument that complex systems have an unpredictability in their behaviour which needs to be taken into account by strategic management. The institutions and organisations which will best survive the potentially traumatic period of global reconstruction which has only just begun, and even thrive during it, will be those which have the best understanding of the changing position of English in local markets, which can adapt the products and services they offer most quickly and effectively and which know how to establish appropriate alliances and partnerships.

But the function of strategic management can extend beyond ensuring either survival or the effective exploitation of changing conditions in the marketplace. In complex systems, small forces, strategically placed, can lead to large global effects. There is no way, at present, of knowing what nudges placed where will have what consequences. But careful strategic planning, far-sighted management, thoughtful preparation and focused action now could indeed help secure a position for British English language services in the 21st century.

[. . .]

The indications are that English will enjoy a special position in the multilingual society of the 21st century: it will be the only language to appear in the language mix in every part of the world. This, however, does not call for an unproblematic celebration by native speakers of English. Yesterday it was the world's poor who were multilingual; tomorrow it will also be the global elite. So we must not be hypnotised by the fact that this elite will speak English: the more significant fact may be that, unlike the majority of present-day native English speakers, they will also speak at least one other language – probably more fluently and with greater cultural loyalty.

ISSUES TO CONSIDER

At the end of the book, I leave you with more questions than answers. You can probably do little more than make educated guesses in relation to some of these topics and (those of you young enough to do so) wait and see what happens.

❑ Graddol's book was published in 1997. To what extent do you believe the situation has already changed since then? Have any of Graddol's predictions been proved or disproved, or the indications become any clearer?

❑ *The Future of English?* was commissioned by the British Council. Do you think this had any 'softening' influence on the position adopted by Graddol regarding the role of Britain in the global English enterprise?

❏ The main focus of Graddol's book is on the implications for British English. If the same questions were to be applied to American English, how similar or different, in your view, would the answers be?

❏ In strand 6, I referred to the 'Blair Initiative', that is, the British prime minister Tony Blair's drive to promote the use of English as the global *lingua franca* and to persuade the British to capitalise on their advantages as native speakers of the language. In the light of Graddol's point that English monolingualism may not be advantageous for much longer, and bearing in mind the points I made in C8, do you think the Blair Initiative has any chance of success? Why, or why not?

❏ How do *you* see the future of English?

FURTHER READING

ENGLISH AND COLONIALISM

❑ For detailed information on the historical background, see Bailey (1991), Crystal (1997), McCrum *et al.* (1992), Watts and Trudgill (eds) (2002).

❑ Much has been written about current social, cultural and political issues. See, for example: Bamgboṣe (1998), Brutt-Griffler (2002), Cheshire (ed.) (1991), Fishman (1999, especially Chapters 14 and 29), Kachru (1986, 1992 (ed.), 1996), Kachru and Nelson (1996), Leith (1996), McArthur (1998, 2002), Pennycook (1994, 1998), Phillipson (1992).

❑ On 'English Only' in the US, the following will be useful: Baugh (2000), Bourhis and Marshall (1999), Dicker (2000), Fishman (1999, Chapter 17), Hinton (1999), Kubota (2001), L. Milroy (1999), Milroy and Milroy (1999).

❑ English in Africa and other developing countries is discussed in: Bisong (1995), Burke, Crowley and Girvin (eds) (2000: 416–43), Canagarajah (1999), de Klerk (1999), Granville *et al.* (1998), McArthur (1999), Obeng and Adegbija (1999), Pennycook (1994), Phillipson (1992), Titlestad (1998).

❑ Norton (2000) investigates the place of identity in English language learning.

PIDGINS AND CREOLES

❑ The following provide more detailed accounts of theories of pidgin and creole development (including some not covered in A2) and analyses of their characteristics: Hall (1966), Holm (1988, 1989, 2000), Le Page and Tabouret-Keller (1985), Mufwene (2001), Mühlhäusler 1997, Romaine (1988), Sebba (1997), Singh (2001) and Thomason and Kaufman (1988). There are also useful chapters in Aitchison (1991), McArthur (1998), Wardhaugh (2002).

❑ On Black English in general and London Jamaican in particular, see: Edwards (1986), Hewitt (1986), Sebba (1993), Sutcliffe (1982). On accent see Wells (1973, 1982).

❑ Pidgin and creole resources are also available on a number of websites. You can access many of these via the *Creole Database Project*: http//:www.ling.su.se:80/creole

THE OWNERSHIP OF ENGLISH

❑ Further contributions to the *English Today* debate were made by Christensen (1992) and Tripathi (1992).

❑ On native/non-native teachers see Arva and Medgyes (2000), Braine (ed.) (1999), Medgyes (1992, 1994), Samimy and Brutt-Griffler (1999), Seidlhofer (1999).

❏   On teaching methods and materials see: Canagarajah (1999, especially Chapters 4, 5 and 6), Holliday (1994), Kachru and Nelson (1996), Pennycook (1989, 1994, especially Chapter 5, 2001).

❏   On testing English see: Davies (1995), Lowenberg (1992, 2000).

VARIETIES OF ENGLISH

❏   On postcolonial issues including the extent to which the English language does or does not serve its speakers in the former colonies, see these two collections of articles: Ashcroft, Griffiths and Tiffin (eds) (1995), Burke *et al.* (eds) (2000).

❏   On postcolonial literature, see: Carter and McRae (2001), B. Kachru (1992, 1995), Lowry (1992), Thumboo (1992).

❏   On Singlish, see Gupta (1999), Lee-Wong (2001), Pakir (1993, 1995). Brown (2000) is a study of the sources of tongue slips in Singaporean English.

❏   On Estuary English consult the University College London Estuary English website: http://www.phon.ucl.ac.uk/home/estuary – which contains an extensive collection of papers on the subject including a number which are sceptical of the existence of Estuary English as a new variety of English. The Wells and Maidment articles are both posted there. See also Coggle (1993). Chia and Brown (2002) is an interesting study of Singaporeans' views on Estuary English.

❏   For a number of perspectives on cross-cultural pragmatics, see Spencer-Oatey (2000).

'STANDARD' ENGLISHES

❏   Among the many works taking a critical look at standard language ideology are: Aitchison (1997), Bauer and Trudgill (eds) (1998), Bex and Watts (eds) (1999), Milroy and Milroy (1999).

❏   Particularly political in their perspectives are: Cameron (1995, especially Chapter 5), Holborow (1999), Parakrama (1995), Pennycook (2001).

❏   For arguments in support of standard language ideology, see Honey (1997).

❏   To find out more about the processes involved in standardisation, see the classic work: Haugen (1966).

❏   Refer to Baron (2000) for more information on the development of writing, differences between speech and writing, and e-discourse. See Carter and McCarthy (1995) on the grammar of spoken English.

❏   We have not considered contrastive rhetoric in strand 4, but if you want to explore the field, useful texts include: Connor (1996), Y. Kachru (1992, 1997a, 1997b).

ENGLISH AS AN INTERNATIONAL LANGUAGE

❏   For earlier perspectives on EIL see: Brumfit (1982), Gimson (1978), Quirk (1982), Quirk and Widdowson (eds) (1985), Smith (ed.) (1983), Strevens (1980).

❏   The following are among the many recent works on EIL and on its implications for English language teaching and testing: Gnutzmann (ed.) (1999), Jenkins (1998, 2000), McKay (2002), Willis (2003).

❏ While many writers currently use the terms EIL and ELF interchangeably, some regard ELF as being in some way distinct, because they treat it as an emerging *variety* of English as well as a context of use, and one in which native speakers cannot, by definition, participate. For further discussion of ELF, see: James (2000), Jenkins *et al.* (2001), Knapp and Meierkord (eds) (2002), Seidlhofer (2001a, 2001b).

❏ Some of the discussion of EIL focuses on the problem of international intelligibility. The main older sources which consider intelligibility from a non-native listener perspective as well as a native one are: Smith and Bisazza (1982), Smith and Rafiqzad (1979) and, a little later, Smith (1992). More recent work in this area includes Jenkins (2000) which is concerned with the intelligibility of accents, and Nelson (1995) which takes a broader perspective.

❏ To follow up the debate on native and non-native speakers of English, see: Block and Cameron (2002), Brutt-Griffler and Samimy (2001), Davies (1991, 1995), Leung *et al.* (1997), Medgyes (1994), Norton (1997), Rampton (1990), Tsuda (1997).

ASIAN ENGLISHES

❏ On Indian English see: Bailey (1991, Chapters 5 and 6), D'souza (2001), Krishnaswamy and Burde (1998), Parasher (1998, 2001).

❏ On the emergence of Hong Kong English see: Benson (2001), Bolton (ed.) (2000, 2002), Bolton and Lim (2000), Boyle (1998), Evans (2000), Gisborne (2000), Hung (2000), Li (2000), Pennington (1998).

❏ Although not much has yet been written on what is becoming known as 'Euro-English', you can follow up the European material in A7 and B7 in: Berns (1995), Cheshire (2002), Hoffmann (2000), House (2001), James (2000), Jenkins and Seidlhofer (2001), Jenkins *et al.* (2001), Phillipson (2003), Preisler (1999), Viereck (1996).

❏ For more detail on the Outer Circle interlanguage/fossilisation controversy, see: Brutt-Griffler (2002), Ho and Wong (2002), Kachru and Nelson (1996), Kirkpatrick (2002), Sridhar and Sridhar (1992).

WORLD ENGLISHES IN THE FUTURE

❏ The final chapter of McArthur (2002) provides a wide range of perspectives on likely future developments in World Englishes.

❏ Crystal (1999) covers similar ground, focusing in particular on the issue of international intelligibility and the possible development of a World Standard Spoken English.

❏ To keep abreast of contemporary developments in World Englishes, it is worth consulting journals in the field. I recommend two in particular: *World Englishes* (published by Blackwell) provides lengthy, detailed studies of individual Englishes, while *English Today* (published by Cambridge University Press) contains shorter, less complex, but equally relevant discussions of changes in the language(s).

REFERENCES

Achebe, C. (1965) 'English and the African writer', *Transition* 18.

—— (1975) 'The African Writer and the English Language', in *Morning Yet on Creation Day*, New York: Anchor.

Ager, D. (2001) *Motivation in Language Planning and Language Policy*, Clevedon, UK: Multilingual Matters.

Ahulu, S. (1997) 'General English', *English Today* 13/1: 17–23.

—— (1998) 'Lexical variation in international English', *English Today* 14/3: 29–34.

Aitchison, J. (1991) *Language Change: Progress or Decay?*, 2nd edn, Cambridge: Cambridge University Press.

—— (1996) *The Seeds of Speech*, Cambridge: Cambridge University Press.

—— (1997) *The Language Web*, Cambridge: Cambridge University Press.

Alobwede Charles d'Epie (1998) 'Banning Pidgin English in Cameroon?', *English Today* 14/1: 54–60.

Ammon, U. (1989) 'Die Schwerigkeiten der deutschen Sprachgemeinschaft aufgrund der Dominanz der englischen Sprache', *Zeitschrift für Sprachwissenschaft* 8/2: 257–72.

—— (1990) 'German or English? The problems of language choice experienced by German-speaking scientists' in P. Nelde (ed.) *Language Conflict and Minorities*, Bonn: Dümmler.

—— (1996) 'The European Union (EU – formerly European Community): status change of English during the last fifty years', in J. Fishman, A. Conrad and A. Rubal-Lopez (eds) *1996 Post-Imperial English*, Berlin: Mouton de Gruyter.

—— (1998) *Ist Deutsch noch internationale Wissenschaftssprache? Englisch auch für die Lehre an den deutschprachigen Hochschulen*, Berlin and New York: de Gruyter.

—— (2000) 'Towards more fairness in International English: linguistic rights of non-native speakers?' in Phillipson (ed.) 2000.

Anderson, B. (1983) *Imagined Communities*, London: Verso.

Andreasson, A-M. (1994) 'Norm as a pedagogical paradigm', *World Englishes* 13/3: 395–409.

Arva, V. and Medgyes, P. (2000) 'Native and non-native teachers in the classroom', *System* 28: 355–72.

Ashcroft, B., Griffiths, G. and Tiffin, H. (eds) (1995) *The Post-Colonial Studies Reader*, London: Routledge.

—— (eds) (2000) *Post-Colonial Studies*, London: Routledge.

Bailey, R. (1991) *Images of English*, Cambridge: Cambridge University Press.

Bamgboṣe, A. (1998) 'Torn between the norms: innovations in world Englishes', *World Englishes* 17/1: 1–14.

Bansal, R. (1990) 'The pronunciation of English in India', in S. Ramsaran (ed.) 1990.

Barber, B. (1996) *Jihad vs McWorld*, New York: Ballantine Books.

Baron, N. (2000) *Alphabet to Email*, London: Routledge.

Bauer, L. and Trudgill, P. (eds) (1998) *Language Myths*, London: Penguin.

Baugh, J. (2000) 'Educational malpractice and the miseducation of language minority students', in J. Hall and W. Eggington (eds) 2000.

Bautista, M. (1998) 'Tagalog-English code-switching and the lexicon of Philippine English', *Asian Englishes* 1/1: 51–67.

Benson, P. (2000) 'Hong Kong words: variation and context', *World Englishes* 19/3: 373–80.

Berns, M. (1995) 'English in the European Union', *English Today* 11/3: 3–11.

Berns, M. *et al.* (1998) '(Re)experiencing hegemony: the linguistic imperialism of Robert Phillipson', *International Journal of Applied Linguistics* 8/2: 271–82.

Bex, T. and Watts, R. (eds) (1999) *Standard English. The widening debate*, London: Routledge.

Bickerton, D. (1981) *Roots of Language*, Ann Arbor: Karoma.

—— (1984) 'The language bioprogram hypothesis', *The Behavioral and Brain Sciences* 7: 173–88.

Bisong, J. (1995) 'Language choice and cultural imperialism: a Nigerian perspective', *ELT Journal* 49/2: 122–32.

Block, D. and Cameron, D. (eds) (2002) *Globalization and Language Teaching*, London: Routledge.

Bloodworth, D. (2001) 'Go on, dare to boldly split the infinitive', *Straits Times*, 17 May.

Bolton, K. (2000) 'The sociolinguistics of Hong Kong and the space for Hong Kong English', *World Englishes* 19/3: 265–85.

—— (ed.) (2002) *Hong Kong English: Autonomy and Creativity*, Hong Kong: Hong Kong University Press.

Bolton, K. and Lim, S. (2000) 'Futures for Hong Kong English', *World Englishes* 19/3: 429–43.

Bourhis, R. and Marshall, D. (1999) 'The United States and Canada', in J. Fishman (ed.) 1999.

Boyle, J. (1998) 'What hope for a trilingual Hong Kong?' *English Today* 14/4: 34–43.

Braine, G. (ed.) (1999) *Non-Native Educators in English Language Teaching*, Mahwah, NJ: Lawrence Erlbaum Associates.

Brown, A. (2000) 'Tongue slips and Singapore English pronunciation', *English Today* 16/3: 31–6.

Brumfit, C. (ed.) (1982) *English for International Communication*, Oxford: Pergamon Press.

—— (1995) 'The role of English in a changing Europe: where do we go from here?', *Best of ELTECS*, The British Council.

—— (2002) 'Has everything changed?', *EL Gazette* No.265, February 2002: 11.

Brutt-Griffler, J. (2002) *World English. A Study of its Development*, Clevedon, UK: Multilingual Matters.

Brutt-Griffler, J. and Samimy, K. (2001) 'Transcending the nativeness paradigm', *World Englishes* 20/1: 99–106.

Bryson, B. (1990) *Mother Tongue: The English Language*, London: Hamish Hamilton.

Burke, L., Crowley, T. and Girvin, A. (eds) (2000) *The Routledge Language and Cultural Theory Reader*, London: Routledge.

Burnett, L. (1962) *The Treasure of our Tongue*, London: Secker and Warburg.

Butler, S. (1997) 'World Englishes in the Asian context: why a dictionary is important', in L. Smith and M. Forman (eds) 1997.

Cameron, D. (1995) *Verbal Hygiene*, London: Routledge.

Canagarajah, A.S. (1999) *Resisting Linguistic Imperialism in English Teaching*, Oxford: Oxford University Press.

Carter, R. (1999) 'Standard grammars, spoken grammars: some educational implications', in T. Bex and R. Watts (eds) 1999.

Carter, R. and McCarthy, M. (1995) 'Grammar and the spoken language', *Applied Linguistics* 16/2: 141–58.

Carter, R. and McRae, J. (2001) *The Routledge History of Literature in English*, London: Routledge.

Celente, G. (1997) *Trends 2000: How to Prepare for and Profit from The Changes of the 21st Century*, New York: Warner Books.

Cenoz, J. and Jessner, U. (eds) (2000) *English in Europe. The Acquisition of a Third Language*, Clevedon, UK: Multilingual Matters.

Chamoiseau, P. (1998) *School Days*, translated by Linda Coverdale, London: Granta Books.

Cheshire, J. (ed.) (1991) *English Around the World*, Cambridge: Cambridge University Press.

—— (1999) 'Spoken standard English', in T. Bex and R. Watts (eds) 1999.

—— (2002) 'Who we are and where we're going', in P. Gubbins and M. Holt (eds) *Beyond Boundaries*, Clevedon, UK: Multilingual Matters.

Chia, B. and Brown, A. (2002) 'Singaporeans' reactions to Estuary English', *English Today* 18/2: 33–8.

Christensen, T. (1992) 'Standard English and the EFL classroom', *English Today* 8/3: 11–15.

Claiborne, R. (1983) *The Life and Times of the English Language: The History of our Marvellous Tongue*, London: Bloomsbury.

Clyne, M. (1981) 'Culture and discourse structure', *Journal of Pragmatics* 5: 61–6.

—— (1987) 'Cultural differences in the organization of academic texts', *Journal of Pragmatics* 11: 211–47.

Coggle, P. (1993) *Do you speak Estuary?* London: Bloomsbury.

Collins, B. and Mees, I. (1999) *The Real Professor Higgins*, Berlin: Mouton de Gruyter.

—— (forthcoming) *Phonology and Phonetics*, London: Routledge.

Connor, U. (1996) *Contrastive Rhetoric*, Cambridge: Cambridge University Press.

Cook, G. and Seidlhofer, B. (eds) (1995) *Principle and Practice in Applied Linguistics. Studies in honour of H.G. Widdowson*, Oxford: Oxford University Press.

Coppieters, R. (1987) 'Competence differences between native and near-native speakers', *Language* 63: 544–73.

Coulmas, G. (1987) 'Why speak English?', in K. Knapp, E. Werner and A. Knapp-Potthoff (eds) *Analyzing Intercultural Communication*, Berlin: Mouton de Gruyter.

Crowley, T. (1989) *The Politics of Discourse: The Standard Language Question in British Cultural Debates*, London: Macmillan.

Crystal, D. (1987) *The Cambridge Encyclopedia of Language*, New York: Cambridge University Press.

—— (1995) *The Cambridge Encyclopedia of the English Language*, Cambridge: Cambridge University Press.

—— (1997) *English as a Global Language*, Cambridge: Cambridge University Press.

—— (1999) 'The future of Englishes', *English Today* 15/2: 10–20.

—— (2000) *Language Death*, Cambridge: Cambridge University Press.

—— (2001) *Language and the Internet*, Cambridge: Cambridge University Press.

—— (2002) 'Broadcasting the nonstandard message', in R. Watts and P. Trudgill (eds) 2002.

Davies, A. (1991) *The Native Speaker in Applied Linguistics*, Edinburgh: Edinburgh University Press.

—— (1995) 'Proficiency or the native speaker: what are we trying to achieve in ELT?', in G. Cook and B. Seidlhofer (eds) 1995.

de Klerk, V. (1999) 'Black South African English: where to from here?', *World Englishes* 18/2: 311–24.

Deneire, M. and Goethals, M. (eds) (1997) *World Englishes* 16/1. Special Issue on English in Europe.

de Quincey, T. (1862) *Recollections of the Lakes and the Lake Poets*, Edinburgh: Adam and Charles Black.

Dicker, S. (2000) 'Official English and bilingual Education: the controversy over language pluralism in U.S. society', in J. Hall and W. Eggington (eds) 2000.

Di Pietro, R. (1990) Review of Ulrich Ammon (ed.) 'Status and function of languages and language varieties', *Language Problems and Language Planning* 14: 288–91.

Dorian, N. (1998) 'Western language ideologies and small-language prospects', in L. Grenoble and L. Whaley (eds) (1998) *Endangered Languages*, Cambridge: Cambridge University Press.

D'souza, J. (1999) 'Afterword', *World Englishes* 18/2: 271–74.

—— (2001) 'Contextualizing range and depth in Indian English', *World Englishes* 20/2: 145–59.

Edwards, J. (1994) *Multilingualism*, London: Routledge.

Edwards, V. (1986) *Language in a Black Community*, Clevedon, UK: Multilingual Matters.

Ellis, R. (1994) *The Study of Second Language Acquisition*, Oxford: Oxford University Press.

Elmes, S. (2001) *The Routes of English 4*, London: BBC.

Evans, S. (2000) 'Hong Kong's new English language policy in education', *World Englishes* 19/2: 185–204.

Fairclough, N. (1989) *Language and Power*, London: Longman.

Fippula, M. (1991) 'Urban and rural varieties of Hiberno-English', in J. Cheshire (ed.) 1991.

Fishman, J. (1971) 'National languages and languages of wider communication in developing nations', in W.H. Whiteley (ed.) *Language Use and Social Change*, Oxford: Oxford University Press.

Fishman, J. (ed.) (1999) *Handbook of Language and Ethnicity*, Oxford: Oxford University Press.

—— (2001) 'Why is it so hard to save a threatened language?', in J. Fishman (ed.) (2001) *Can threatened languages be saved?*, Clevedon, UK: Multilingual Matters.

Friel, B. (1988) *Translations*, London: Faber and Faber.

George, J. (1867) *The Mission of Great Britain to the World, or Some of the Lessons which She is now Teaching*, Toronto: Dudley and Burns.

Gimson, A.C. (1978) 'Towards an international pronunciation of English', in P. Strevens (ed.) *In Honour of A.S. Hornby*, Oxford: Oxford University Press.

—— (2001) *Gimson's Pronunciation of English*, 6th edn, revised by A. Cruttenden, London: Arnold.

Gisborne, N. (2000) 'Relative clauses in Hong Kong English', *World Englishes* 19/3: 357–71.

Gnutzmann, C. (1999) *Teaching and Learning English as a Global Language*, Tübingen: Stauffenberg Verlag.

Gomez de Matos, F. (1998) 'Learners' pronunciation rights', *Braz-TESOL Newsletter* (September): 14–15.

Gordon, E. and Sudbury, A. (2002) 'The history of southern hemisphere Englishes', in R. Watts and P. Trudgill (eds) 2002.

Görlach, M. (1988) 'The development of Standard Englishes', in M. Görlach (1990) *Studies in the History of the English Language*, Heidlberg: Carl Winter.

Graddol, D. (1997) *The Future of English?*, London: The British Council.

—— (1999) 'The decline of the native speaker', *AILA Review* 13, The English Company (UK) Ltd.

Graham, L. (2000) 'Talkin' Jamaican', unpublished Master's dissertation, King's College London.

Gramley, S. (2001) *The Vocabulary of World English*, London: Arnold.

Granville, S. *et al.* (1998) 'English with or without g(u)ilt: a position paper on language in education policy for South Africa', *Language and Education* 12/4: 254–72.

Grenoble, L. and Whaley, L. (eds) (1998) *Endangered Languages*, Cambridge: Cambridge University Press.

Gupta, A. (1999) 'Standard Englishes, contact varieties and Singapore Englishes', in C. Gnutzmann (ed.) 1999.

Haarmann, H. (1997) 'On European identity, fanciful cosmopolitanism and problems of modern nationalism', *Sociolinguistica* 11: 142–52.

Haberland, H. (1989) 'Whose English, nobody's business', *Journal of Pragmatics* 13: 927–38.

Hall, J. and Eggington, W. (eds) (2000) *The Sociopolitics of English Language Teaching*, Clevedon, UK: Multilingual Matters.

Hall, R. (1966) *Pidgin and Creole Languages*, Ithaca and London: Cornell University Press.

Hartmann, R. (ed.) (1996) *English Language in Europe*, Oxford: Intellect.

Haugen, E. (1966) 'Dialect, language and nation', *American Anthropologist* 68: 922–35, in J. Pride and J. Holmes (eds) (1972) *Sociolinguistics: Selected Readings*, Harmondsworth, UK: Penguin Books.

Hewitt, R. (1986) *White Talk Black Talk*, Cambridge: Cambridge University Press.

Hinton, L. (1999) 'Trading tongues: loss of heritage languages in the United States', *English Today* 15/4: 21–30.

Ho, W.K. and Wong, R. (eds) (2002) *English Language Teaching in East Asia Today*, Singapore: Times Academic Press.

Holborow, M. (1999) *The Politics of English*, London: Sage Publications.

Holliday, A. (1994) *Appropriate Methodology and Social Context*, Cambridge: Cambridge University Press.

Holm, J. (1988) *Pidgins and Creoles*, Vol.1., Cambridge: Cambridge University Press.

—— (1989) *Pidgins and Creoles*, Vol.2., Cambridge: Cambridge University Press.

—— (2000) *An Introduction to Pidgins and Creoles*, Cambridge: Cambridge University Press.

Honey, J. (1997) *Language is Power*, London: Faber and Faber.

Honna, N. (1995) 'English in Japanese society: language within language', *Journal of Multilingual and Multicultural Development* 16/1 and 2: 45–62.

—— (1997) 'English as a language for international communication: an Asian perspective', paper presented at the Second Symposium on Intercultural Communication, Beijing, October 10–15, 1997.

House, J. (2001) 'A "stateless" language that Europe should embrace', *Guardian Weekly, Learning English Supplement*, April 2001: 1–3.

Hudson, R. (1996) *Sociolinguistics*, 2nd edn, Cambridge: Cambridge University Press.

Hughes, A. and Trudgill, P. (1979) *English Accents and Dialects*, London: Arnold.

Hung, T. (2000) 'Towards a phonology of Hong Kong English', *World Englishes* 19/3: 337–56.

James, A. (2000) 'English as a European lingua franca: current realities and existing dichotomies', in J. Cenoz and U. Jessner (eds) 2000.

Jenkins, J. (1996) 'Native speaker, non-native speaker and English as a foreign language: time for a change', *IATEFL Newsletter* 131: 10–11.

—— (1998) 'Which pronunciation norms and models for English as an International Language?', *ELT Journal* 52/2: 119–26.

—— (2000) *The Phonology of English as an International Language*, Oxford: Oxford University Press.

—— (2002) 'A sociolinguistically based, empirically researched pronunciation syllabus for English as an international language', *Applied Linguistics* 23/1: 83–103.

Jenkins, J. and Seidlhofer, B. (2001) 'Be proud of your lingua franca', *Guardian Weekly, Learning English Supplement*, April 2001: 3.

Jenkins, J., Modiano, M. and Seidlhofer, B. (2001) 'Euro-English', *English Today* 17/4: 13–19.

Jenkins, S. (1995) 'The triumph of English', *The Times*, 25 February.

Jenner, B. (1997) 'International English: an alternative view', *Speak Out!* Newsletter of the IATEFL Pronunciation Special Interest Group, No.21: 10–14.

Jesperson, O. (1938/1982) *Growth and Structure of the English Language*, Oxford: Basil Blackwell.

Johnson, R. (1990) 'International English: towards an acceptable teaching target variety', *World Englishes* 9/3: 301–15.

Jones, G.M. (1997) 'Immersion programs in Brunei', in *Bilingual Education*, Vol.5 of J. Cummins and D. Corson (eds) *Encyclopedia of Language and Education*, Dordrecht: Kluwer Academic Publishers.

Joyce, J. (1969) *Portrait of the Artist as a Young Man*, Harmondsworth: Penguin Modern Classics.

Kachru, B. (1986) *The Alchemy of English: The Spread, Functions and Models of Non-native Englishes*, Oxford: Pergamon Press, reprinted 1990, Urbana: University of Illinois Press.

—— (1991) 'Liberation linguistics and the Quirk concern', *English Today* 25: 3–13.

—— (1982/1992) 'Models for non-native Englishes', in B. Kachru (ed.) (1992).

—— (1992) 'Teaching world Englishes', in B. Kachru (ed.) 1992.

—— (ed.) (1992) *The Other Tongue. English Across Cultures*, 2nd edn, Urbana, IL: University of Illinois Press.

—— (1995) 'Transcultural creativity in world Englishes and literary canons', in G. Cook and B. Seidlhofer (eds) 1995.

—— (1996) 'The paradigms of marginality', *World Englishes* 15/3: 241–55.

—— (1997) 'World Englishes 2000: Resources for research and teaching', in L. Smith and M. Forman (eds) 1997.

Kachru, B. and Nelson, C. (1996) 'World Englishes', in S. McKay and N. Hornberger (eds) 1996.

Kachru, Y. (1992) 'Culture, style, and discourse: expanding noetics of English', in B. Kachru (ed.) 1992.

—— (1993) 'Interlanguage and language acquisition research', review of L. Selinker, *Rediscovering Interlanguage. World Englishes* 12/1: 265–68.

—— (1997a) 'Culture and argumentative writing in world Englishes', in L. Smith and M. Forman (eds) 1997.

—— (1997b) 'Cultural meaning in contrastive rhetoric in English education', *World Englishes* 16/3: 337–50.

Kandiah, T. (1991) 'South Asia', in J. Cheshire (ed.) 1991.

—— (1995) 'Forward' to Parakrama, A., 1995.

Kasper, G. and Schmidt, R. (1996) 'Developmental issues in interlanguage pragmatics', *Studies in Second Language Acquisition* 18: 149–69.

Kaye, A.S. (1999) 'Reply to Modiano', *English Today* 15/2: 31–3.

Kfua, B. (1996) 'Time is up for Pidgin English', in (the Cameroon bi-weekly) *The Herald*, 359, 20–22 September.

Kiernan, V. (1969) *The Lords of Human Kind: European Attitudes Towards the Outside World in the Imperial Age*, London: Weidenfeld and Nicholson.

Kirkpatrick, A. (ed.) (2002) *Englishes in Asia*, Melbourne: Language Australia Ltd.

Knapp, K. and Meierkord, C. (eds) (2002) *Lingua Franca Communication*, Frankfurt, Peter Lang.

Koenig, E., Chia, E. and Povey, J. (eds) (1983) *A Sociolinguistic Profile of Urban Centres in Cameroon*, Los Angeles: Crossroads Press, University of California.

Kramsch, C. (1998) 'The privilege of the intercultural speaker', in M. Byram and M. Fleming (eds) (1998) *Language Learning in Intercultural Perspective*, Cambridge: Cambridge University Press.

Krishnaswamy, N. and Burde, S. (1998) *The Politics of India's English*, Delhi: Oxford University Press.

Kubota, R. (2001) 'Teaching world Englishes to native speakers of English in the USA', *World Englishes* 20/1: 47–64.

Lanham, L. (1990) 'Stress and intonation and the intelligibility of South African Black English', in S. Ramsaran (ed.) 1990.

Lee, A. (2001) 'English to get English Lessons', *Straits Times*, 15 May.

Leech, G., Deuchar, M. and Hoogenraad, R. (1982) *English Grammar for Today*, Houndmills, Basingstoke: Macmillan.

Lee-Wong, S.M. (2001) 'The polemics of Singlish', *English Today* 17/1: 39–45.

Leith, D. (1996) 'English – colonial to postcolonial', in D. Graddol, D. Leith and J. Swann (eds) *English History, Diversity and Change*, London: Routledge.

Le Page, R. and Tabouret-Keller, A. (1985) *Acts of Identity*, Cambridge: Cambridge University Press.

Leung, C., Harris, R. and Rampton, B. (1997) 'The idealised native speaker; reified ethnicities, and classroom realities', *TESOL Quarterly* 31/3: 543–60.

Li, D. (1996) *Issues in Bilingualism and Biculturalism: A Hong Kong Case Study*, New York: Peter Lang.

—— (1998) 'Incorporating L1 pragmatic norms and cultural values in L2: developing English Language curriculum for EIL in the Asia-Pacific region', *Asian Englishes* 1/1: 39–46.

—— (2000) 'Cantonese-English code-switching research in Hong Kong: a Y2K review', *World Englishes* 19/3: 305–22.

Lightbown, P. and Spada, N. (1999) *How Languages are Learned*, 2nd edn, Oxford: Oxford University Press.

Li L (2000) 'Email: a challenge to Standard English?', *English Today* 16/4: 23–9.

Li Y (2000) 'Surfing e-mails', *English Today* 16/4: 30–40.

Lii-Shih, Y.E. (1994) *Conversational Politeness and Foreign Language Teaching*, Taipei: The Crane Publishing Co. Ltd.

Lindquist, H., Klintborg, S., Levin, M. and Estling, M. (eds) (1998) *The Major Varieties of English. Papers from MAVEN 97*, Växjö: Acta Wexionensia.

Lippi-Green, R. (1997) *English with an Accent*, London: Routledge.

Lowenberg, P. (1992) 'Testing English as a world language: issues in assessing non-native proficiency', in B. Kachru (ed.) 1992.

—— (2000) 'Non-native varieties and the sociopolitics of English proficiency assessment', in J. Hall and W. Eggington (eds) 2000.

Lowry, A. (1992) 'Style range in New English literatures', in B. Kachru (ed.) 1992.

McArthur, A. (1987) 'The English languages?', *English Today* 11: 9–13.

—— (1998) *The English Languages*, Cambridge: Cambridge University Press.

—— (1999) 'English in the world, in Africa, and in South Africa', *English Today* 15/1: 11–16.

—— (2002) *The Oxford Guide to World English*, Oxford: Oxford University Press.

McCarthy, M. and Carter, R. (1994) *Language as Discourse*, London: Longman.

McCarty, T. and Zepeda, O. (1999) 'Amerindians', in J. Fishman (ed.) 1999.

McCrum, R., MacNeil, R. and Cran, W. (1992) *The Story of English*, 2nd edn, London: Faber and Faber.

McKay, S. (2002) *Teaching English as an International Language*, Oxford: Oxford University Press.

McKay, S. and Hornberger, N. (1996) *Sociolinguistics and Language Teaching*, Cambridge: Cambridge University Press.

Maidment, J. (1994) 'Estuary English: hybrid or hype', paper presented at the 4th New Zealand Conference on Language and Society, Lincoln University, Christchurch, New Zealand, August 1994. Available on: http://www.phon.uck.ac.uk/home/estuary/maidment.htm

Maley, A. (1997) 'I so blur, you know', *IATEFL Newsletter* No.135: 16–17.

Matalene, C. (1985) 'Contrastive rhetoric: an American writing teacher in China', *College English* 47/8: 789–808.

Matsuda, A. (2000) 'The use of English among Japanese returnees', *English Today* 16/4: 49–55.

Mbassi-Manga, F. (1973) 'English in Cameroon: a study of historical contacts, patterns of usage and current trends', unpublished PhD thesis, University of Leeds.

Medgyes, P. (1992) 'Native or non-native: who's worth more?', *ELT Journal* 46/4: 340–9.

—— (1994) *The Non-Native Teacher*, London: Macmillan.

Mesthrie, R. (2002) 'Building a new English dialect', in R. Watts and P. Trudgill (eds) (2002) *Alternative Histories of English*, London: Routledge.

Metcalf, T. (1995) *Ideologies of the Raj*, Cambridge: Cambridge University Press (Indian edition, New Delhi: Foundation Books).

Milroy, J. and Milroy, L. (1999) *Authority in Language. Investigating Standard English*, London: Routledge.

Milroy, L. (1985) 'Social network and language maintenance', in A.K. Pugh, V.J. Lee and J. Swann (eds) *Language and Language Use*, London and Milton Keynes: Heinemann Educational Books and The Open University Press.

—— (1998) 'Bad Grammar is slovenly', in L. Bauer and P. Trudgill (eds) 1998.

—— (1999) 'Standard English and language ideology in Britain and the United States', in T. Bex and R. Watts (eds) 1999.

Mitchell, R. (1993) 'Diversity or uniformity? Multilingualism and the English teacher in the 1990s', *IATEFL Annual Conference Report. Plenaries 1993*: 9–16.

Modiano, M. (1999a) 'International English in the global village', *English Today* 15/2: 22–34.

—— (1999b) 'Standard English(es) and educational practices for the world's lingua franca', *English Today* 15/4: 3–13.

—— (2000) 'Rethinking ELT', *English Today*, 16/2: 30–4.

Mufwene, S. (1997) 'The legitimate and illegitimate offspring of English', in L. Smith and M. Forman 1997.

Mufwene, S. (2001) *The Ecology of Language Evolution*, Cambridge: Cambridge University Press.

Mugglestone, L. (1995) *'Talking Proper'. The Rise of Accent as Social Symbol*, Oxford: Clarendon Press.

Mühlhäusler, P. (1997) *Pidgin and Creole Linguistics*, London: University of Westminster Press.

Murray, H. and Dingwall, S. (1997) 'English for scientific communication at Swiss universities: God helps those who help themselves', *Babylonia* 4: 54–9.

Nayar, P.B. (1998) 'Variants and varieties of English: dialectology or linguistic politics?', in H. Lindquist *et al.* 1998.

Nelson, C. (1982) 'Intelligibility and non-native varieties of English', in B.B. Kachru (ed.) (1982) *The Other Tongue. English across Cultures*, Urbana, IL: University of Illinois Press.

Nettle, D. and Romaine, S. (2000) *Vanishing Voices*, Oxford: Oxford University Press.

Ngũgĩ wa Thiong'o (1986) *Decolonising the Mind: The Politics of Language in African Literature*, London: James Currey.

Norton, B. (1997) 'Language, identity, and the ownership of English', *TESOL Quarterly* 31/3: 409–29.

——— (2000) *Identity and Language Learning*, London: Longman.

Nylenna, M., Riis, P. and Karlsson, Y. (1994) 'Multiple blinded reviews of the same two manuscripts. Effects of reference characteristics and publication language', *The Journal of the American Medical Association* 272/2: 149–51.

Obeng, S. and Adegbija, E. (1999) 'Sub-Saharan Africa', in J. Fishman (ed.) 1999.

Odlin, T. (1992) 'Transferability and linguistic substrates', *Second Language Research* 8: 171–202.

Omoniyi, T. (1999) 'Afro-Asian rural border areas', in J. Fishman 1999.

Pakir, A. (1991) 'The range and depth of English-knowing bilinguals', *World Englishes* 10/2: 167–79.

——— (1993) 'Spoken and written English in Singapore: the differences', in A. Pakir (ed.) (1993) *The English Language in Singapore*, Singapore: SAAL.

——— (1995) 'Expanding triangles of English expression in Singapore', in Teng Su Ching and Ho Mian Lian (eds) *The English Language in Singapore. Implications for Teaching*, Singapore: SAAL.

——— (1997) 'Standards and codification for World Englishes', in L. Smith and M. Forman (eds) 1997.

Parakrama, A. (1995) *De-hegemonizing language standards*, London: Macmillan.

Parasher, S. (1980) 'Mother-tongue English diglossia: a case study of educated English bilinguals' language use', *Anthropological Linguistics* 22: 151–68.

——— (1998) 'Language policy in a multilingual setting: the Indian scenario', *Asian Englishes* 1/1: 92–116.

——— (2001) 'Communication in multilingual India: a sociolinguistic perspective for the 21st century, *AILA Review* 14, The English Company (UK) Ltd.

Pennington, M. (1998) 'The folly of language planning: or, a brief history of the English language in Hong Kong', *English Today* 14/2: 25–30.

Pennycook, A. (1989) 'The concept of method, interested knowledge and the politics of language teaching', *TESOL Quarterly* 23/4: 589–619.

—— (1994) *The Cultural Politics of English as an International Language*, London: Longman.

—— (1998) *English and the Discourses of Colonialism*, London: Routledge.

—— (2001) *Critical Applied Linguistics: A Critical Introduction*, Mahwah, NJ: Lawrence Erlbaum Associates.

Phillipson, R. (1992) *Linguistic Imperialism*, Oxford: Oxford University Press.

—— (1996) 'Linguistic imperialism: African perspectives', *ELT Journal* 50/2: 160–67.

—— (ed.) (2000) *Rights to Language: Equity, Power, and Education*, Mahweh, NJ: Lawrence Erlbaum.

Phillipson, R. (2003) *English-Only Europe? Challenging Language Policy*, London: Routledge.

Pinker, S. (1994) *The Language Instinct*, London: Penguin.

Platt, J., Weber, H. and Ho, M.L. (1984) *The New Englishes*, London: Routledge and Kegan Paul.

Preisler, B. (1999) 'Functions and forms of English in a European EFL country', in T. Bex and R. Watts (eds) 1999.

Prodromou, L. (1997) 'From corpus to octopus', *IATEFL Newsletter* No.137: 18–21.

Quirk, R. (1982) 'International communication and the concept of nuclear English', in C. Brumfit (ed.) 1982.

—— (1990) 'Language varieties and standard language', *English Today* 21: 3–10.

Quirk, R. and Widdowson, H. (eds) (1985) *English in the World: Teaching and Learning the Language and Literature*, Cambridge: Cambridge University Press.

Rao, R. (ed.) (1947) *Kanthapura*, Oxford: Oxford University Press.

Rampton, B. (1990) 'Displacing the "native speaker": expertise, affiliation and inheritance', *ELT Journal* 44/2: 97–101.

—— (1995) *Crossing: Language and Ethnicity Among Adolescents*, London: Longman.

Ramsaran, S. (ed.) (1990) *Studies in the Pronunciation of English: A Commemorative Volume in Honour of A.C. Gimson*, London: Routledge.

Rolleston, C. (1911) *The Age of Folly: A Study of Imperial Needs, Duties, and Warning*, London: John Milne.

Romaine, S. (1988) *Pidgin and Creole Languages*, London: Longman.

Rosewarne, D. (1996) 'Changes in English pronunciation and some implications for teachers and non-native learners', *Speak Out!* Newsletter of the IATEFL Pronunciation Special Interest Group, No.18, Summer 1996: 15–21.

Samimy, K. and Brutt-Griffler, J. (1999) 'To be a native or non-native speaker: perceptions of "non-native" students in a graduate TESOL program', in G. Braine (ed.) 1999.

Scollon, R. (1997) 'Contrastive rhetoric, contrastive poetics, or perhaps something else', *Language in Society* 24/1: 1–28.

Sebba, M. (1993) *London Jamaican*, London: Longman.

—— (1997) *Contact Languages*, London: Macmillan.

Seidlhofer, B. (1999) 'Double standards: teacher education in the Expanding Circle', *World Englishes* 18/2: 233–45.

—— (2001a) 'Brave New English?', *The European English Messenger* X/1: 43–8.

—— (2001b) 'Closing a conceptual gap: the case for a description of English as a lingua franca', *International Journal of Applied Linguistics* 11/2: 133–58.

Selinker, L. (1972) 'Interlanguage', *International Review of Applied Linguistics* 10: 209–31.

Siegel, J. (1991) 'Variation in Fiji English', in J. Cheshire (ed.) 1991.

Siegel, M. (1996) 'The role of learner subjectivity in second language sociolinguistic competency: western women learning Japanese', *Applied Linguistics* 17/3: 3356–82.

Singh, I. (2001) *Pidgins and Creoles*, London: Arnold.

Skuttnab-Kangas, T. (1999) 'What fate awaits the world's languages?', *Media Development*, Journal of the World Association for Christian Communication Vol.XLVI 4/1999: 3–7.

Skuttnab-Kangas, T. and Phillipson, R. (1994) 'Linguistic human rights, past and present', in T. Skuttnab-Kangas and R. Phillipson (eds) (1994) *Linguistic Human Rights. Overcoming Linguistic Discrimination*, Berlin and New York: Mouton de Gruyter.

—— (1996) 'Linguicide and linguicism' in G. Hans *et al.* (eds) *Kontaktlinguistic/ Contact Linguistics/Linguistique de contact*, Vol.1. Berlin and New York: de Gruyter.

Smith, L. (ed.) (1983) *Readings in English as an International Language*, Oxford: Pergamon Press.

—— (1992) 'Spread of English and issues of intelligibility', in B. Kachru (ed.) 1992.

Smith, L. and Bisazza, J. (1982) 'The comprehensibility of three varieties of English for college students in seven countries', *Language Learning* 32: 259–70.

Smith, L. and Forman, M. (eds) (1997) *World Englishes 2000*, Honolulu, Hawai'i: University of Hawai'i Press.

Smith, L. and Rafiqzad, K. (1979) 'English for cross-cultural communication: the question of intelligibility', *TESOL Quarterly* 13/3: 371–80.

Spencer-Oatey, H. (ed.) (2000) *Culturally Speaking. Managing Rapport through Talk across Cultures*, London: Continuum.

Sridhar, K. and Sridhar, S. (1992) 'Bridging the paradigm gap: second-language acquisition theory and indigenized varieties of English', in B. Kachru (ed.) 1992.

Steiner, G. (1975) *After Babel: Aspects of Language and Translation*, Oxford: Oxford University Press.

Strevens, P. (1980) *Teaching English as an International Language*, Oxford: Pergamon Press.

—— (1985) 'Standards and the standard language', *English Today* No.1/2: 5–8.

—— (1992) 'English as an international language: directions in the 1990s', in B. Kachru, (ed.) 1992.

Stubbs, M. (1986) *Educational Linguistics*, Oxford: Blackwell.

Sutcliffe, D. (1982) *British Black English*, Oxford: Blackwell.

Takahashi, S. (1996) 'Pragmatic transferability', *Studies in Second Language Acquisition* 18: 189–223.

Tay, M. (1991) 'Southeast Asia and Hongkong', in J. Cheshire (ed.) 1991.

Thomas, J. (1983) 'Cross-cultural pragmatic failure', *Applied Linguistics* 4/2: 91–112.

Thomason, S. and Kaufman, T. (1988) *Language Contact, Creolization and Genetic Linguistics*, Berkeley: University of California Press.

Thumboo, E. (1992) 'The literary dimension of the spread of English', in B. Kachru (ed.) 1992.

Tiffen, B. (1992) 'A study of the intelligibility of Nigerian English', in A. van Essen and E. Burkart (eds) *Homage to W.R. Lee. Essays in English as a Foreign and Second Language*, Dordrecht: Foris.

Titlestad, P. (1998) 'South Africa's language ghosts', *English Today* 14/2: 33–9.

Todd, L. (1990) *Pidgins and Creoles*, 2nd edn, London: Routledge.

—— (1997) 'Ebonics: an evaluation', *English Today* 13/3: 13–17.

—— (1999) 'Reply to Modiano', *English Today* 15/2: 30–1.

Toolan, M. (1997) 'Recentring English: New English and Global', *English Today* 13/4: 3–10.

Tripathi, P. (1992) 'English: "the chosen tongue"', *English Today* 32: 3–11.

—— (1998) 'Redefining Kachru's "outer circle" of English', *English Today* 14/4: 55–8.

Trosberg, A. (1995) *Interlanguage Pragmatics: Requests, Complaints and Apologies*, Berlin: Mouton de Gruyter.

Trudgill, P. (1984) *Language in the British Isles*, Cambridge: Cambridge University Press.

—— (1998) 'World Englishes: convergence or divergence?', in H. Lindquist *et al.* (eds) 1998.

—— (1999) 'Standard English: what it isn't', in T. Bex and R. Watts (eds) 1999.

—— (2001) *Sociolinguistic Variation and Change*, Edinburgh: Edinburgh University Press.

Trudgill, P. and Chambers, J.K. (1991) 'Introduction: English dialect grammar', in J.K. Chambers and P. Trudgill (eds) *Dialects of English*, London: Longman.

Trudgill, P. and J. Hannah (1994) *International English*, 3rd edn, London: Arnold.

—— (2002) *International English*, 4th edn, London: Arnold.

Tsuda, Y. (1997) 'Hegemony of English vs ecology of language: building equality in international communication', in L. Smith and M. Forman (eds) 1997.

Tsui, A. and Bunton, D. (2000) 'The discourse and attitudes of English language teachers in Hong Kong', *World Englishes* 19/3: 287–303.

Ufomata, T. (1990) 'Acceptable models for TEFL (with special reference to Nigeria)', in S. Ramsaran (ed.) 1990.

Vandenbroucke, J.P. (1989) 'On not being born a native speaker of English', *British Medical Journal* 298: 1461–2.

van Els, T. (2000) 'The European Union, its institutions and its languages', public lecture given at the University of Nijmegen, the Netherlands on 22 September 2000.

Viereck, W. (1996) 'English in Europe: its nativisation and use as a lingua franca, with special reference to German-speaking countries', in R. Hartmann (ed.) 1996 *English Language in Europe*, Oxford: Intellect.

Wardhaugh, R. (2002) *An Introduction to Sociolinguistics*, 4th edn, Oxford: Blackwell.

Watts, R. and Trudgill, P. (eds) (2002) *Alternative Histories of English*, London: Routledge.

Wells, J. (1973) *Jamaican Pronunciation in London*, Oxford: Basil Blackwell.

—— (1982) *Accents of English*, Cambridge: Cambridge University Press.

—— (1994) 'Transcribing Estuary English: a discussion document', Speech Hearing and Language: UCL Work in Progress, Vol.8: 259–67. Also available on: http://www.phon.ucl.ac.uk/home/estuary/wells.htm

Wesley-Smith, P. (1994) 'Anti-Chinese legislation in Hong Kong', in M.K. Chan (ed.) *Precarious Balance: Hong Kong between China and Britain, 1842–1992*, Hong Kong: Hong Kong University Press.

Widdowson, H.G. (1993) 'The ownership of English', IATEFL Annual Conference Report, Plenaries 1993.

—— (1994) 'Pragmatics and the pedagogic competence of language teachers', in T. Sebbage and S. Sebbage (eds) *Proceedings of the 4th International NELLE Conference*, Hamburg: NELLE.

—— (1997) 'EIL, ESL, EFL: global issues and local interests', *World Englishes* 16/1: 135–46.

Willis, D. (1996) 'Accuracy, fluency and conformity', in J. Willis and D. Willis (eds) 1996 *Challenge and Change in Language Teaching*, London: Macmillan Heinemann.

Willis, D. with Jenkins, J. (1999) 'From pronunciation to lexicogrammar', talk given at International House Teacher Training Conference London, February 1999.

Willis, D. (2003) *Rules, Patterns and Words: Language Description for Language Teaching*, Cambridge: Cambridge University Press.

Wolfram, W. and Schilling-Estes, N. (1998) *American English*, Oxford: Blackwell.

Wolfson, N. (1989) *Perspectives: Sociolinguistics and TESOL*, New York: Newbury House.

Yano, Y. (2001) 'World Englishes in 2000 and beyond', *World Englishes* 20/2: 119–31.

GLOSSARIAL INDEX

The glossarial index is based on significant terms used in the text. Page numbers in bold refer to explanations or significant information.